# PLAYING FOR REAL

## RePlaying the Game of Life

*Play as if your life depends on it – it does!*

O. Fred Donaldson, Ph.D.

No matter how adult you are, sometimes all it takes to become human again is for a child to take you by the hand.

Peace is already in the child, who takes nothing more seriously than what adults dismiss as sentimental and childish.

The human addiction to contest makes original play necessary; our capacity for kindness makes original play possible.

*For David,*

*You defined original play as no one else has.*

*For Paul,*

*You showed me that life is for loving not for fearing.*

*For Katie,*

*You giggled your face of God to me.*

*For Insui,*

*You kept the spirit of play alive.*

# Contents

# Introduction: *Changing The Game*

*"The die has been cast."*

Julius Caesar—William Shakespeare

*"In this situation there is no game."*

—Michal Graczykowski

The two statements above portray the tragedy and the hope of humankind. These two statements also hint at the purpose of this book. On the one hand, we have been given Creation's Gift of Life to be lived as One. On the other hand, humans have misinterpreted this message as life is to be won. This distinction is at the very foundation of life itself. Is the purpose of life to be one or is it to be won? We have locked ourselves in a perverse game of survival we feel must be lived as won. The message of this book is that we can change the game of life. By playing for real we can become the humans we are meant to be. Make no mistake this is an entirely new adventure. It will be controversial. The reward is a new living paradigm.

On a recent trip to South Africa, Michal, age 11, and his sister Magda, age 13, created a board game. When it was ready they, their mother, and I sat down to play. Michal laid out a large sheet of paper he had colored green. He placed four reddish rocks on the corners to hold down the field of combat. He had created four armies of paper men. He carefully arranged each army in one of the four corners of the green field

I was amazed at how Michal had worked out the complicated procedures by which the armies were to engage each other. For example, the men of each army, some mounted on horses, had different kinds of weapons. Winning and losing individual combat was decided by a complex arrangement that ended with a throw of the die. I did not understand exactly how this happened, but it became clear that rolling a six guaranteed a win.

My strategy of letting the other three armies fight it out worked well until it came down to Michal and I. He quickly dispatched my men and won the game. Trying to make me feel better, Michal told me that

1

"Coming in second is good, too."

I woke up the next morning at 3:30 with Michal's game still on my mind. The game of Chinese baseball described by R.G.H. Siu is played almost exactly like American baseball—the same field, players, bats, and balls, method of scoring, and so on. The batter stands in the batter's box as usual. The pitcher stands on the pitcher's mound as usual. He winds up, as usual, and zips the ball down the alley. There is only one difference, and that is: After the ball leaves the pitcher's hands, and as long as the ball is in the air, anyone can move any of the bases anywhere. The bases that in American baseball are solidly fastened to the ground are movable. This changes the game creating the potential for new possibilities outside the reality of traditional baseball.

That's it! Suppose... I were to change Michal's game. We would play on the same board with the same four contesting armies. The game would be played as before with the same fundamental assumption that each interaction is based on self-defense. Just as before members of each of the four armies enter the game with a known skill set. In Michal's game there is only one winner; everyone else loses. The game is played for keeps. But suppose a fifth person from an unknown land enters the game with a different assumption of engagement. Realizing that self-defense is a limiting behavioral set this new participant plays the game rather than competes the game. This new player is not a contestant; and is not restricted by the limitations imposed by self-defense. Unrestricted by the old rules this new player carries his own die that has a six on every face. In a game of limits the new player enters without limits. This new player is not playing for keeps, but rather playing for real.

When I suggested this modification to Michal and asked him to think about its consequences. It didn't take him long to reply, "It's not good for the game." He added, "In this situation there is no game." Michal is right. Implicit in the game's routine is the assumption that life is a commodity to be won and lost. The new player quietly makes the game's routine impossible. Suppose we can transfer this modification from a board game to real life. I'm proposing an order of magnitude improvement of the evolutionary dead-end within which humanity has been trapped. Why do we continue to engage life as a dead end game? Because it's the *only* game we know. We dedicate ourselves to contests and in doing so, we refuse to become who we can be. Philip Bobbitt points out that, "The looming combination of a global terrorist network, weapons of mass destruction, and the heightening vulnerability of enormous numbers of civilians emphatically require a basic transformation of the conventional wisdom in international security." He says later that, "...it is precisely our old idea of war that must be adjusted." An "adjustment" is far too meager a change. *We must play a new game one that shifts from a war to a peace story, and from a dying world story to a living world story.* This possibility is neither mere sentimentality nor is it just theoretical. This book challenges the old certainties that humans have lived with for centuries and in doing so ignites childhood's fire that remains an ember beneath the ashes of adult lives.

We assume and expect that children will somehow discover peace from the games of their warring seniors. Imagine our shock to learn that these same warring seniors can, on the other hand, learn peace from children.

Children's gift is not to try to coax peace out of war; it is, rather, the skill of giving and receiving love anew each day without hiding in the transient refuge of fear.

I join with the world's children in tugging at your hearts, minds, and bodies in the hope that you will listen and act. My aim is not merely to share interesting stories of my play experiences, but to present a vital message for our times. *Playing For Real* proposes a profound and until now unheeded cry for a behavioral paradigm shift from a contest world of *won* to a playful world of *one*. Although I did not know it at the time I was beginning an adventure in search of love. This is a book about who we are meant to be. I am fortunate, to say the least, to be able to participate in one of the most extraordinary adventures in the history of humankind. This is as deChardin exclaimed when we harness the energies of love we will have for the second time discovered fire. Can we change not only our minds, but our hearts and brains as well? Isn't there a way of discovering a sustainable peace?

Peace must be an experience, not merely an ideal. This peace is felt in particular lives and is of perennial importance. Immediately, original play presents us with a problem— how do we use cultural strategies to go beyond culture? We don't. The purpose of this book is to present a new game plan and in so doing change how we play the game of life. This new game plan is described in a deceptively simple sentence—peace is child's play. My intent in this book is threefold: (1) suggest that our contest model of life is a dead-end; (2) propose an alternative game plan based not on surviving but thriving; (3) to reveal that this new model of living is encrypted as a behavioral code of peace in the original play of childhood.

Humans have lived as if we have no choice but to live life as a game to be won. Like dairy cows chained to milking stanchions, we are incarcerated in catastrophic contests, because we know no other alternative. We live as if the fix is in and life must be played for keeps. Julius Caesar, was succinct, "The die has been cast." Despite the efforts of our best and brightest we continue to participate in the collective psychosis of contest, which has us all in its lethal grip. The game not only defines who we are, but who we can become. We are dead wrong! What makes our cycles of war and peace inevitable is our belief that they are. We're still following Aristotle's thought that, "We make war so that we may live in peace." General Omar Bradley, thinks that, "We know more about war than we know about peace, more about killing than we know about living." Barbara Tuchman questions, "Why do we invest all our skills and resources in a contest for armed superiority which can never be attained for long enough to make it worth having, rather than in an effort to find a *modus vivendi* with our antagonist—that it is to say, a way of living, not dying?"

French novelist Anatole France wrote that,"War will disappear only when men shall take no part whatever in violence and shall be ready to suffer every persecution that their abstention will bring them." Will and Ariel Durant went further and wrote that it would take interplanetary war to make the earth one. Azar Gat, ends his massive study of war by saying that, "How future developments will affect the use of wide scale violence... is anybody's guess." At the conclusion of her history of governmental policy *The March of Folly,* Barbara Tuchman laments that we can only "muddle on" as we've done for thousands of years. However far our "muddling" has gotten us, it is not far enough. Our belief in the validity of our contest approach to life keeps us from developing new ways of thinking and acting. In desperation it seems the best we can do is leave solutions to our problems of war and peace to aliens, guesswork, or "muddling on." It never occurs to us, of course, that our very assumptions, roles, and stories are the problem. Virginia Woolf asked a question in the 1930's that we still don't know how to answer: "What sort of education will teach the young to hate war?" She points out that we teach them not how to hate force, but how to use it.

We believe in and are living a dead end. We give our allegiance to the very perverse game that endangers us. Not surprisingly, however, we tend to resist the idea that our approach to the game of life is a delusion. Self-defense is self-defeating. John Keegan, the military historian put it this way, "a cultural transformation from our warrior past demands a break from the past for which there are no precedents." John W. Dower points out that overcoming our psychological and institutional pathologies "requires faith and reason of a radically different sort." To abandon our delusion no matter how illusory it may be is asking a great deal from human beings who believe that to do so would leave them alone adrift in a hostile world.

But suppose the *fix* is not in. Albert Einstein said, "No problem can be solved from the same consciousness that created it—we must learn to see the world anew." Original play is not a childish distraction but a choice that makes everything else more vital. Imagine we can press the re-play button. *Playing for Real* is life's way of replaying the game of life.

Recall that the caterpillar yells up to the butterfly, "you're never going to get me up there!" The caterpillar is correct; a metamorphosis is necessary in order to become a butterfly. Likewise a metamorphosis is required for us to truly play the game of life. Mathematical cosmologist Dr. Brian Swimme puts it this way, "We need to put our energy into inventing new cultural forms for initiating ourselves into an ecstatic sense of involvement with the community of beings that is the very universe."

Humans have lost our place in the scheme of things; consequently we no longer feel our sense of place in the world. What is required is a metamorphosis, a transformation, a break from the past with no precedents, a radically different faith and reason, and an ecstatic sense of involvement. That is a tall order for humanity. I'm suggesting nothing less than the making of a new species of human—the one we are meant to be. This new person has recently been described by the term "anthropocene" from the Greek "anthropo" meaning human and "cene" meaning new. It is a name coined in 2000 by Nobel Laureate Paul Crutzen for the present geological epoch defined by the massive impact of humans on the earth. Paul Crutzen asked, "Can We Survive the "Anthropocene Period?" Yes, but survival is the old game based on an outdated story. We have been mired in this story, unable to free ourselves as if it is quicksand. The greatest hunger in our world is for neither security nor food but for belonging. We must do more than survive; we must thrive. Suppose that the *anthropocene* is a time of a profoundly innovative human, one with a brain not limited by fear in a struggle to survive, but rather a human whose mind opens to the potential to thrive.

What we are searching for really is a new order of relationship in which a will to play with life replaces the fear of contesting with life. In pressing the **re-play** button we activate the transformative energies necessary to reconnect with our original sense of belonging to all life. This transformation makes routine competitive acts impossible; it makes conflict obsolete. It makes possible the strength and sense of meaning we wanted but couldn't find in our contests. Only then can we realize that the purpose of life is to be *One*, not *Won*.

Where are we going to discover such a new human? The answer is much closer than we imagine. We have been given a myriad of clues, some more evident than others. We have, however, been unable or unwilling to follow them. By neither recognizing that we are lost, nor that children can be guides, we've ignored their telltale signs. Fortunately, like bread crumbs strewn along humanity's path, sages have repeatedly told us to go to the children. Jesus, Buddha, Lao-tzu, Gandhi, Black Elk among others have suggested that children have something important to offer us. Janusz Korczak wrote that children could indeed be "the salvation of the world." Graca Machel has called children "the nucleus of sustainable human development." What are they getting at? The implications of this question are far more profound than we have dared to imagine. Children considered being nothing more than ciphers turn out to be the bearers of life's most important promise—peace. It seems like an absurd idea that *Peace is child's play.* But as Einstein once remarked, "If an idea is not at first absurd, there's no hope for it." But perhaps the degree of this absurdity is only exceeded by the our ridiculous belief that war creates peace, which is the definition of an ignorance that is conventional, criminal, and suicidal.

*Playing For Real* is neither a conventional book about peace nor a book about conventional play. Do not expect much in the way of convention, for my intent is to hint at something over there, seen briefly, like a shooting star, and if not attended to, not seen at all.

Every once in a while something happens in science that opens doors that were either closed or presumed not to exist. Suddenly a discovery is made that allows or forces us to change or enlarge our view of the world. Sometimes what we discover has been right in front of us all the time waiting for our exploration. Like so many adults I was prodigal; it was time for me to find my way back to the gifts of childhood. Over the past forty years I have been initiated into a unique relationship with children and animals. I call it *Original Play.* Original play creates a right-of-way by which we can return to our abandoned childhoods. This relationship has challenged not only my ideas about life but more importantly my place on earth.

Before being tugged to the ground I had never taken children's play any more seriously than other adults. I assumed, like other adults, that child's play was nothing more than random acts of childishness, at best merely for entertainment value. I could not have been more wrong. I came to realize that in children's play, a new world of possibilities was being revealed. *Playing For Real* presents a point of departure, a direction of spirit. Over the past forty years I have been in the presence of a great many children but I've felt the absence of childhood. This is like the pain one feels but cannot explain where it hurts. I've learned that the world may look at children but we do not care about the hopes, dreams, and grace of childhood. It is as simple and cruel as that.

We must re-imagine childhood. We are unable to imagine alternatives to our approach to children and childhood that must be "cost-effective", "accountable", and "realistic". Such "in the box" thinking leads to rationalization, disengagement, and cynicism. The approach outlined in this book requires that we "get down and dirty" with children. It is not enough to keep our distance, emotionally and physically, while writing reports as children remain passive subjects of our studies. We will only learn what we need to know by playing with children. Only then can we join the preemptive kindness necessary to disable the crippling effects of fear and aggression.

*Playing For Real* is a *How-to-Be... so-Play-will-Happen-with-You* book. A narrow cultural approach to children's play obscures the nature of its potential, thereby enfeebling our best responses to it. This book's insights, like hot cocoa on a cold day, are best felt from the inside out. But however warm this book may make the reader, it is not meant to be a substitute for a child. This book is not so much written about children and animals as it is written with their energy, trust, touch, and love. This is a book written not from the point of view of someone interested in child development, nor in having an animal guide, nor in peace as an utopian vision, or play as a bizarre peak experience, not by someone who learns by observing and analyzing children, nor thinking about peace, but from the conviction of someone who has lived peace in a forty year apprenticeship with thousands of children and animals.

This book is about a choice that children opened to me—a choice I never knew I had. A choice to make my human existence the sacrament it is meant to be. Children care for me as if they are performing a kind of graceful triage as they teach me again and again to widen my circle of compassion to embrace all life. Sometimes children break into my life with shattering impact, tearing open a gash in the hard worked fabric of adulthood and liberating my spirit from its cultural tyrannies. Children dare to beckon me to go further than I have ever gone before. I recall holding Magda, a four-month-old girl in a Polish orphanage, whose eyes like dark matter had a gravitational pull on me. She dared to disturb my cultural moorings with the light of an evocative presence. In doing so she reminded me that as Pirkei Avoth put it, "In a place with no people, try to be a person." Magda showed me that I am not who I think I am, but rather who I pretend I cannot become. And by that I am made greater in my imagination and my humanity. Her simple expression of love is Creation's gift, childhood's dream, and the plot of our new living world story. Children are harbingers of a conspiracy of which I was unaware.

We are what we know and what we know is fear. Primitive, medieval, and modern humans all "know" that the world is a series of contests governed by the fixed and natural laws of survival. In *Playing For Real* I argue that this is not the whole truth. We not only have a choice, but we have inherited an as yet undiscovered behavioral antidote that makes real peace possible. This is indeed a provocative and revolutionary thesis. *Playing For Real* is a pioneering book, doing what humans have assumed cannot be done—it demonstrates not only that we can choose love over fear, this much is a profound advancement for human beings, but it is not enough. What makes *Playing For Real* a truly original book is that it goes beyond being a conceptual leap to presenting an innovative, universal, and tangible practice to achieve peace. In original play structural violence is replaced by structural kindness. By making peace readily accessible *Playing For Real* changes everything.

This book is a guide to a necessary, far-reaching, and subversive journey. If you choose to embark on this ambitious quest you will ultimately discover for yourself the *choice* to love instead of fear, liberating *your* spirit from the tyrannies of fear that have haunted human beings for generations. Jeremy Rivkin in his radical new view of civilization points out that, "Play then is far from a trivial pursuit. It is where we stretch our empathic consciousness and learn to become truly human." *One of the most important messages of this book is that we, each of us, has a choice about disengaging from the contests of our lives.* Despite the fact that we are human such a choice is ours; and, because we are human such a choice is ours. Go ahead, go out and play with the world. If nothing else it may make you think, or better yet, stop your thinking altogether.

This book has taken twenty years to write. The further my exploration proceeded the more clearly two things emerged. The first was that there are two fundamental stories of life, one that has been told repeatedly and another that has not yet been imagined.

The second was that in exploring a new story I discovered that the old ways of storytelling simply failed utterly to be able to tell the new story. I was uncovering nothing less than a gateway to a hidden universal form of communication: a pattern of intention and practice which are the very stuff of human wholeheartedness.

Before we embark on the journey that is this book I will set out a brief route-map. The most important ideas are presented as *keepsakes*.

# Keepsakes

I remember as a young boy my mother scooping up my jeans from the floor to put in the wash. She had learned to check my pockets first. "Fred, come in here." I would come into the laundry room to collect the latest pile of souvenirs of my travels in the woods, pastures, and ponds of the farm—stones, arrowheads, bones, marbles, horseshoe nails. I gathered up my treasures and deposited them in a cigar box for safe keeping.

Here are a few such mementos from the pockets of my mind. These are some important keepsakes transported home from my forty years of playing with people and animals. It is important to be acutely conscious while reading these points that original play cannot be reduced to an explanation. To reduce original play to words cannot even suggest its passion and compassion, hardships and pains , unknowns and mysteries. The truth of original play is a love not of this world and yet entirely of it.

- *Humans have been devoted to a dying world story, a tale of tragic distortion of consciousness in which we believe ourselves to be strangers in a dangerous world where our only hope for survival is self-defense.*

- *The dying world story is based on the Duchess' Game, a culture of war in which fear is the organizing principle and life is a contest for survival accepted not only as normal and natural, but necessary.*

- *In the Duchess' Game a Faustian bargain is made between adults and children and in the process life's original play is adulterated into cultural play.*

- *In the Duchess' Game children are expendable and childhood is null and void.*

- *But we have an unexplored choice of a living world story in which we can choose to thrive not merely survive. This is a profound shift in human consciousness, unlike any that has come before.*

- *The living world story is based on a conspiracy hidden within childhood that restructures the social contract between humans and life.*

- *Children's enthusiasm delivers Creation's message—life is to be lived as one. This pact with the divine is the genesis of original play in which the divine and human meet as the pattern that connects, a secret sympathy, hidden in the profusion and diversity of life, and so pledged to reproduce its underlying connective pattern, on however small a scale, so that the original design is there for the spirit to discover and follow.*

- *Original play is a code of peace whose wisdom is at once biological and spiritual, ecological, and ecumenical.*

- *Original play's breathtakingly ingenious neural pattern recognition system is an innate ecological intelligence or pattern of kindfullness that not only recognizes that all life is of only one kind, but embodies an emergent pattern of behavior that sustains this sense of life's deep belonging.*

- *Original play is an ongoing process of open-heart surgery in which whole-hearted practice as well as a set of heartfelt principles enable us to feel the underlying unity beneath life's diversity.*

- *Original play bestows upon children a latitude of freedom that they know exactly what to do with. Come join them and play as if your life depends upon it—it does.*

# How To Read This Book

Original play rearranges the patterns of our minds, bodies and hearts. It is a total endeavor requiring a transformation of your entire being. This book has taken 20 years to write; it will take more than a reading, more than a workshop to rediscover that the practice of Original Play® is based on your heart's intention.

*Do not read this book as you would a novel for entertainment. Do not read this book as a "how to do it" manual as if you are searching for the rules of a game.* You may, instead, approach it as you would read a Haiku poem or look at a Chinese landscape painting; much is left open for you to fill in.

*Original play must be experienced to be realized.* I am often asked why I don't put exercises in the book. Why I don't write out clear and precise formats and rules for others to follow. Original play is not learned by following pre-established formats. I place a great deal of responsibility upon you, the reader, to not only thoughtfully assess my ideas, but to add your own play experiences. Many of the ideas in this book will require playing to fully understand what I have written.

*You must make the choice to play in order to understand the lessons of original play.* I cannot do that for you. I can, however, invite and guide. I can hold your hand, provoke your mind, and inspire your heart.

*For that purpose, I invite you to join me and re-play your life.* The more you play the more this book will make sense. As your practice changes you this book will change along with you. You can find out more about Original Play® and my lectures, workshops, and seminars by contacting me at either ofreddybear@aol.com or www.originalplay.eu.

# Prologue: The Name of the Game

*How easy it is to become learned,*
*How difficult it is to become human.*
— Nur Ali Elahi

*"Man is a messenger who forgot the message."*
— Abraham Joshua Heschel

*"God has imprinted on man's heart a Law which his conscience*
*enjoins him to obey."*
— Pope John XXIII

*"...I learned that all human stories in this world contain*
*many lost or unwritten or unreadable or unwritable pages*
*and that the truth about us, though it must exist,*
*though it must lie around us every day, is mostly hidden*
*from us, like bird's nests in the woods."*
— Wendell Berry

*Playing For Real* is about two stories of the game of life. Both stories begin the same. "Once upon a time.... But they quickly and starkly diverge into very different plots. Here are two such stories, one allegory, one true, one traditional, one modern, depicting the choice between the dying and living worlds. Fauliot shares an old Japanese tale.

"One day a samurai came to see the Zen master Hakuin and asked him,"Is there truly a heaven and hell?"

"Who are you?" the master asked.

"I am the samurai..."

"You, a soldier!" Hakuin exclaimed. "Just look at yourself. What lord would want you in his service? You look like a beggar."

The samurai grew angry and drew his sword. Hakuin continued: "Oh, good you even have a sword! But you are certainly too clumsy to cut off my head with it."

Losing all self-control, the samurai raised his sword, ready to strike the master. At that very moment the latter spoke, saying, "Here is where the

12

gates to hell open."

Surprised by the monk's air of calm assurance, the samurai sheathed his sword and bowed before him.

"This is where the gates of heaven open," the master then said.

We now move from traditional Japan to modern New York City. A young man confronts the same issue as that faced by the samurai. "A young man pleads with me, can you help me not to fight? When someone even touches me I hit without thinking. I'm tired of fighting and being in the principal's office every day. I'm tired of having to talk with the police."

The speaker is an eighteen-year-old gang member in a New York City workshop I gave for gang leaders. He stopped me during a break to talk. I asked him if he would come up in front of the others with me after the break. He shrugged and agreed. After the break we stood facing each other about a foot apart. I whispered to him, "Can I push you?" He nodded yes. I put my hand on his shoulder and pushed him sideways. He hardly shifted his feet. He is about six feet and around 200 pounds. I whispered, "Can I push you harder?" He shrugged and nodded. I shoved him harder this time. Reflexively his right fist came toward my face. I deflected his fist with the back of my right hand as it neared my left cheek. I spiraled it away in an "S" motion bringing it down to my chest where I held it softly against me. I looked in his eyes and released his hand. We hugged and sat down.

When I sat down the young woman sitting next to me whispered, "Did you see his eyes?"

"Yes, I know." I nodded. He was crying.

Like the samurai, the teenager's reflexive response to a conflict was aggression. Also like the samurai, the teenager was then presented with an unprecedented reaction. The teenage gang member punched but there was no victim, no aggressor, no blame, no fault, no revenge. This is the promise of original play—the possibility of dissolving aggression and victimization, that seems improbable, if not impossible. When the twenty-five gang leaders and I were saying goodbye on the street after the play session the young man came up to me.

"Can I learn to do this with children?"

"Of course," I said. We hugged again and went our separate ways. But not as separate as before.

The samurai and the teenager experienced the choice between the living and dying world stories. In both stories attack was the habitual response to threat, perceived or real. In both cases the intended victim disappeared as a victim. Original play creates a deep sense of belonging in which there is no difference that makes a difference. This is the moment when a playground is created, an "out-of-this-world" time space within which two people have the opportunity to create a new relationship of belonging that is literally outside the categories of their normal worlds. It's not that they don't acknowledge the cultural world, it's that they don't accept the consequences of thinking in its categories.

> *Out beyond ideas of wrongdoing and rightdoing, there is a field.*
> *I'll meet you there.* – Rumi

I experienced both types of stories in my childhood. One tale I was taught by my culture. In this story the name of the game is *Won* and it is played for keeps. This is by far the more common story. When I was a young boy the world was full of contests in my family, school, and neighborhood. I saw movies of cowboys and Indians every Saturday. I played war games outside in the neighborhood and with tiny soldiers in my room. I played baseball, football, and ice hockey. Contests shaped my attitudes, and provided me with purpose.

## *Fred, there's nothing to be afraid of.*

I was fortunate as a child to have exposure to a different kind of story. When I was young my mother taught on a Native American reservation. Some days she would take me with her. I would join the kids in the one-room school house. After school I would play with them. One day I was taken for a walk by one of the elders. I called him Grandfather. I never knew what to expect when this happened. Our walks were usually silent. There was no fuss about him; it was just the way he was. On this day in his soft voice he whispered, "Fred, There's nothing to be afraid of." He spoke as if he was bypassing my mind and speaking directly to my heart. I'm sure he could tell that my mind could not grasp what he was saying. I wondered what world he lived in. I could think of many things to be afraid of in my world. He was quietly hinting at another kind of story. It was to take over twenty years before his hint had any meaning for me. Then I would discover the coherence of the world in which he belonged. In his story the name of the game is one and it is played for real. This is the story I was to be shown by the children.

What this book sets out to demonstrate is that there are two stories which we can use to guide our lives. The one with which we are all familiar, I call a dying world story. The one which remains largely unheard and unexperienced, I call a living world story. The patterns of life the latter story tells serve a far deeper and more significant purpose in our lives than we have realized; indeed this importance could not be more profound. We have a choice of which story to live.

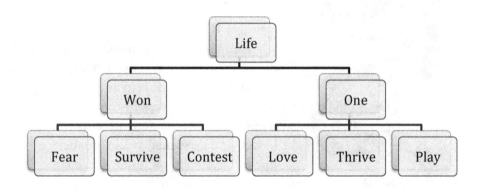

*Figure 1: Two Stories of Life*

"Once upon a time..." At first, *Creation* was reluctant to reveal the mysteries of its intoxicating, sacred processes to humankind. Eventually, however, for unclear reasons, under unknown circumstances, God yielded and divulged secrets. One of these messages was especially guarded because it penetrated secrets that were engraved at the very heart of the universe. Humans were granted this message knowing that it would engender human wisdom, but if misunderstood, would result in malice, cunning, and revenge. Though Creation gave humans the message, it trembled as it considered humankind's potential for misunderstanding.

# Be as quiet as you can.

If you listen very carefully you can hear it—a story more ancient than the human race. When your body grows weary for the night and the darkness rises around you, the stars are shooting, and from across whirling light years Creation calls your name and whispers, "I have endowed you with a gift— I tell you that life is to be lived as *One*." Did you hear correctly? Is the game of life to be played as *One*, or is it to be played as *Won*?

Stages of *Playing for Real*

The burden of these messages is always the same. Someone gets the message wrong. We hear, "Life is to be lived as *Won*." Then the inevitablity of conflict is mistakenly written into our script. In fact we believe that, as Christopher Booker writes without some measure of conflict there cannot be a story. Our error seems impossible to correct. The entire edifice of human life is built upon the misunderstanding on one small word— *One*. Our misinterpretation of the message opens the way for struggle, conflict, and war to intrude into the world. And intrude they do.

An ancient version of this story is found in a tale told among the Bushmen of the Kalahari. It seems that in the beginning the moon looked down upon the earth and saw that everyone was afraid of death. The moon out of unfailing love choose the hare, because he was the swiftest, to go and tell all people on earth to look up at the moon and know that as I am dying I am renewed, as they will be. The hare was in such a hurry that it got the message wrong and told the people of the earth: "Unlike the moon who in dying is renewed, you will not be renewed again." The moon was so furious with the hare that it bit it on the lip. That is why the hare still has a split lip, as a sign that he gave the wrong message regarding a universal promise.

Creation was right to be concerned. Humans are in just as much of a hurry as the hare. As Winston Churchill commented, "Certain it is that while men are gathering knowledge and power with ever increasing and measureless speed, their virtues and their wisdom has not shown any notable improvement as the centuries have rolled." Like the hare humans misinterpret Creation's message: "Life is to be lived as *One*." In their haste what humans hear is "Life is to be lived as *Won*." Such a small word, but it has made all the difference in the world.

Many historians and social scientists, including van Crefeld, Keegan, Hillman, and Stevens have pointed out that conflict and war play a critical role in human culture. Others, including Heraclitus, Augustine, Hegel, Marx, Jung, Lorenz, Ardrey, deChardin, and Prigogine believe, for example, that conflict produces our immense material and biological creativity. The game of war, for example, is thought by van Creveld to be "the greatest joy of all." Others proclaim that war and fighting are sublime, lovely and "like kids letting loose, fighting is the way we learn to be who we are." As Evan Thomas puts it, "War has been, for almost all peoples and all times, the purest test of manhood." Thomas describes Theodore Roosevelt as a "true war lover" who wanted to test himself in the crucible of battle." U.S. Supreme Court Justice Oliver Wendell Holmes Jr. lectured Harvard students that "war was 'divine,' not to be missed." Combat is a game and like kids' games the point is to win. Our "wars" are simply the normal outgrowths of our "every person for themselves" ideology. There is a story about Alfred van Schlieffen, the German Chief of Staff who summed up the purpose of war, "Yes... it all comes down to this foolish question, how to win." As General Thomas Powell, SAC commander has said regarding nuclear war, if "two Americans are left, to one Russian, we win."

This shrinking can reach the point where people will choose to live with a known tyranny rather than to escape to an unknown freedom.

We have accepted the game of won and its story as natural and necessary parts of our lives and interpreted our survival in their terms. And in turn we have created societies that worshop *Won* and have forgotten the gift of *One*. The result is a distortion of consciousness in which we believe that we are strangers in a dangerous world in which our only hope of survival is self-defense. Unable to perceive beyond our fearful categories we have shrunk the world to meet our fears. Like some naïve observer blindly watching a magic show, fooled by culture's slight of mind, confused by its elaborate array of dazzling categories—we are misdirected and misled into thinking that it is the game of *Won* and its dying world story itself that is the basis of life, its moral order and cohesion, as well as the source of its vitality and creative powers. The result is a homespun tale of elemental and global violence.

There has been and remains only one war. While the characters change, the plot remains the same. Our dying world story is a kind of monster story, but not just another fairy tale to frighten children. Booker points out that, "There are few cultures in the world which have not produced some version of the overcoming the monster story." These are alpha predator contests in which a superhuman embodiment of evil power threatens a community, kingdom, or the world. For example, the first part of the earliest written story in human history, dating back to the dawn of civilization, the Sumerian Epic of Gilgamesh tells of how the kingdom of Uruk had fallen under the shadow of a great and mysterious evil figure, Humbaba. Later we have St. George versus the dragon, Theseus versus the Minotaur, Odysseus versus Polyphemus, Beowuf versus Grendel, to name just a few of our legendary contests. The hero of the epic must confront the monster in a fight to the death. Eventually the power of the creature must be confronted and overthrown. Such monsters are potent creatures, whether they dwell in our imaginations or our environments, in our closets or our oceans, they remind us of our story's inescapable theme of our struggle with a hostile world.

Like other fairy tales, we pass our monster story on to our children as if it were some priceless heirloom. Our monster story is different; it is not embodied in a mythical or metaphorical *alpha* predator, nor does it hide in a closet nor under the bed. But there is a profound difference between our monster and all the others—unlike dragons and goblins, we believe in this one. Our monster is an idea that we have become as attached to as barnacles on a ship's hull. This story tells of an unfriendly universe in which we must constantly struggle to survive. As a world view, our monster story severely limits our ability to sustain life on earth. Contest, struggle, and cruelty we are told, are part of nature and the source of our development, intelligence, and strength. Without them we believe that we could not meet life's challenges.

A deep crisis occurs when a people's story becomes inadequate to meet their needs. Our story traps us in a sort of moral twilight. In such a fog we no longer are, nor do we know how to be, the people we are meant to be. Tagore correctly described this as, "a perilously losing game, in which man stakes his all, to gain a part." In our rest periods that we call peace, we persuade ourselves that we are civilized until the next version of our wars makes quaint the one that went before. As Thomas Merton put it, "In such a situation we speak peace with our lips but the answer in the heart is war, and war only."

Our current story is normative, but inadequate to meet our needs. While we firmly believe in it and act according to its dictates, our dying world story is dysfunctional. The dying world story is one part of a complex of elements that together sever the ecological mind disconnecting us from our original sense of belonging. We are victims of a misunderstanding of which we imagine ourselves to be beneficiaries. Our lack of awareness in the consequences of our story is expressed in an anecdote of the Second World War in which a German officer visited Picasso in his Paris studio. The officer saw Guernica and shocked at the modernest "chaos" of the painting, asked Picasso: 'Did you do this?" Picasso calmly replied,: 'No, *you* did this! " In the Bushmen's story the hare's penalty is a split lip. Our legacy is a poverty of spirit that touches everyone.

Ernest Becker has written that, "There is simply no way to transcend the limits of the human condition or to change the psychological structural conditions that make humanity possible." Living with the dying world story, however, we have no idea what humanity's limits and structural conditions really are. "What if," asks Albert Camus, "these forces wind up in a dead end, what if that logic of history on which so many now rely turns out to be a will o' the wisp?"

Fortunately, there is another story to be told with a new plot for living which transforms every aspect of human life, our social and cultural forms, and the underlying pattern and purpose of our individual lives. If we listen again with new ears perhaps we can hear it. With new voices we can begin to pass on a living world story.

## Again be as quiet as you can.

If you listen very carefully you can hear it—a story more ancient than the human race. When your body grows weary for the night and the darkness rises around you, the stars are shooting, and from across whirling light years Creation calls your name and whispers, "I have endowed you with a gift— I tell you that Life is to be lived as *One*." This time we hear correctly. The real game of life is to be played as *One*.

"Once upon a time..." Having whispered the secret to us God returns to the task at hand—so to speak. God had his hands full making all the really big things like stars, planets, and the cosmos. Then God made all the smaller things, mountains, oceans, and trees. After that came all the animals. What a "fun time" God had fashioning all the different shapes of animals... like the giraffe, butterfly, and manta ray. Finally, on the seventh day, God got around to people. While God was busy working on the complicated body, a rush of wings startled him. Being so engrossed by making people, God had forgotten all about the Earth. Meanwhile, a little bird, probably a chickadee, was fluttering hither and yon over the Earth as though it were frightened. Forgetting that at the angel's request God had made birds with wings—so that there would be something like angels on earth, God smiled and said, "The birds are always flying about. Can someone help him find his way home?""

God soon forgot the bird and re-immersed herself in making a person. Before God knew it, St. Nicholas, who stands especially high in God's esteem, came up and said through his great white beard; "I'll help. Oh, by the way, unlike the birds, your lions are sitting quite still, and very haughty beasts they are, I must say."

Looking down and contemplating his handiwork on earth and seeing the teeming life of plants and animals, God replied to St. Nicholas, You think lions should fly? If you don't like my lions, you try and make some yourself."

Well, while God's attention was diverted to look at the lions on earth, his hands continued working on the person. Suddenly out of the corner of his eye God saw something small falling through space. He called to his hands, who were all smeared with clay.

"Where is my person?" God thundered. "Oops," said the right hand

20

to the left, "We dropped it." "What do you mean, we?" responded the left hand.

So, people, rendered as only Creation can, fell to earth unfinished. We are outsourced by Creation. This may seem like a crisis, but, as the Chinese calligraphy for crisis suggests, this is instead both a challenge and an opportunity.

How wonderful that we are challenged to be who we are meant to be and simultaneously given the opportunity to share in our creation. The future unfolding of the possible human depends upon the finishing job done by human hands which helps explain original play's role in the creation of a human being.

When I use the words *Creation* or *God* throughout this book I am referring to the ineffable presence that goes by many names including, *God, Allah, Great Spirit, One, Logos, Tao, Brahman, Buddha, Krishna, Wakan Tanka, The Universal Spirit or Principle.*

Thus begins an entirely new story of human life. *Playing for Real* is childhood's dream and a living world story revealing our astonishing, genuine, and intimate connection with all life. This story is written with the soul's calligraphy. Its words are merely rough notations whose meanings are known only to the heart. It's mysteries, both our most demanding and most rewarding work in this world, must be lived to be known. For if they are not they remain dusty archives in a museum of the never lived and nothing more.

This is a story told, but not yet heard. There is no way around it, living this story runs counter to much of what we have accepted as true. The nature of the change required of us demands a creative leap of imagination as well as a giant step into a new way of living. Should we falter on our path, and we surely will, some angels will grumble, but will support us nonetheless for they know that we are trudging along the best we can. For as much as they might moan over our bumbling, our efforts always make them laugh. And they shout along with children, "Please come out and play, for then perhaps you'll meet God."

# Part I:

---

## The World As Won: Childhood's Dream Deferred

*And there went out another horse that was red: and power was given to him that sat thereon to take peace from the earth, and that they should kill one another.*
—Revelation 6:4

*We have forgotten most of our childhood, not only its contents but its flavor...*
—R.D. Laing

*"I was eleven years old, but I no longer knew how to play. What I wanted and needed was warmth and loving care."*
—Eva Mozes Kor,

*"Can God fight?"*
—Five-year-old Teddy's question to his father
Theodore Roosevelt

# CHAPTER 1:

# The Nightfall of the Human Spirit:
# The Pathogenesis of Won

*"Man exists only in so far as he is opposed."*
—George Hegel

*"Hate came, I don't know from where."*
—19-year-old Tarja Krehic, Bosnia

*The taking of a single life is equivalent to the destruction of the world.*
—Qur'an 5:32

*Between two groups of men that want to make inconsistent kinds of worlds I see no remedy except force...*
*It seems to me that every society rests on the death of men."*
—Oliver Wendell Holmes

# The Time of the Hyena

*"What a long train of dead bodies follows in
the wake of a single living person!"*
—Chao-chou

*"Must man always be brute first and man after, if at all?"*
—Paramahansa Yogananda

*Alas, do all living creatures kill one another?*
—Gautama Buddha

"Hello, out there! God, This is us."

"Who?"

"Us, you know. We are praying again to you for peace."

"What is it this time? Are you looking for heavenly disaster relief yet again?"

"You have not answered our many prayers. Help us find peace."

"But I have, on the off chance that you might listen. A shaky assumption I admit.

Help Us!"

God thunders in response. "You think of yourselves as so important that I can stop whatever I'm doing to care for you? Such vanity! I try to help you, but you don't listen. You act as if peace is an aberration and war is supposed to be the norm. You may ask for peace, but you live for war. You are always telling me what I want as if you know what is best for me. You are a nuisance. Sometimes I think you are a disgrace to the human race." Sadly, as if having lost faith in his work, God laments, "I continually send you my message but you refuse to listen or repeatedly misinterpret it into what you want to hear. Anyway, I'm really tired of being on everyone's side." What would you do with yourselves if you spent all of your time being kind rather than fighting? Then almost as an afterthought God adds, "You do everything you think I say and nothing I actually say. One thing I have no worry about is whether there is intelligent life in the universe. But it has occurred to me that it isn't you. I'm thinking that because of your behavioral defects, I will conduct a massive recall."

In the above dialogue God senses that our minds have been invaded by the darkness described by Laurens van der Post in the Bushman expression, "the time of the hyena," when "the light of the mind is invaded by darkness." The time of the hyena is the nightfall of the human spirit. In this darkness wisdom is destroyed by fear and life loses it's preciousness. Pressed into service of fear, life is stripped of its vitalizing capacity, making wisdom and the ecological mind impossible. Hallie shares the darkness of our plight as shown in the words of a child who was going into the Nazi gas chambers with her mother. Her child says, "'Mother it's dark, it's so dark, and I was being so good."

Do human beings exist? Not yet. This process is not only the death of a living being, of a living process, not just the death of a process, but in its extreme expression of *the* living process. We become deadened to the extent that our abnormal reactions to abnormal events become normalized. With fear as the organizing principle of life humans are "taken out of context." We no longer feel our original state of belonging to all life. In its place we have assumed that contest whether on the battlefield, in the courtroom, boardroom, or playground is the crucible for human behavior. Benjamin Franklin explained that, "The problem of war was essentially a competitive race to the bottom, a problem of pathological and ultimately fruitless competition among nations." Our assumptions about life as a contest are so widespread and habitual that it is very difficult to escape them. Most of us assume that there is no alternative to self-defense as a moral code just as we assume that there is no alternative to survival as the biological imperative. Our sickness, however, is so prevalent that it is not recognized as an ailment. Our minds are circumscribed within the narrow limits inposed by our habitual belief in contests as our only way of life. It is as if we are suffering from a form of collective anosognosia, a condition in which a person, in our case a species, suffers a disability but is unaware of the existence of their disability. For such a person living a widespread malaise or cultural autism, it makes no sense at all to talk about peace, it simply does not exist. The result is that we are living what Edward Abbey called "the ideology of the cancer cell." We may be able to survive in such a world, but we cannot thrive.

*"War is desired by men, deliberately, in defiance of the most sacred laws. That is what makes it so evil."*
—Pope John XXIII

The "time of the hyena" is a profound narrowing of consciousness, in which a person lives a partial life and calls it whole. It's as if one of life's most worthwhile experiences is cathartic destruction. What we lack in integrity and compassion we think we make up for with self defense skills. We are no longer aware of the importance of what we must know in other ways, of the living experience existing before and beyond our fears. Stripped as we are of our natural armaments we must defend ourselves. Without an enemy such a person loses their bearing, and all sense of proportion. For example, Steinberg writes that in the world of Pollsmoor Prison in Cape Town, South Africa this pathology was described by a warder as "a world of all against all." This internal world is described by Steinberg as, "a violent game between captors and convicts."

> *And fastened to a dying animal*
> *It knows not what it is...*
> —W.B. Yeats, "Sailing To Byzantium"

As Yeats points out we are duped by our contests into becoming unknowing "dying animals." A "dying animal" attracts predators. Our hearts are destroyed suppressing our inner need to trust life and each other. In the process we lose our heart's compass, our moral direction. We become someone other than the humans we are meant to be. Annihilated as people, we are no longer able to recognize humanity in ourselves or others. For example, when First Platoon members murdered an Iraqi family and raped their teenage daughter in March 2006, Sergeant Diem described them as "becoming something monstrous." We may be sane, but we are certainly not in our right minds.

There are five major themes that form the time of the hyena. Together they create an ethos of beliefs, aspirations, and practices that combine to form a vicious spiral of individual and structural violence with extensive areas of overlap. In fact, they rarely are separate. Their redundancy makes them very dangerous. A small escalation in one theme is amplified by other themes creating a cascade effect as the situation grows continually worse. At each increasing level of escalation one's satisfaction must be re-calibrated. What satisfied yesterday is meager today. The pathogenesis of won becomes its own nuclear reactor in which the dying world story creates the small cage habit, which generates the Duchess' game, which forms the Faustian bargain, which produces the nullification of childhood, which recreates the dying world story. In the Game's vicious spiral whatever is necessary to survive or vindicate one's right is acceptable. For despite all of the suffering resulting from the moral contest between ends and means, very few people are interested enough and willing to dismantle the infrastructure of war. If life can only be lived in this way then contest is an addiction and death begins to have a strange charm. This results in a profound moral failure —when we play to win every victory is a funeral.

- First, we are told a *dying world story* admonishing us of the necessity of competing for survival in a world of contest.

- Second, tricked into a world of conflict, isolation, and separation we disconnect and learn self-defense which disables our ability to accurately perceive options even when they are available to us. I call this the *Small Cage Habit*.

- Third, this habit is a fear based system of contest behavior in which life is a contest for survival called *the Duchess' Game*.

- Fourth, to maintain the continuity of the game children are forced to trade their original sense of belonging to all life for membership in a culture. I call this *The Faustain Bargain*

- Fifth, in this bargain childhood is adulterated and children become commodities, cannon fodder, and ciphers. Childhood becomes *null and void*.

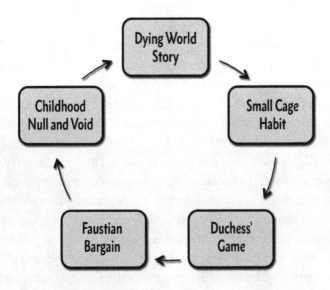

*Figure 2: The Pathogenesis of Won*

28

# The Metastasis from the Small Cage Habit To The Duchess' Game

*A warrior lives on his wars... and he suffers a collapse if he finds that his warring capacity is no longer wanted."*
—Mohandas K. Gandhi

O nce there was a bear that lived in a zoo in a mid-western town in America. He was a large bear living in a small cage. When the bear wasn't eating or sleeping he was pacing ten steps one way and ten steps back the other way, back and forth all day long. Anyone who has spent time visiting a zoo is familiar with this scene.

One day two children, named Magda and Michal, visited the zoo and watched the bear pace back and forth. They felt very sorry for the bear. They looked at each other and knew what they must do. They ran to the zookeeper and asked if a bigger enclosure could be built for the sad bear. He told them that the zoo didn't have enough money. So the next day Magda and Michal went to see the mayor. It was the same story. He told them that he was sorry, but it was a small zoo in a small town and there was no money for a bigger cage.

Michal and Magda decided to help the bear. They went around the town collecting money to build a bigger cage for the bear. They gave the money to the mayor who designated it for the new bear enclosure. The zookeeper built a large, open space for the bear. When the new enclosure was completed there was great excitement in the small town. All the townspeople showed up for the opening. The mayor gave a speech. Magda and Michal were asked to lead the ceremony and help the zookeeper open the small cage so the bear could walk into his new space. The crowd was quiet with anticipation as the large bear stepped out of his small cage. The sad bear looked out and slowly took one step, two, three, seven, ten and then... the bear turned around and paced back ten steps. To the shocked amazement of the crowd, the mayor, the zookeeper, and especially Michal and Magda that bear paced over and over the same ten steps in his large space that he had done in his small cage. Ten steps. This is all the bear knew. Even when placed in a much larger environment he could revert only to the habit he knew — ten steps.

* I'm told that the original version of the story is credited to Dr. Harry Emerson Fosdick, a minister, author, and radio personality in St. Louis. In

the 1920's he visited the St. Louis zoo and watched a polar bear pace back and forth. When he asked the zoo keeper about it he called it the small cage habit. This story appeared in the Journal of Creative Behavior. V. 14 (2), 75-76, 1980.

Humans are like the bear in the story. Like the bear our habits limit our reality even when the limits that created the habits are taken away. We contest with the world even when we don't have to. For example, framing life as a fearful contest is a symptom of a vast biological malignancy and has a great deal to do with our inability to thrive. We suffer from a massive failure of imagination. We become hemmed in, confined by the hard, unyielding ideas of our contest habits. At first unknowingly, but when we grow accustomed to our boundaries we are terrified that these may break apart and leave us alone, helpless and gasping for air like a fish out of water.

Unlike the bear cage, our enclosure is not made of bars but of ideas. Make no mistake these ideas create a cage of the most dangerous kind—a myopia that confines us in endless cycles of pathological aggression and revenge based on ideas such as war is necessary; contests are natural; fear helps us stay alive; winning is most important; men need to fight; and revenge brings closure. This attitude towards war has been likened by Tom Christie a Pentagon weapons tester to a sexual drive, "Persistent, urgent and natural." Constructed of such ideas the small cage habit confines minds in what William Blake called, "mind-forged manacles." J. Dee Higley relates that, "Now we know that if you keep a primate in a single cage, you are very likely to have an abnormal animal." We may still think of ourselves as human, but we are less humane.

Eventually our ability for self-integration, our attachment capabilities to others, and our decision-making capacities are disrupted. For example, Steiner writes about Lydia, a Jewish girl of the Vilna ghetto in Poland who exclaims, "I am nothing. I am neither girl nor woman. I am only hate. I live only for vengeance." This is the posture of someone who feels basically threatened and insecure, who has nothing to gain and therefore nothing to lose. The essence of this process is self-defense. The price we pay for this contest created self is the necessity to prolong and defend it endlessly from all assaults, real and imagined, in order to survive and keep from being undervalued personally and by the group. Our psychic and physical energy is depleted by such conflicts. With time a small cage habit metastasizes into what I call the Duchess' Game.

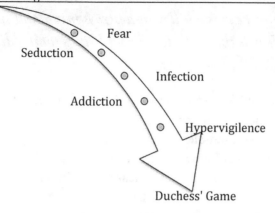

**Figure 3: The Metastatic Process From The Small Cage Habit To The Duchess' Game**

Like a cancer cell the game multiplies as if it is genetically programmed to do so. The malignancy of the small cage habit progresses through five stages to reach the Duchess' Game. These are: fear, seduction, infection, addiction, and hypervigilance. Together they form a deadly spiral made up of countless individual choices, actions, evasions, rationalizations, and compromises. The habit metastasizes throughout a body of culture, sustained by patterns of thought and behavior enshrined in a code of contest ethics found in socioeconomic, political, educational, and healthcare systems.

## Fear

*"I was once a little child,*
*Three years ago,*
*That child who longed for other worlds.*
*But now I am no more a child*
*For I have learned to hate.*
*I am a grown-up person now,*
*I have known fear."*

—Hanus Hachenburg, (died December 18, 1943, in Auschwitz)

*"I must not fear. Fear is a killer; it destroys mind and spirit, as well as body. "Fear is the little death that brings total obliteration."*
—Frank Herbert

The small cage habit's deadly spiral is rooted in fear. Fear is considered a natural emotion and a necessary component of survival. According to the I-Ching No. 51, for example, "All things in the cosmos will be aroused to movement through fear." Fear seems to be our most potent emotion and is programmed into our DNA. This fear is lived in our hearts, minds and bodies, mutating us into beings far less than who we are meant to be. Karen Armstrong writes that, "every single fundamentalist movement that I have studied in Judaism, Christianity and Islam is rooted in fear."

The small cage habit of fear is dangerously insular. Contest pathology affects not only the way information is processed in the brain but how we respond to that information making it difficult to sense the world without fear. Ashley Montagu adds that, "the unloved person, taken at any age, is likely to be a very different biochemical entity from those who have been adequately loved." In fact, a sustained self-defense response inhibits the creation of life-sustaining energy. Ellis Amdur points out that, "Knowledge learned in a state of fear then requires fear as a component when used in another setting."

Separated as we are from our sense of belonging to all life, we feel that we must constantly defend ourselves in order to survive. A fearful person often has impaired judgment, a low tolerance for frustration, a willingness to do whatever is necessary for group acceptance, a sense of entitlement, and a capacity to distance oneself from violence, particularly that which they inflict. But the longer one stays in self defense the more necessary it seems and the more growth is compromised. Rees points out, for example, that many people who decried violence in Germany in the rise of Hitler came to support and even welcome it when they saw it as giving them a sense of peace and security.

As contests become our habitual response to the world they disappear into the white noise of cultural background. Such fear is often institutionalized. As James Carroll describes, "Leaders who are afraid do terrible things, not least by making their nations afraid."

For example, Mun Chol, a resident of Pyongyang, North Korea, declared following his country's third nuclear test, "Now we have nothing to be afraid of in the world." In the United States, for example, fear of outsiders has spawned a vast Homeland Security industry. In 1999 there were nine companies with federal homeland security contracts; in 2003 there were 3,512, and in 2006 there were 33,890 such companies. Fear is more than a thriving business. In 2008 Scurlock points out that fear took over as the basis for the world economy.

Neither the meaning of our being nor the possibility of our spirit can be expressed or created by the means that we use to win our way through life. Furthermore, the concepts on which we base our actions are unworthy of the being that clamors to be released. A fearful, unloved human remains in silence, the silence that falls when all connection is broken between one and another. The result is a psychosis of fear which is all the more debilitating when it is not objectively justified, leading then to a mythification of power. In such cases fear becomes a permanent menace attaining exaggerated proportions simply because of its invisibility.

## Seduction

Being such fearful creatures we are easily seduced into believing that our contests will provide us with the security that we crave. It is so much a part of who we are and what we do that we don't question its morality or efficacy. Behind this claim of "is" lies the self-justifying claim of "ought." We have created, however, a fearful cage that is a catch 22, a paradoxical situation in which we depend upon a system of thought to change our dependence upon a way of thinking that we believe cannot be changed. For example, while we want peace, we believe that the conditions that would lead to peace cannot be obtained except through war. We follow the Roman Senate's principle as if it was indelibly imprinted in our hearts, "If you want peace, prepare for war." During the Cold War, for example, our "normality led to a lethal exchange of nuclear growth between the USA and the Soviet Union called MAD (Mutual Assured Destruction). In this game expediency trumps wisdom as evil outcomes are morally permissible. Legitimacy is achieved by assertion and deception. Arms control means weapons accumulation. The result is that we have a commitment to a contest order believing it to be a lifeline, when in actuality it is a deathtrap.

The small cage habit arranges the world in such a way that we don't have to experience the consequences of our actions. This small cage habit requires that we must learn to disengage ourselves from others and our inner sense of well being. Having made one false move, we are led into another and another in an increasingly desperate bid to shore up our defenses. This must not be recognized as being bad, but rather merely living by the rules. One is just doing his job. We also must believe that what we are doing makes good, logical sense and is the authentic experience of our sense of self. Our deceit must be flawless, the last thing we must do is admit that our participation in contests is meaningless. I witnessed such a lesson in contest etiquette with a special needs boy in California. It was at a staff review for Danny. Danny was a five year old abused child with I had been playing for about nine months. At the time Danny lived in a residential care facility. There were fifteen adults in this meeting, thirteen were staff of the center, myself and my Director. I normally did not attend them, but my Director thought it would be good for me to experience such a meeting.

At one point in the meeting a staff member described a race she had organized for the kids in her unit, which included Danny. She was concerned about Danny's "refusal to play" with the other children in the race. She said with a mocking laugh, "He didn't even know how to race." She said that he ran along with the others laughing and going in all directions instead of straight to the finish line like the other children." She recorded on his chart that "He refused to play."

Jan, my director smiled at me and put her hand on my arm, telling me to be quiet. I now understood why she wanted me to attend and why I didn't want to go. There was no place in the woman's competitive mind or her chart for Danny's play. He knew how to play; he just didn't know that in the adult world in order to play he had to compete.

The game's seduction demands a very high price. The Duchess' Game makes its pathology seem normal. The Game's effects are not accidental nor are they random in effect. Yet there is the feeling that the Game is something that happens to us, not something that we do. Inequalities may be unfortunate; victims may be unlucky but not unjust—just part of the Game.

# Infection

Seduced by our contests the dying world story implants fear within us that acts like a cancerous tumor, infecting us with the seeds of a parasitic relationship that metastasizes and infects our entire life cycle. This fear acts like a parasite, perfectly designed to infiltrate human hosts. For the most part this conviction of the world as a contest for survival pitting one against all is thought to lie deep within us like some kind of latent infection. The result is an pandemic pathology, usually defined as a disease that is a deviation from the normal. But in this case the pathology is the normal. As Ernest Becker points out, "If everybody lives roughly the same lies about the same things, there is no one to call them liars: they jointly establish their own sanity and call themselves normal." In the game we normalize what isn't normal to cope or survive the game's brutality.

In time the abnormal becomes the norm. But it is more than individuals pursuing their personal eccentricities. In time the small cage habit becomes an undetected learning disability, a habit of body, mind and spirit that channels a deep personal insecurity into a fearful culture forming legacy. There is no wisdom in our small cage behavior. We squander our moral capital on our competitive competence. As Bruce Lipton points out, "The simple truth is when you're frightened you're dumber." It is much easier to know what is right than to put it into practice.

## Addiction

The Duchess' Game requires a great deal from its participants. We must give our allegiance to a contest system devoted to the creation and maintenance of false selves. In this process we are able to sustain such a minimal amount of self-esteem that we must seek our security from outside sources. Others must lose so that we can win. This cage is very difficult to recognize largely because we don't see it as a cage. We accept our contest model of life as a factual explanation of the universe. The result is that people no longer see contest for what it is, a deceptive addiction, but accept it for what it isn't, a harmless game. Recently I saw an ad on Swedish TV for a video war game. It was described as addictive. This is, of course, seen as a positive attribute of the war game. Joel Bakan says, "addiction' has become the gold standard of gaming, the true mark of a game worth playing." Our extraction from our original world of play is so complete that we lose all contact with that childhood self and discredit the instincts through which it was sustained.

What makes contest's small cage so dangerous is that it's very difficult to compete just once. Contest is our foremost addiction. Contest is an enticing elixir that hides a lethal addiction raised to an article of faith. Like a hand that falls asleep, we become out of touch, experiencing a sensory cut off which results in difficulty in connecting with ourselves or others. The impulses are not correctly given or received. Like powerful narcotics, contests promise to solve all of our problems, but instead reinforce the very disease they profess to counteract. We have assumed that a failure in contest at one level can be remedied later by a larger contest. As every addict knows, "You can't win just once." So, like other addictions we must constantly "up the dose" in order to sustain the gratification. Each time we feel a mini-climax, which cannot lead to satisfaction, it requires something stronger to achieve the next surge. Like the addict who pays dearly for the source of his own death we stumble forward into the addict's downward spiral. Nobody has to hate us, because we've beat them to it. We continue to defend and attack because we must press upon others that we are not the failures whom we think others think we are. This becomes the sane well-adjusted person. Such a person is like Adolf Eichmann, well adapted to the needs and dictates of the social system which he or she carries out in an orderly, cool fashion.

Like addicts everywhere contestants think of themselves as impervious to the Game's victimization. We believe so steadfastly in the efficacy of contests that we pursue the Duchess' Game endlessly in the vain hope that its bribes, membership, money, position and trinkets, awards and prizes are the stuff that satisfies the soul. The result is a person who is vision less yet wholly image, with a storm in his or her heart that rages over the earth. But there are no winners. In its extreme the Duchess' Game is genocide. Hatzfeld shares, for example, that Pio, one of the killers in Rwanda in 1994 describes the cause of his and others actions in killing as "the desire to win the game for good." Of course, what Pio, and so many others entranced and deluded by the game never realize is that the game *cannot be won for good*.

## Hyperviligance

Hypervigilance can reach a point when without realizing it people internalize the grim spirit of contest's small cage habit. In the anguish of a human life unfulfilled fear may solidify into cardiosclerosis, or hardening of the heart, inflicting a mortal wound on life's spirit.

While vigilance is obviously very important hypervigilance, an exaggerated scanning of one's environment for threats, can be a serious problem leading to obsessive behavior patterns, as well as producing difficulties with social interaction and relationships. Seeing dangers were there are none we become like the boy who cried wolf in one of Aesop's fables. We become hypervigilant, constantly on the defensive, defending ourselves from countless attacks, real and imagined. When fear replaces love as our motivation for living we become like muscle fibers out of sync; we are in a constant state of fibrilation, like having a constant mental "charley horse." If the threatening situations occur often enough, the neuromuscular contractions of the reflex become chronically potentiated. One learns to suppress one's inner need to trust life and the heart disappears beneath a dismal swamp of justifications. Our fears and contest ideology so arrange the world so that in order to survive we must see ourselves as alone and threatened. The camps were as Primo Levi described "a struggle of one against all" in which "[s}urvival without renunciation of any part of one's moral world—apart from powerful and direct interventions by fortune—was conceded only to very few superior individuals, made of the stuff of martyrs and saints."

There is no discernible meaning to compensate for the meaninglessness of our contests. They become an orthodoxy in a game of shadows and mirrors, illusion and disillusion to which our very lives become indebted. When this happens bureaucratic language is often used as a shield. No one ever did anything wrong, there were no actors, merely actions or facts. As a Japanese radiologist sarcastically commented after Hiroshima, "I did the experiment years ago, but only on a few rats. But you Americans— you are wonderful. You have made the human experiment." Now it seems remarkable as Van De Mark adds that the conferees who discussed dropping the atomic bombs on Japan at a meeting on May 31, 1945 in the Pentagon "never seriously contemplated not dropping it. He adds, "Ethical and moral concerns had been eclipsed by their emotional and psychological investment and the intensity they brought to problem solving. It was easy for the scientists to think of the Japanese as "the other." More recently, John Holmes, the United Nations humanitarian coordinator spoke of the 2010 hunger situation in Niger as not yet "catastrophic." If your child dies of hunger it is indeed catastrophic. Hunger is a "situation" that *no one* commits. The moral link between acts and consequences is severed. In such a diseased state we tacitly consent to the injustice obscured by an elaborate etiquette that permits us to participate in what we know is wrong.

This is a fundamental moral disengagement of humans from being humane. Consciences are eroded, life is devalued, and truth is evaded. One is no longer able to feel one's humanity nor can one feel the humanity of others. As R.D. Laing put it, "if our experience is destroyed, our behavior will be destructive." Consequently, the link between acts and their consequences—which is, after all, what we mean by moral consciousness—is severed. We commit atrocities against one another which at the time we regard not as crimes. These events are so much a part of our lives that we do not notice them for the destructive forces that they are. When this happens humanity is lost in the calculus of destruction. William Shirer writes, for example, in *The Rise and Fall of The Third Reich* that he could find no one in Berlin, "even among those who don't like the regime, who sees anything wrong in the German destruction of Poland." More recently, Arthur Compton, one of the physicists who worked on and decided to drop the atomic bombs on Hiroshima and Nagasaki, expressed his regret for the enormous human suffering caused by the bomb and in accepting his share of responsibility, declared, "We made the best choice for man's future that we knew how to make."

The Duchess' Game is a shared value system among fearful people who need a symbolically and externally constituted sense of self worth and a society which, by granting it to them, reduces them to objects. Perhaps nothing is more symptomatic of our pathology than that we must deny our humanity in order to do what must be done. Having depersonalized ourselves we go about depersonalizing others. People become epithets, euphemisms, and abstractions. As Alena Synkovd, one of the 100 surviving of 15,000 children under the age of fifteen who passed through Theresienstadt transport camp, writes, "I've met enough people. Seldom a human being."

The issue becomes then not the violence done only by individuals outside the accepted social boundaries, but when these boundaries are drawn so widely they include as appropriate an enormous range of aggression and violence by everyone as legitimate behavior. Everyone becomes hypervigilant in their fear behaving with the calm assurance of people doing what everyone else is doing. For example, Levi points out that it was the "everyday duty" for the SS aggressors to knock Jews to the ground. Which is exactly how Hutus described their participation in the genocide in Rwanda in 1994. In his book, *Machete Season* Jean Hatzfeld interviews ten men who killed in the 100 days of genocide in Rwanda in 1994. When these men speak about "the killing season" they talk about it as ordinary life. They get up early, have breakfast, meet friends, and go to work of killing as just another day in the fields and marshes. Fulgence adds, "'We became more and more cruel, more and more calm, more and more bloody. But we did not see that we were becoming more and more killers. The more we cut, the more cutting became *child's play* to us (italics mine). For a few it turned into a treat, if I may say so."

Intimidation and violence are internalized in the reflexive habits of a lifetime's experiences and expectations of aggression and victimization, of us and them, of kill and destroy. Consequently, we must learn to suppress our inner need to trust life. Caught between the arbitrary alternatives of winning and losing, we are unable to conceive or to develop the trust or kindness necessary to remake our lives, and in the process we waste our own lives and pass on a devastating heritage to our children. "My dear little Daddy, bad news: After my aunt , it's my turn to leave." Friedlander adds that seventeen year old Louise Jacobson was murdered in Auschwitz the day after writing this to her father.

> *Tweedledum and Tweedleedee*
> *Agreed to have a battle;*
> *For Tweedledum said Tweedledee*
> *Had spoiled his nice new rattle.*
> —Lewis Carroll

The schism in consciousness required by the process of metastasis from small cage to the Duchess' Game breaks more than "rattles." The Game's fundamental deceit lies in the assumption that winners can be conceptually separated from losers. At every level of success the ratio of losers to winners increases. Consequently, in order not to be thrown back on our own meager resources we cling desperately to a membership that requires having an enemy. The foundation of contest relationships is that in order to experience oneself as a winner, one has to suppress one's awareness of our contingency, our need for losers; and, the game's need for losers is insatiable. Victims must themselves search for victims. Langer writes, for example, that "one of the bitterest truths we encounter in these ghetto records[Holocaust] is how easily the concept of one's own' shrank into the narrow identity of one's self."

# The Duchess Game

*Greed is finally being recognized as a virtue..."*
—William Safire

*Greed is good.*
(Ad in the WSJ April 8, 2008)

The Duchess' Game is a way of being and acting based on the Duchess' Law from *Alice In Wonderland*. The moral of the Duchess' Law states, "The more there is of mine, the less there is of yours." The Duchess' Game is not a natural disaster; it is, rather, a largely "man-made"(here I'm being gender specific) disaster. Filtered through cultural traditions, the Duchess' game isn't merely a metaphor. It is a zero-sum game in which everything, including life itself can be won, lost, possessed, and awarded. It is played anywhere and everywhere, at anytime, with balls, guns, and words and on sports fields, international battlegrounds, corporate boardrooms, and family living rooms. The Duchess' Game is a social contract lived and obeyed largely without conscious recognition. As a social contract the Duchess' Game is realized emotionally and physically, millions of times over, as a process in the nervous systems of individual people splintering consciousness and atrophying or disrupting the natural pathways of connection whose finely tuned integrity is necessary to maintain the dynamic processes that sustain personal health and social well being.

Just as grammar gives order to our words, so culture's consensual forms organize and give meaning to everyday life. The Duchess' Game has many forms from seemingly harmless teasing to bullying and war.

Having wrapped ourselves in the game's dogma we try to protect ourselves from the harsh coldness of its lies and atrocities. The Game defines people as splinter individuals and dutiful members who acquiesce to the group's definition and responsibilities of membership. Deprived of our own sense of self we can inflate ourselves with the honor, glory, and revenge of the group. We continually propagate the belief that contest's revenge cruelty, hate, brutality, sadism, and destruction bring out the best in us. Like historical cultures that performed sacrifice to propitiate their gods, we take that which kills us and elevate it. It is a hallmark of the

40

Duchess' Game that we are not prepared to right what we know is wrong. The game's routine allows people to escape the responsibilities for their knowledge of what they will do or what they've done.

The act of participating in the Duchess' Game places oneself in the extremely vulnerable position of pinning his or her happiness and well being to the precarious nature of the arbitrariness of the game's dehumanizing order. In such a Game fear acquires its own momentum and logic. Self-defense gives immediate and tangible reinforcement for the continued need for fear draining all energy in a struggle to survive.

The Duchess' Game is played for keeps. The devastating nature of the Duchess' Game has has been described by Dennis Overbye as The Three Laws of Thermodynamics:

1. You can't win.

2. You can't break even.

3. You can't get out of the game.

The game is also accurately interpreted as "Toddler Property Laws" as follows:

4. If I like it, it's mine.

5. If it's in my hand, it's mine.

6. If I can take it from you, it's mine.

7. If I had it a little while ago, it's mine.

8. If it's mine it must never appear to be yours in any way.

9. If I'm doing or building something, all the pieces are mine.

10. If it looks just like mine, it is mine.

11. If I saw it first it's mine.

12. If you are playing with something and you put it down, it automatically becomes mine.

13. If it's broken it's yours.

The Duchess' Game puts a premium on scarcity. The game prescribes that all things of value including feelings such as loyalty, trust, and love are limited goods and therefore subject to the rules of the game—that is they can be won and lost. In such a world of scarcity it becomes difficult to give away what you believe you don't have enough of. This results in a vicious spiral of fear and self-defense in which individuals feel alone and isolated when they attempt to solve social problems. Teachers, for example, are often called upon to solve problems of aggression for which they have no training.

My sister Ann and I had our own version of the Duchess' Game that we played whenever our Mother brought candy home for us from the grocery store. Ann would eat all of hers very quickly. I ate mine very slowly. Which meant that after hers was finished I still had some. Ann would say to our Mother that I was teasing her by eating mine in front of her. Our mother then intervened and said that I must share mine with Ann. Of course, I yelled that it wasn't fair. Ann was then going to get more candy than me. Mother came into the living room and took my candy and shared it with Ann who smiled behind our Mother's back.

Angrily I stormed out of the room. On my way out I "touched" Ann. She cried that I hit her. Our Mother returned and scowled at me. I yelled out that, "She started it."

That didn't help. I was sent to my room with only a fraction of my candy. I suspect that anyone who was raised with brothers and sisters recognizes this game. But on the streets the stakes are often measured in more than pieces of chocolate.

In the normal course of our experience kids in my neighborhood, like children everywhere, become contestants in the Duchess' Game.

## Chicken

Chicken is one common version of the Duchess' Game.
"Oh Yeah!'
"Yeah!"
"You wanna make somethin' of it?"
"Yeah. What you gonna do about it?"
This was one of the ways that the Duchess' Game started in my Detroit neighborhood in the 1950's. It was called chicken. Chicken had many variations, from verbal taunting to physical torture, all of which were designed to maintain some semblance of order in the constantly shifting contests of our young lives. However it was played, it was a game of domination and the target was always someone's mind. In the normal course of growing up male I was becoming a contestant. I was learning the Duchess' Game.

Our games of chicken were usually initiated by taunting. This taunting reminded me of the little rhyme I was taught as a child—"Sticks and stones may break my bones, but names will never hurt me." The rhyme was wrong because it did not take into account the emotional attack of words, nor did it recognize the escalation clause inherent in contest behavior.

No one wanted to give in and be branded a coward. The Duchess' Game required that we maintain the illusion that we could keep our contests from crossing some ill defined boundary.

But our games easily escalated. Initial taunts were followed by derogatory sexually charged put-downs directed at the other guy's sister or mother. This was never play, never in jest. It was always an attempt to bait the other guy into losing his cool. Which someone usually did. Being "cool" was image and image was everything. I recently saw two ads in the Stockholm subway that reminded me of this aspect of my childhood. They were large posters for TV movies with the headline, "Welcome to Showtime! A World of Action." In one ad Micky Rourke says, "Better be dead and cool than alive and uncool." In the other ad Bruce Willis says, "You don't just go around punching people. You have to say something cool first."

Taunting can easily escalate into pushing and shoving. We had a number of these contests to choose from. In one version we would punch each other in the shoulder until one gave up. In a variation we wet our fingers and snapped them on another's forearm. A third game was to hold another's forearm in two hands and twist the hands in opposite directions. When these became tame we played stretch. We played this facing each other with knives. One at a time we threw our knives toward the other's boy's feet. If the knife stuck in the ground he had to stretch a foot to that spot. Since we weren't good at knife throwing and we used ordinary jack knives which weren't weighted for throwing, there was always the possibility a knife would stick in your foot.

These games could sometimes escalate into what we called "playfighting." There was nothing playful about these interactions. In my neighborhood these play fights were only fought with fists and were sporadic and quickly settled. Bloody noses were the worst injuries.

In some neighborhoods, however, these games were much more dangerous than in my neighborhood. Lorenzo Carcaterra, for example, describes getting ready for a fight in his neighborhood, "'everybody checkin' out everybody. If they even thought you were scared it was over. It was a game, like Cowboys and Indians. Except, instead of us havin' bows and arrows, we had knives, pipes, and guns." Brinkley describes variations played in Haifa and Tel Aviv. In one, children lie down in the street as a car comes toward them. The last one up wins.

Such games of chicken are taken for granted as "boys will be boys" behavior in which kids test their skills and "manhood."

Chicken's games are more than kid's stuff. When boys become men they continue to play the same worthless no-win games. But, of course, the stakes are higher. During the second world war, for example, Russian soldiers played a type of chicken called "cuckoo." The players stood around the walls of a darkened room with loaded pistols. Each in turn, cried out "cuckoo" and the others fired at the sound of the voice. During the Vietnam war American soldiers played cowboy, trying to outdraw each other. These men had specially made holsters. In the first four months of 1968 Davies points out that sixty men were killed in this game.

Chicken is also popular among politicians. A Harvard researcher, Dr. Gary King found, for example, that in 2011 members of Congress spent 27% of their time taunting each other. In October,1962 Kennedy and Khruschev held the world hostage to see who would blink in their game of nuclear chicken over the Soviet Union's decision to deploy rockets in Cuba. According to Dobbs, Khruschev chortled, "'The Americans have chickened out...'" The same game of nuclear chicken was later played by the Soviet Union and the United State in October,1969 and later in the 1980's.

> *"Nuclear war was the ultimate game of chicken."*
> –Dobbs

# The Bully System

> *The only thing necessary for the triumph of evil*
> *is for good men to do nothing.*
> —Edmund Burke

> *"I was a human being, and I became a devil.*
> *But I was made into one."*
> —Hajime Kondo

Bullying is another form of the Duchess' Game. Children are conscripted early and bullied into the violence of the Duchess' Game. Like chicken, bullying, or mobbing as it is called in Europe, is often regarded as a childhood rite of passage. Bullying is often excused as a normal and necessary process of growing up and learning how to play the Duchess'

Game. In the DR Congo, for example, Allen writes that 13-year-old
Ndungutsa signed up to be a soldier with the militia after he witnessed
them shooting his brother who refused to join. Ndungutsa puts it clearly,
"'They asked me if I was ready to sign, so what could I do—I didn't want
to die.'"

In Ghana, Severik writes that nine year old Mercy Sonahe is another
victim of the adult game's routine violence. She is kidnapped, bound,
beaten, and raped and held captive for sixteen years to atone for her
grandmother's stealing of an earring.

Bullying is more than the random acting out of a few individuals. It
is more than "kid's stuff." Bullying is repeated aggression, either physical
or verbal, done intentionally or unintentionally to hurt another person.
The degree of aggression and violence in bullying varies considerably, from
teasing to ostracism to physical injury and even death. In 2002 Lemonick
points out that the American Medical Association warned that bullying is
a public health issue with long-term mental health consequences for both
bullies and victims. Wilkins reveals that children ages 8-15 ranked teasing
and bullying as the top tough issue they face. In a recent study reported
in the *Journal of Pediatric Psychology* Dr. Erich Storch writes that, "about
one in five children is chronically bullied." With the aid of technology the
problem extends from personal to cyberspace. According to WiredSafety.
org half of 3,000 children surveyed in the six months between October,
2004 and March, 2005 were victims of cyber bullying.

Bullying was a ceremony of natural selection in my high school gym
classes. Bullying was so normal that I never thought about it. It was how
things were done. We didn't seem like villains. The entire system was made
up of well-intentioned or unknowing participants making well-motivated,
defensible decisions within a socially accepted system called high school
physical education —all with the effect of demeaning human beings.

Here is how it worked. There was a cruel hierarchy disguised as team
play and sportsmanship. What mattered in gym class was one's position
in the hierarchy of choosing. Choosing up sides to play a game was a food
chain with the PE teachers at the top. This pitiless selection process was
organized by the PE teachers. They chose the team captains. These were
always the varsity football players. Other athletes were chosen next. Then
came the non-athletes. Finally there were the last chosen. Everyone knew
who these kids were. Sometimes they weren't even chosen, just abandoned
to the bench. It didn't really matter whose team they were on because they

never got to participate. I recall looking at these boys and being thankful that I was on the varsity football team. This ceremony of choosing extracted from the last chosen, through painful humiliation, undeniable proof of the rightness of their lowly status.

This ceremony of degradation has been described in professional football by Steve Smith. He describes the Baltimore Raven defensive philosophy as: "we build bullies... we take your lunch box. we take your sandwich. We take your juice box. We take your apple sauce. And we take your spork and break it. And we leave you with an empty lunch. that's the Baltimore Raven way. That's the bully way. And that's football."

This painful process is described in a Calvin and Hobbs cartoon. Calvin is proud because he catches a fly ball in the outfield. What he doesn't realize is that it is a fly ball from a hitter on his own team. He was left in the outfield when the teams changed at bats and no one noticed. (This was common in our high school games.) His joy at making a catch quickly changes to sadness as he is harassed by his teammates. They yell at him, "Hey stupid. If you're going to get our guys out, why don't you join the other team?" And another, "Who taught you to play anyway? Your grandmother.(This is an example of the escalation in the taunting process described earlier.)" When Calvin replies that, "C'mon guys, it's just a game. This is supposed to be fun!" Another teammate angrily points his finger saying," Games are only fun when you win, bonehead! You're goin' make us lose." Calvin walks away dejectedly telling the coach, "Mr. Lockjaw, I don't want to play anymore. There's too much team spirit." The coach replies, "OK, Quitter! Goodbye."

It's not just lack of athletic ability that can be used as an excuse for bullying. Any difference can be used to isolate and victimize a person. Bullying contains the numbing certainty that one can be mistreated for your difference. Hall points out, for example, that Gandhi ran home every day "lest someone would poke fun at him" because of his frail body. Children with learning disabilities and medical conditions are more likely to be victimized by their peers according to Dawkins.

Hammer discovered that children evacuated from Fukushima prefecture in Japan following the 2011 earthquake, tidal wave and nuclear disaster were singled out, shunned, and taunted as being "irradiated."

We must rethink what we know about bullying. Bullying is a fear based system of terror with four interacting parts: a bully, a victim, bystanders, and a supportive infrastructure. In bullying our humanity is lessened as we pull down in others the very thing that we ourselves need to elevate.

Because we promote the contests that perpetuate the violence we denounce, it is difficult to know where to draw the line between what is and is not acceptable aggression. As one mother put it after her son was bullied, "I knew that boys will be boys and tease each other but I never expected my son to be really physically hurt. This supposed "line" between acceptable and unacceptable aggression is also a part of life in Pollsmoor Prison in Cape Town, South Africa. A warder, Andrew Bosch described the game played between warders and convicts with regard to prisoner communication. The warders job is to keep communication closed, but not too closed. As Bosch put it, "'It's difficult to know where the line should be drawn.'"

In the Duchess' Game code of ethics there is no such line. This code is regularly violated, corrupted and discarded. Escalation is inherent in the game and is considered normal. The words of Rev. Martin Niemöller, a German anti-Nazi pastor describes our confusion well., "'First they came for the socialists, and I did not speak out —because I was not a socialist. Then they came for the trade unionists, and I did not speak out —because I was not a trade unionist. Then they came for the Jews, and I did not speak out —because I was not a Jew. Then they came for me and there was no one left to speak for me."

Stopping bullying is difficult not only because people feel that it is normal but also that it is necessary. I experienced two mothers who felt that they were forced to be accomplices in the violence experienced by their children. In a parent meeting in Southern California I was asked what I felt about spanking. I replied that I consider it violence and do not see any excuse for it. She became upset and replied that she sometimes spanked her daughter when she didn't do what she was repeatedly asked to do. The mother cried and said that she didn't want to do it but felt compelled by her husband and her in-laws who told her that her daughter needed to learn "who's boss". She felt that she was being bullied into being a bully.

A mother in rural South Africa felt enormous pressure from her son, husband and her community to agree to what she felt was abuse of her son. We were having tea one afternoon when her eight year old son came home from school. He was very excited and wanted to share his day with his mother. He told her that he missed a number of words on his spelling test. The penalty for a misspelled word is getting hit with a cane rod across his hand. But instead of getting all of the hits at once he was allowed to "bank" some of them for later punishment. She hugged her son and he ran off to play. When he left she shared her sadness and frustration. She wanted to go to the headmaster and have the abuse stopped, which she could have done. But both her son and husband told her not to go. Her son said that the other kids would humiliate him if she did that. Her husband agreed with the punishment and warned her that her interference would create hardships for his business in the small community. She felt bullied into allowing the abuse of her son to continue.

Bullying is an aspect of the psychic and social numbing inherent in the Duchess' Game. Self anesthesia does not allow the bully to recognize the humanity of his victims. To see the truth of one's actions can not be tolerated; it is inadmissible blindness. Peck reports that what happened in My Lai, Viet Nam, "was covered up for a year primarily because the troops of Task Force Barker did not know that they had done something radically wrong ..." Christopher Browning points out that many of the ordinary German men of Police Battalion 101 who took part in the killing of Jews, "Simply did not know any better." Killing Vietnamese or Jews did not conflict with the value system that these men had grown up in.

Bullies are seduced and often exhilarated by their violence and the intoxicating freedom from restraint. This psychic numbing may go so far that ones destructive actions are considered fun. For example, Lt. Gen. James, USMC, expresses, "It's fun to shoot some people." Bakan reports that the same delight is expressed by a twelve year old boy playing the computer game Halo. The boy exclaims, "It's fun blowing people up." But in reality it's not always such fun. Moreno, a soldier in Afghanistan said to Junger, "'Dude, it's difficult when you see your best friend lying there dead. You think you're a badass until you've seen a fallen soldier lying there not breathing anymore and then it's a different fucking story.'"

I am often asked to solve a problem of bullying in schools. If possible I prefer to work with all four parts of the problem: bully, victim, bystanders, infrastructure. But, more often than not I only have access to the victim.

A few years ago in southern Poland a mother and her ten year old son came to me. The mother said that her son wanted to ask for my help but he didn't speak English. So she would translate. Her son was being bullied at school by a larger boy. He would push her son down. He was not hurt but he was embarrassed. In the beginning he had told the adults at school but that only made things worse. He was now called a tattletale. He didn't want to fight, but he doesn't know what else to do.

I invited him to stand up with me. I explained that the first lesson was knowing how to fall down. I said that it is important to know how to fall, but even more important was getting up. I related that when I began playing I had to relearn how to fall and get up. He seemed surprised by my words. I said that like other adults I at first fell over like a tree. The idea is to fall down, not over. I told him that I first learned this from a boy with autism. Then I practiced it in my aikido classes.

I asked him to push me down exactly the way he was pushed at school. I received his push, went down and rolled backwards. I had him push me a number of times. He seemed to enjoy pushing me down.

Then it was his turn. We took this slowly step by step. First, he was waiting to be pushed down. I suggested that instead of waiting he would step forward, entering into the push. He was no longer going to be a passive victim. As he stepped forward he raised his arms and lightly touched the underside of my arms as I pushed him. This almost invisible action does two things. First, it raises the attackers arms. At the same time it changes the angle of contact with the shoulder. The result is that the force of the push is directed up and away from the shoulder.

Then lesson two was how to fall down and not over. We repeated many times the back fall and roll from aikido until he felt comfortable with it.

Then there is step three. When he is on the ground he is to reach up immediately to the boy who pushed him. When this occurs quickly enough the boy responds reflexively and reaches out to help him up. No victim, no attack.

When we finished our mat time I told him that for the next couple of weeks whenever I saw him I was going to come up and push him down. Anytime, anywhere. He smiled and seemed delighted by this as if he was looking forward to being pushed.

Together we accomplished two things. First, we changed his mind about falling. Secondly, we gave him the skills to receive the push. He had now a different emotional framework and skill set with which to engage with the bully. Not being a victim creates a different kind of relationship.

# CHAPTER 2

# Foul Play: The Dogs of War

*"Caesar's spirit, raging for revenge with Ate by his side, shall cry 'Havoc' and let slip the dogs of war."*
—Brutus' vision, Julius Caesar, Act. 3 Sc.1. Shakespeare

*"Well, of course, They're Marines. They're dogs of war. It's what they do."*
—Marc Chretien

Sometimes I wonder if God put all of humanity into a particle accelerator to see what would happen. Then God pumped up the energy and it was like Einstein suggested, "General annihilation beckons." We became like subatomic particles as we were sent crashing into one another in a mindless Big Bang! Ever since we have been searching through the chaos of the result for hints about the fundamental nature of life. Crashing about in the moral dark we've come up with the Duchess' Game as humanity's default behavior system. Like moral eunuchs we slip into contest thinking as if we had no choice. Martin van Cleveld for example, believes that, "war and its culture form an integral element of human history and human life and are likely to do so for all future to come." In his prize winning essay on war and peace Michael Howard, for example, points out that "Peace, as we have seen, is not an order natural to mankind."

I sometimes begin a lecture on original play with an exercise that demonstrates the reflexive nature of our urge to compete. The exercise is called "when push comes to shove." Here's how it goes. I ask participants to face a partner. One partner puts up a fist and the other one touches the fist with the palm of an open hand. Then I say, "The person with the fist push hard." After a couple of moments I tell them to stop and reverse roles. I repeat, "The person with the fist push hard." After a couple of moments I say stop.

I ask everyone to listen to the directions again. I repeat, "The person with the fist push hard." There are a few smiles and quiet laughs from people who suddenly realize what they had done. Then I ask, "What did the person with the open hand do?" Now there are more smiles and louder laughter as more people realize that the person with the open hand pushed back without being told to do so. I ask then if they recognize this pattern of behavior. Their smiles and nodding heads confirm their recognition of the Duchess' Game.

In this exercise there is no threat, no objective reason to push back, but when "push comes to shove" you push back even when it is unnecessary. This reflexive response mirrors the deadly pattern of the Duchess' Game. The Duchess Game is a non-self-correcting pattern that functions like a complementary *schizogenesis* or a rift that escalates and eventually feeds on itself.

"Snakes don't bite people. Snakes bite what people think." I remember being told this by a Native American elder. Like so many other lessons I received from Native Americans, this one was succinct and clear. The elder felt no need to elaborate. It was my thoughts about snakes that were so dangerous for them and me. At first his words didn't make sense. It was as if he knew that I had killed a snake years earlier. I wrote about this incident in *Playing By Heart*. One day I killed a snake while playing war in the little mounds, holes, and weeds of an abandoned construction site near my apartment in Detroit, Michigan. As I recall it must have been either a garter snake or what we called a blue racer. It was between two and three feet long. I saw it moving amidst the weeds and managed to catch it. I don't recall exactly how the next events unfolded but I placed the snake on the side of a small mound of dirt and ran away a few yards. As it slithered away I threw my "spear"( a three foot long piece of pipe I had found in the grass) at the snake. I missed. I quickly ran to the hill and grabbed the snake before it could get too far away, pulled my spear from the ground and repeated my throw. I repeated this until after a number of attempts hit the snake with my pipe spear. It writhed around the pipe until it died. Until the actual death I had felt excited and heroic. Gardner explains, after all, fear of snakes is universal and hardwired. So I was, accordingly, excused for just acting out of my genetic predisposition to fear snakes.

Something happened to me when I saw the snake die. I was startled into an awareness of the living spirit of the snake. I ran home. I was too ashamed to tell my parents what I had done. I know they would have been disappointed in me. I returned the next day to the vacant lot. My spear was still there impaling the dead snake. I apologized, buried the snake, and threw the spear into the weeds.

We have organized our personal and collective lives around the Duchess' Game whose pattern of fear, violence, and revenge has been accepted as not only normal and natural, but necessary. The Game is made up of a complex network of formal and informal habits, small affronts and great losses all bundled together into a body of evidence or meta-rules, which I call the "dogs of war." These "dogs of war" are the corrosive fine print of the Duchess' Game, learned through both conscious and unconscious practice until they become default behavior. These rules are not only individual reflexes but are also embedded in institutional systems which have the capacity to sustain the game in ways that transcend the wills and purposes of individuals. Humans do not question the authority of that which we raise to godlike status.

The "dogs of war" aren't written down; you won't find them in Grotius' *Law of War and Peace*, Lieber and Lincoln's *1863 Code of War*, nor are they in the more modern *Laws of Armed Conflict*, nor in the Geneva Conventions. A major problem with such legal codes is that they rest on the conviction that one form of contest, *law,* will erase another form of contest, *war.* Our laws are often nothing more than moral disguises behind which we continue our conflicts. Invoking the laws of war, we remain unsure of our agreement with their premises. We struggle with a seeming paradox with no way out: We must win at any cost, but there is a line that must not be crossed. Fairness, humanity, moderation are constrained only by the law of victory. Witt points out that some military men have worried it is impossible to simultaneously successfully conduct a war and follow the laws of war. Of course, there is only one just side in a conflict. This is not just a problem of moral gymnastics for nations and armies, but also for parents and children.

Unlike laws, the dogs of war don't need to be written—they become repetitive gestures born of habit, because everyone accepts the morass of the game. The dogs of war form a kind of logic, that is the cultural feedback loop built into our fundamental concepts of both how we view our nature and the nature of life on earth. The Duchess' Game becomes a culture, what military historian Martin van Creveld has called *The Culture of War.* This game is played for keeps.

There are six meta-rules or "dogs of war" in the Duchess' Game.

## The Dogs of War

- The Chameleon Principle: The Game is not what it seems to be
- No Choice: The Duchess' Game is the only game in town
- Play to win... And Every Victory Is A Funeral.
- Us and them.
- Revenge is sweet: The Game's Escalation Clause,
- All's fair in...

*Figure 4: The Dogs of War*

While it is easy to dismiss the dogs of war as only characteristic of demented individuals like Stalin, Pol Pot, and Hitler and large-scale or endemic violence as in Darfor, Rwanda, Nazi Germany, gangs in Los Angeles or Rio De Janerio. That would be a mistake. From the writings of the Greeks, to the founding fathers of America to a current "guide to the social game of everyday life" life is described as "endless battle and conflict." To John Adams, power must be apposed to power. Alexander Hamilton wrote that "the fiery and destructive passions of war reign in the human breast with much more sway than the mild and beneficent sentiments of peace." James Madison concurred, "the latent causes of faction are sown in the nature of man." Thomas Jefferson made the matter clear saying that, "The Revolution was nothing less that a bold and doubtful choice between submission, or the sword."

The language of this logic is basic masculine, managerial narcissism. It is apt to be antiseptic, business-like, and uncontaminated by sentiment, masking the cruel, inhumane, and detached nature of the game. When repeated over and over the Game's language begins to resemble truth. In this system one proves one's virality and toughness by "playing" with the lives of others. One must not acknowledge that one's own success is based on the failure of others. This moral ambiguity masks the ultimate logic that allows the game to continue. We approach our struggles as if killing is our foremost problem solver, a necessary and unavoidable evil. That is the great tragedy. It is also the monstrous delusion of the Duchess' Game.

The "dogs of war" are system archetypes or generic structures which are embedded in the Duchess' game. It is important to realize that it's very difficult to compete just once. In time the contest habit becomes a pattern of body, mind, and spirit that channels a deep personal insecurity into a fearful culture forming legacy. Nothing is more symptomatic of this state than knowing clearly the right things to do, and consistently doing the wrong ones.

Because they can be so subtle and so commonplace we often don't see these processes for what they are. The Duchess' Game cannot take place without the tacit and complicit support of ordinary people who are "just doing their jobs." For example, Friedlander points out that the extermination system in Germany during World War II would not have worked were it not for the people at several levels of organization, including, of course, those who directly implemented the killing. They could not have done those "jobs" had not they been so effectively trained to do things that were inhumane. In fact the system worked so well that Rees declares that 85% of the SS who worked at Auschwitz escaped all punishment because they had not personally killed anyone. It was the gas chambers that killed! As Bakan states strange as this may sound it is not different from the the general legal standing of corporations whose boards, directors and executives are protected from legal liability. Judge Frank Easterbrook and law professor Daniel Fishel wrote that, "Only people have moral obligations. Corporations can no more be said to have a moral obligation than does a building, an organization chart, or a contract." Or a concentration camp. Dr. Mukherjee points out that, "many of the cigarette makers had not only known about the cancer risks of tobacco and the potent addictive properties of nicotine, but had also actively tried to quash internal research that proved it." More recently CNN reports, in the Spring of 2010 Trans Ocean Ltd. Owner of the Gulf of Mexico oil rig that exploded, killing eleven workers and injuring seventeen others as well as causing a huge environmental catastrophe has awarded its top executives large bonuses and raises calling 2010 "the best year in safety performance in our company's history." The pathology of won creates a *Catch-22* in which the process we revere as the basis of our survival is actually a threat to our survival and no one is responsible for the destruction of anyone.

The dogs of war create a pathological synergism of fear that quickly spins out of control in a deadening spiral burying so much of the fragile fabric of life.

# Breaking News From the War: WAR WINS!

## Play To Win... And Every Victory is a Funeral

*"Force is as pitiless to the man who possesses it, or thinks he does, as it is to its victims; the second it crushes, the first it intoxicates."*
—Simone Weil

*"It is not enough for me to win—the other must lose."*
—Gore Vidal

In a comic strip six-year-old Calvin, having beaten his stuffed tiger Hobbes in a game of checkers, goes berserk, as he usually does, shouting,"I won! I did it! I won! I won! I'm the champion! I'm the best there is! I'm the top of the heap!" Suddenly he looks around and senses the emptiness of his winning. He asks, "Is that all there is?"

Yes, Calvin. That's all there is. Disenchanted, no amount of winning can heal Calvin's disappointment. Like Calvin we are caught between the arbitrary alternatives of winning and losing. Like people the world over when faced with shiny trinkets neither the meaning of his being nor the possibility of his spirit can be expressed or created by the means that

Calvin uses to win his game. The trinkets of the Game are needed just as a drug addict needs cocaine.

It is very seductive to be a winner. And as every addict knows, "You can't win just once." Once success is achieved, it must again be achieved at a higher level. Not everyone can win. In fact, by definition, most people must be losers. Without losers winners are deflated and their fitness for life is lessened. Losers, on the other hand, are supposed to feel that it is not who wins but how the game is played that is important. We must not, however, admit this lie. The game's need for losers is insatiable. At every level of contest the ratio of losers to winners increases. This is the way the game is set up, like house rules in a casino—the house wins. Speaking of his neighborhood Lorenzo Carcaterra said that, "The street had won. The street would always win." Consequently, though our addiction keeps us from realizing it we lose even when we win.

Winning, of course, is much more than theories, slogans and headlines. Winning is a serious business. As football coach Vince Lombardi once put it, "It is and always has been an American zeal to be first in anything we do, and to win and to win and to win." Sportswriter Mark Maske points out that the owners of National Football teams were not just interested in the amounts of money they made. "Wealth wasn't enough. The owners wanted the extra boost that came from winning football games."

In the world of contest winning is synonymous with strength, losing with weakness. Israeli lawmaker, Michael Eitan states that, for example, "I am strong and you are weak.' is part of Israel's political discourse." He could have been speaking not only for the world's political leaders, but for all of us who engage in contests. Nobody wants to be a loser or seen to be weak. For presidents, just as it is for citizens, weakness is the last thing one must admit. Contests are often seen as a political style of presidents who want to establish themselves as tough. At various times this was true for Presidents Eisenhower, John F. Kennedy, Lyndon Johnson and George Bush. None of them could afford to look feeble and soft. In a 2003 phone conversation released in a British document, Jehl declares, for example, President Bush is quoted saying that "His biggest concern was looking weak." Everyone wants to "play" the game but, of course, no one wants to lose!

*We know not how to advance; they know not how to retreat.*
—Edmund Burke

Sooner or later we are faced with the truth of the Game: winning and losing are not merely abstract nor are they merely matters of money, but may very well be a terrifying, calculated matter of life and death. A young Elie Wiesel recalls, for example, that the head of the block in which he was interred with his father talked him into not giving his bread to Elie's father but keeping it for himself. The head of the block said, "listen to me boy. Don't forget that you're in a concentration camp. Here, every man has to fight for himself and not think of anyone else even of his father. Here there are no fathers, no brothers, no friends. Everyone lives and dies for himself alone."

The Duchess' Game can be a blood sport. For example, the founder of Opus Dei, Monsignor Josemaria Escriva wrote that "holy coercion is necessary... When a person does not have the zeal to win others, he is dead." This is how the game is played. As Rwandan leader Paul Kagame told Romeo Dallaire in a meeting in January, 1994, "If things continue as they are, we are going to face the situation where someone is going to have to emerge as a winner." By that time 800,000 people had already lost their lives.

We become our games. We live in them and they feed on us. The game has no heart. There is no moral brake on the game. Contest social responsibilty is an oxymoron. The Game depends upon honorable people agreeing to participate in a dishonorable process. For example, Bakan reports that both General Motors and IBM worked with the Nazi's; unconcerned with the morality of the Nazis; they did so because it was profitable. Like a cancer cell the game multiplies as if it is genetically programmed to do so. The game is a shared value system in which our contests infect the spirit with deep metaphysical doubt. The game creates an inner turmoil, a gnawing sense that one's actions did not live up to one's own moral code. Winners require losers. This "winner take all" approach to power was evident in the struggle for survival in Auschwitz where survival often depended upon edging away from the brink of death by edging past others. As Olga Lengyel, a prisoner in Auschwitz put it, "It seemed as though the Germans constantly sought to pit us against each other, to make us competitive, spiteful, and hateful."

As contestants we sell our birthrights for a mess of mush. In such a situation all tragedies are seen as possible, perhaps even welcomed. When dreams are demolished some prefer, not merely to die, but to kill. One's worthiness becomes madness.

Consequently, we live in what Joseph Chilton Pearce has called "a mutually shared anxiety state." The Duchess' Game is essentially ego-centered self-indulgence. The Game requires that we give our allegiance to a process devoted to the creation and maintenance of a false self cut off from being and condemned to ceaseless contesting. One is beside oneself. The Duchess Game splits the human consciousness—one must fight to attain acceptance, while at the same time ignore that my acceptance is based on another's loss. That is the psychic split between doing the right thing and the behavior required by the game. Like Calvin, we cannot acknowledge the empty meaning of such a victory.

We have a basic need to defend the psychic split of the Duchess' Game because winners, like vacuum cleaners, must ceaselessly suck in losers as personal ballast to keep from losing or disappearing themselves. The Game provides so little real substance to the self that any sense of internal steadiness must come from external sources. The stoking of self-esteem produces a psychic inflation that must continually be fed. This process of personal decline is described by Booker as follows, "The difference between Beethoven and his successors... was that Beethoven believed in God, Brahms believed in Beethoven and Wagner believed in Wagner."

The Duchess' Game allows boys to look like men and men to act like boys. It is often argued, for example, that the discipline of the game within a framework of rules subordinates the individuals to something higher than themselves. This is the Game's deception; it subordinates the human to something lower than oneself. Living by the game's whims and expediency betrays one's inner moral compass. One is able to perform the most violent acts without *apparent* emotional damage to oneself. But that is a delusion. There has only been one war as if it were humanity's perdition. We merely change uniforms and weapons. A fearful, unloved human remains in silence, the silence that falls when all connection is broken between one and another. Only the dead have seen the end of war. You see Calvin, "When you play to win every victory is a funeral.

## The Chameleon Principle

*"Peace Is Our Profession"*
—stencil on the side of SAC bombers

*"War is peace."*
—George Orwell

A child asks, "If everybody in the world says they want peace, how can we still sell guns? Somebody must be lying" Yes, someone is lying. Just as the chameleon can change colors to blend in with its environment the first lesson that must be learned in the Duchess' Game is that the game is not what it seems to be. Lying is the Game's camouflage. Sociologist Charles B. Perrow found in his study of large bureaucracies that run high-risk systems that they practiced deception and downright lying.

To tell the truth is to destroy the Game. Such deceit is the first step in contest mental health. Vaclav Havel calls this "'living within the lie."

As a child I remember getting a magic set for my birthday. I read the little book and practiced the misdirection necessary for a magician to fool an audience. I practiced the slight of hand to focus my audience's (my sister) attention on one hand while I performed the trick with the other. I never got the trick to work because my sister always looked at the truth in my other hand. It's not just in children's magic sets that slight of hand and mind is performed. Just as in my magic set the goal in the Duchess' Game is to perform a slight of mind, getting the person to focus on one idea while the real objective remains unobserved. For example, we speak peace, but we act war. President Teddy Roosevelt received the Nobel Peace Prize, while proclaiming, "No triumph of peace is quite so great as the supreme triumph of war."

The pathological nature of the Duchess' Game depends upon allegiance to its lies. We must believe and learn to live the lies of the Game as the *Truth*. The truth was turned upside down; for example, in 1939 when children with serious disorders were required to be registered in Germany. About 5,000 children were murdered; their fate was marked by a + for death and a – for life on their registration forms. "Killing had become a positive outcome" adds Stargardt. That there is an ethical problem embedded in this slight of mind must be ignored.

The same game replete with double meanings is played in business, war and politics. In contests, winning is often disguised for excellence and truth, authority disguised for expertize, and might stands for right.

As Orwell pointed out, "Political language is designed to make lies sound truthful and murder respectable, and to give an appearance of solidity to pure wind." For example, lies masquerade as the truth and the truth is concealed in lies in the "creative accounting" in the 2010 nuclear pact between Russia and the United States. As arms researcher Pavel Podvig points out, "'they found a way of making reductions without actually making them ....'" Secretary of Defense Robert Gates points out that, "Most governments lie to each other. That's the way business gets done."

Normal foreign policy is a matter of creating an illusion of activity and concern, while doing nothing. Kofi Annan described the situation in Darfur as "a rather cynical game where everybody is coming to the African Union knowing full well they don't have the capacity, but at least your conscience is clear that someone is doing it." The 2008 Peace Nobelist, Martti Ahtisaari said recently that it is a disgrace that the international community has not managed to resolve the conflict in the Middle East. "How can we, year after year, seriously say that we are trying to reach a solution when we aren't? " he asked. Like the leaders whom they serve, Fisk, declares,"Ambassadors are expected to lie for their country."

> *Language is war by other means.*
>
> —E.L. Doctorow

Our language becomes a victim of the Game's pathology. To play the game we must speak one meaning and mean another meaning. For example, the MX missile is called the *Peacekeeper*. The language of the chameleon principle has one purpose above all: to permit the game to continue. But lies cannot be called lies, so we hide behind words and phrases "spin," double-talk, ambiguous political cliché, disinformation, and perception management—all jargon that goes with the game and masks a total callousness, contempt, and moral insensitivity. The problem with verbal communication is not the lack of words or of media, but the fact that words and media are used so commonly and so systematically to deceive. Even as wonderful a document as the United States Declaration of Independence did not mean what it said. *We hold these truths to be self-evident, that all men are created equal, that they are endowed by their Creator with certain unalienable Rights, that among these are Life, Liberty and the pursuit of Happiness.* This sentence is perhaps the best known in the English language, certainly one of the most potent. And yet the men who wrote it did not mean "all men" in either the generic sense of humans nor the more specific sense of males.

The Duchess' Game is a master of disguise. To play the game successfully we must learn to disguise oneself without anyone noticing; and we must speak one meaning and mean another meaning. The Duchess' Game is one of massive fraud, robbing people of their ability to separate illusion from truth. The Game allows us to talk and act as if human beings are merely categories of matter in a calculus of destruction. Human beings disappear as people become epithets, abstractions, and euphemisms. War becomes game theory in which civilian casualties are merely collateral damage. "Neutralizing targets," " target-rich environment," "loss of assets," and "plausible deniability" all help to disguise the horrors of modern war. Thomas Merton reminds us that "Ovaltine substitute from the Swiss Red Cross" was really Zyklon B the deadly poison gas used in Auschwitz.

## "I know, but I don't want to know that I know, so I don't know."

The individual suspects this, but he is frightened at finding himself face to face with this terrible reality, and tries to cover it over with a curtain of fantasy, through which everything becomes clear. Such deceit is the initial step to alienation and becomes then the first step in contest mental health. The genius of the Game's language is to carry out this process of dehumanization without our even being consciously aware that our dehumanization of others simultaneously devalues us. Contestants must disengage from a moral sense of connection to others in order to believe that what they do to them makes good logical sense and is also an authentic self expression. This disguise must be flawless; the last thing one wants is to admit that the game is a fraud and one's actions are meaningless. It is easy to become lulled by the deceptive routine until the game becomes a system of acts based on a specious or very subtle argument; a devious and crafty piece of reasoning. While we are told, for example, that our system of law rests on a commitment to "the whole truth and nothing but the truth," Anne Strick says that in the legal system,"When polarity shapes thinking and winning is the orthodoxy to which men chiefly adhere deceit is absolutely justifiable." What seem to be natural and well-meaning intentions lubricate our slide into a quicksand of lies, that cannot be recognized as lies. In fact the lies must be experienced as moral clarity. Emphasizing this point Merton says that the presiding judge at the conclusion of the trial of 22 former SS men remarked that he had, "yet to meet anyone who had done anything at Auschwitz!"

This evasiveness is as much a part of individual fear as it is a function of the cloak of secrecy functioning as an integral part of official bureaucracy and business. When lying is part of the institutional culture the stakes can be so high that any admission of error would be a failure of huge and unacceptable proportions. To lie is to believe and to believe is to make real. More recently, in 2009 the American Medical Association said that it is committed to the goal of affordable health insurance for all, but these health services should be "provided by private markets, as they are currently." What they didn't say, of course, is that if the private markets were providing this insurance, there would be no problem in the first place. Private markets are not designed to meet everyone's health care needs. Market value is an illusion, determined solely by the whims of greed. As Pellegrino wrote regarding health care, "there is no room in a free market for the non-player, the person who can't 'buy-in'—the poor, the uninsured, the uninsurable." When medicine becomes market driven it is a contest system engaged in by investors, bureaucrats, insurers, and employers. The result is a nonhuman core of modern medicine that Dr. Bernard Lown calls "a deadly virus."

How could systematic lying go on undetected? It doesn't. Lies metastasize and we become accustomed to living within the game's deceit. In this, web of lies, participants are to behave as if the illusions they know are false to be true. On April 26, 1986 the Chernobyl nuclear reactor went into meltdown, and the Soviet scientific and political establishments went into patently dishonest denial reports Carroll. This has become what Yallop describes as the Hitler Syndrome—"Tell a lie long enough and loud enough and it becomes the truth." The mental gymnastics required to be a Chameleon splits the self and alienates oneself from others and life itself. We are split and told that the contests of the Duchess' Game will heal our split and compensate us for the loss of our humanity. Unable to see the contradictions, and consistently indoctrinated in the game's deception we continue to befuddle ourselves.

# No Choice: The Only Game In Town

*...if the next war was inevitable, then the last war never ended.*
—Philip Gourevitch

*The person who does not make a choice makes a choice.*
—Jewish proverb

An elderly Catholic nun told me that she was told to imagine tanks and/or great white sharks destroying her cancer cells. She added that she couldn't do this because these images were too violent. But she also couldn't just be passive and die. She didn't know what to do.

"OK, come down on the floor with me." I suggested.

We sat on the carpet together. I described that I was going to be a healthy cell in her body and she was going to be a cancer cell.

"I want you to come at me the way you imagine a cancer cell "attacks" a healthy cell in your body."

She smiled as if she had an idea what I meant.

"I'm going to be a healthy cell and play with you."

"Ready? OK, come and get me"

She came at me with vigor, much more than I imagined from a nun in her 70's. She pushed and jabbed at me continuously until I clapped. We sat and she smiled "Could you feel that I didn't attack you nor did I allow you to hurt me?"

"Yes, I felt that." she responded.

"OK, now we're going to change roles. This time I'm going to be the cancer cell and you are the healthy cell. I'm going to come at you the way I imagine a cancer cell "attacks" a healthy cell. But you, can't fight me. Neither can you be passive. Your task is to play with me. OK? Ready?"

"Yes!"

I came at her with as much energy as I thought she could handle. She smiled, didn't back away and smoothly moved me around her. Each time I tried something different she was ready for me.

"OK, I'm done. You did it." I responded.

After a few minutes we hugged. She smiled saying, "I get it. I don't need tanks and sharks I can change my relationship with cancer cells by playing with them." She redefined her relationship with cancer. She was no longer at war. Rather than narrowly focusing on surviving, she was now focused on thriving—on being alive while she was alive. She learned that she had a choice, she didn't need to fight her cancer, neither did she need to be its victim. Contest wasn't "the only game in town."

\*\*\*

Leggett shares a traditional Chinese martial arts story with the same message. Some time toward the end of the thirteenth century a Chinese official had an interview with a Zen master. From the temple they could see the camps of the Mongol invaders.

"The fighting is endless,' lamented the official. "It goes on and on, and there's no way to stop it."

"Fighting can be stopped," said the Zen master.

"How?'

The teacher came up to him and gave him a backhander on the face. The official was startled and furious... This rude old man!... the old devil... I know I asked him, but what's the point of *that*!... I suppose it's one of their damned Zen riddles... supposed to have some meaning... Idiots!... no, it must have some meaning... there *must* be some meaning in it...

The teacher, who had been looking at him closely, said,

'You stopped it.'

Here are two people, a Chinese official and a Catholic nun, separated by geography and history, but faced with the same problem. Neither is able to perceive a way out of conflict. They feel that they had "no choice" but to fight. Both had learned to defend themselves against the normal repetitive contests of their lives. This is where the sustaining power of the Duchess' Game is developed. Yet, with help both were able to extricate themselves from a seemingly inescapable trap. The nun and the official changed their relationships with life.

But to think we have a choice is heresy—which comes from the Greek *airesis*, "to go one's own way." Such escape is just what the Duchess' Game does not allow. When it came to dropping the atomic bombs on Nagasaki and Hiroshima, for example, from the perspective of the person who ordered it and from most of those who carried out the order there was simply no question about it reports Carroll. "We keep saying, he wrote, we have no other choice" what we should be saying is, "We are not bright enough to see any other course!" This was David Lilenthal, Chairman of the Atomic Energy Commission, in his vote against the development of he H-bomb. It is as Laurens van der Post wrote, "It is the fission in the modern soul which makes nuclear fission so dangerous."

Humans are led to believe that the Duchess' Game is the only game in town. We go to war because we just can't seem to stop ourselves. In fact many believe that conflict, and combat in particular, is one of the most exciting, most stimulating activities that we humans can engage in. Berry reminds us that we are repeatedly told, "[c]onflict is the father of all things." Such a "father" figure can be an unknowingly abusive parent. The Game is so highly prevalent that paradoxically it disappears into the background of the culture. Consequently, we do not see it for what it is. Participation in the Duchess' game is accomplished in such a way that it does not feel imposed but freely chosen. Then the seduction is complete; we are addicted. We are, consequently, trapped in an oxymoron portrayed in the title of Jeanne Kirkpatrick's book, *Making War To Keep Peace*.

The contests of the Duchess' Game aren't merely metaphors; they are realized emotionally and physically repeatedly as a neurophysical process in individuals. The story of Renaissance art, for example, has been described as a contest between Leonardo da Vinci and Michelango Buonarroti. Both masters were employed to create wall murals in the same Great Council Hall in Florence, Italy. The two cartoons Michelango's *The Battle of Cascina* and da Vinci's *The Battle of Anghiari*, were shown side by side in Florence from about 1506 to 1512. This was contest on a grand scale. Not only were the art pieces commissioned to depict real local battles, they were also symbols of the personal battle going on between the two great artists. This was a contest without a formal prize. They were fighting for prestige, for the hearts and minds of the people of Florence. Both were commissioned to glorify war. Michelangelo, being a good citizen, depicted the heroism of war. In fact, as Jones points out, Michelangelo's army of awakened heroes looked very much like a recruiting poster for Machiavelli's militia." Da Vinci's art, on the other hand, was a shocking denunciation of war. The former depicted war as patriotism, the latter saw war as madness. Leonardo in his notebooks explicitly called war a "most bestial madness." Not soon enough we discover that only fools fight while other fools provide them the means.

The destructive nature of the Duchess' Game is hidden behind a toxic belief that contest and its effects are ubiquitous, nonnegotiable, and self-justifying. This assumption of contest's necessity appears so obvious that we are unaware of what we are assuming, because no other way of expressing our reality occurs to us. Dr. W.E. Deming a pioneer in quality management warns that, "We've been sold down the river by competition." It seems that we knowing the right choices constantly choose the wrong ones. There are choices people can make and don't; and there are choices they do not have to make but nevertheless do.

Each generation willingly propagates the Duchess' Game that holds them in bondage. Since everyone plays the Game, no one is able to see through the farce. The Game's sustaining myth of "no choice" is passed on to our children. One day I sat in on a parent-teacher conference in a Head Start classroom. The teacher had asked the mother to stay after class because her son hit another boy. The boy told his mother and teacher that he did it because the other boy teased him repeatedly. He didn't know what else to do. Perhaps feeling a little defensive the teacher answered , "I do not have the time to see what every child is up to all the time." Frustrated the mother replied, "I'm aware of that but how long is my son supposed to be nice and take this teasing?" It seemed to her that talking wasn't working. The mother felt that the boy was justified in his retaliation. "My husband and I told our son that he should try to talk to the boy first but he must stand up for himself and to hit back if necessary." The teacher said, "I do not agree with hitting, but sometimes it is the only way to stop aggression."

"Boys will be boys." The teacher added. The women's only alternative, however unwelcome, was retaliation. That's the best they could do. Because parents and a teacher could not figure out how to create safety at school a four-year-old was urged to fight back. In talking with the Head Start administrators it was clear that they too were unsure what to do. They wanted to support the teacher, but they also didn't want to appear to agree with hitting. This administrator, teacher, and mother are frustrated. But they aren't different from most teachers and parents who believe that sometimes you just have to let them fight it out. The issue these adults faced was no different in essence than that confronted by President Obama in his Nobel Peace Prize acceptance speech. Confronting the necessity of war he said that, " Make no mistake: Evil does exist in the world. A nonviolent movement could not have halted Hitler's armies. Negotiations cannot convince Al Qaeda's leaders to lay down their arms." He continued, "I do not bring with me today a definitive solution to the problems of war." Whether it is administrators, teachers, and parents in Head Start, or international diplomats and presidents, humans just cannot seem to figure out a way to stop aggression without using more aggression. The right of revenge confronts and confounds both parents and presidents with an issue of almost biblical magnitude.

"What else could I have done?" asked the mother, teacher, and administrator. I was a consultant to Head Start and was asked my opinion by the administrators, mother and teacher. I provided an alternative. First, I told them that revenge was not acceptable, so hitting was out. Second, I would take the responsibility of providing the two boys with an alternative relationship that eliminated the teasing in the first place. I would accomplish this not by talking to the boys but by playing with them.

I arranged to come to school the next day and be with the boys. When I arrived the children were outside playing. I went outside and began to play with the two boys. We played on the grass and in the sandbox and later on the carpet in the block area inside. My experience is that children really don't want to fight but they don't know how to safely disengage once a fight begins. I focused their attention on me and simultaneously modeled safe play touch. Original play provided them with a relationship based on positive touch that they can use throughout their day. In my play with the children I became not only a human shock absorber when the interests of the two boys collided, but I modeled the behavior necessary to change their relationship.

Contests express a tragic human destiny: we try desperately to justify ourselves as objects of primary value in a contest universe. Everyone wants to be someone special. As Boo reports the saying in Annawadi, the Mumbai under-city, is everyone wants to go from "zero to hero." In such a system each of us counts more than anyone else. This all takes place under the pretense that each person can achieve their due—a primary sense of human value. This is just what a contest system cannot do. Trapped, we know of no other way to value ourselves other than the standards of the game which requires that our well-being is pinned to the arbitrariness of the contest scheme. We must defend it endlessly from all assaults, real and imagined in order to keep from being under-valued personally and professionally. Our equilibrium is out of our control. We use the contests as self-defense mechanisms to find and display our sense of worth. The fact that this sense of self is based on other's loss must be forgotten. We are fond of stating that our aggressive sports build character, teach teamwork, and instill discipline. Of course these skills are dependent upon having an enemy. But, it is also suggested that since "boys will be boys" the aggression of young men must somehow be managed or all hell breaks lose.

Professional football player Ray Lewis, for example, commenting on the 2011 lockout of players by owners made the following prediction. Lewis told ESPN's Sal Paolantonio: "Do this research if we don't have a season — watch how much evil, which we call crime, watch how much crime picks up, if you take away our game... there's nothing else to do, Sal." Perhaps Ray Lewis read Machiavelli's *The Art of War* in which the author argues that one of the advantages of citizen militias is that it provides young men with something to do. People split in their core may actually know no other way to feel good about themselves other than outward aggression and power over others. A teenage gang member said to me during a workshop, "I didn't know I didn't have to hit." During a play session in the women's section of Pollsmoor prison in Cape Town, South Africa a prisoner admitted that, "Now I know I don't have to hit my child."

Fault lines of conflict criss-cross and rupture across the structure of human life and its institutions. Competition becomes the ruling principle and active ritual in the economic, political, social, and personal aspects of our lives. We become well adapted to the needs and dictates of the contest social system, which we carry out with a terrifying disconnect from the lives we impact. Arthur Levitt, chairman of the Securities and Exchange Commission "warned repeatedly that a 'culture of gamesmanship' was rigging the system with phony numbers, hyped earnings and worthless stock analysis." Such penalties are merely the cost of doing business. For example, Eichmann who along with other Nazi leaders testified at his Nuremberg trial "I was only following orders." Hannah Arendt concludes that Eichmann was so normal that he "commits his crimes under circumstances that make it well-nigh impossible for him to know or feel that he is doing wrong." War is merely the normative extreme sport form of the Duchess' Game.

In a recent, March 16-22, 2009, front page article in the Warsaw Business Review depicted a businessman's fist with the headline, "Fight For Your Rights." Seven months later the same periodical depicted a businesswoman with an upraised fist under a headline reading, "The fight for fairness." Frederick E. Terman, professor, dean of engineering, and provost, said of the game at Stanford, "This game of improving an educational operation is great fun to play because it is so easy to win. Most of the competition just doesn't realize that education is a competitive business, like football, only with no conference rules."

As former insurance executive Wendell Potter points out it is the relentless pressure from Wall Street for health insurance companies to meet earnings expectations not concern for consumer health care that drives these companies. The notion of cost-effectiveness takes the heart out of healing as the market drives health care. When market forces determine who gets healthcare then as Dr. Farmer suggests, "even medicine can constitute a human-rights abuse."

The electing of the Pope and granting of the Nobel prizes are not immune to the Duchess' Game. Sides are chosen. Beneath the robes, tweed jackets, lab coats, and microscopes of the priest, scientist and professor there exists the same need to be a winner and a quest for the thrill of victory. Those who do the choosing of the Pope and Nobel laureates sit astride the complex seismic zone of personal, cultural, and intellectual tremors of conflict. The result is that gate keeping, prejudice, and antagonism leave a clear imprint in science and religion even at the highest levels. It took, for example, seventeen years—from 1905 to 1922 for Albert Einstein to receive the Nobel prize in physics because provincialism, arrogance, and prejudice faced off in a struggle that was as much about the nature of physics as it was about as Einstein's intimidating methods and conclusions.

"Violence sells." Media is part of a belief system that says conflict, not kindness, is the basis of life; it is what attracts viewers and consequently sells products. I experienced first hand that as nature filmmaker Chris Palmer explained, "Television is a money-driven system," he explains, " There are tremendous pressures on wildlife film producers to get dramatic 'money shots.' Some years ago I was interviewed and filmed by a TV crew for a week playing with manatees in Florida, wolves in New Mexico, and Head Start and special needs children in Southern California. During an off camera moment the producer asked, "Why do you play with children and animals?" I smiled and replied, "It's because of the experience of belonging and love that children and animals share with me. This belonging is a feeling of kindness or a connection to all life. It's a feeling of grace." I didn't feel that she understood what I meant, but I hoped that the spirit of original play would be conveyed. I was to discover that not only was the kindness of original play not understood by the producer, but that she was after something quite different. Before the program was to air the producer's assistant phoned me and said that everything I did with manatees, wolves, and children was too gentle for television. I was told that kindness doesn't sell; on TV it is the high-voltage images of conflict that matter. So, she asked if I would return to the wolves and get them to show aggression and attack me. They needed some conflict to catch the audience's attention. I declined the offer to engage in a contest with the wolves so the producer mixed in stock footage of wolves being aggressive with each other. The TV producer choose to portray the wolves she thought fit the image of her viewers. She wanted the "reality" of aggression, even if it wasn't the "reality" we had spent the week filming.

# Crossing The Line: All's Fair in..."

*The barbaric law that has maintained
throughout the ages is that he who wins is just.*
—Daisaku Ikeda

When I played ice hockey in my Detroit neighborhood we had a saying, "we went to a fight and a hockey game broke out." This is a fairly accurate description of our hockey games. In our rough and tumble version of hockey everyone played to win. We didn't worry about fairness, nor did we have some line of violence that we shouldn't cross. Hitting each other with sticks was how we played the game. In our version of hockey we just ignored the inherent crisis of meaning between fairness and winning. Winning trumped fairness.

When our children are young we tell them to "play fair." Then when our child reaches a certain age, we say "Play to win." So, just like in our hockey games playing to win trumps fairness. When the child responds, "It isn't fair!" we admonish them that, "Life isn't fair." It is crucial that this slight of mind characterized by the change in language appears as well intentioned adults doing what makes good logical sense. After all it is the function of befuddled parents and teachers to prepare children for the real world. In the real world of adults play is to win and it isn't fair.

Contests are a lot of things, but fair isn't one of them. Contest mental health requires one to believe that "play to win" is the same as "fair play." Both "fair play" and "play to win" take on mythic proportions in a contest culture. That this is an ethical problem embedded in the very nature of the game is to be forgotten. Fairness is esteemed because it allows us to maintain our illusion. Winning is seductive and doing what's necessary to win is designed to protect and sustain the game. Simon & Burns tell us, for example—Fran has no regrets if someone runs a game on her, because she runs her own games on others in the drug world of the corner in her inner-city neighborhood of Baltimore. Here the corner is the Game. It gives death and it takes life. None of it is fair. In the world of the corner, "Each is to be used, abused, and ultimately devoured with unfailing precision."

While we maintain the illusion of fair play inequalities, cheating, and violence are not only implicit, but necessary to sustain the Duchess' Game.

One of the fundamentals of power is to expect foul play. In speaking about America's conflict in the Middle East, Rami Khouri, director of the Issam Fares Institute of Public Policy and International Affairs at the American University in Beirut, says, "If they (Americans) play by these rules, which are completely unequal, then we'll play by our own rules... If the United States is to survive, long-standing concepts of 'fair-play' must be reconsidered." Glenn Gray points out that, "Even in democratic lands, soldiers are systematically trained to fight dirty."

It's not only in neighborhood "games" that fairness is an illusion. Winning is the first law of the Duchess' Game, whether its played in my neighborhood hockey games or in the larger world of war, politics, sports, and business. We must forget, for example, that cheating is part of the game. If it wasn't we wouldn't need referees in the first place. If it's important enough to play, it's important enough to win. If it's important enough to win, it's important enough to cheat. Cheating is an integral part of the game itself. Sports writer Jim Armstrong tells us, for example, that NASCAR drivers have a saying, "If you ain't cheatin', you ain't competin' or breathin'." Alfie Kohn reports research that "regular sport participants become more committed to winning at any cost and less committed to values of fairness and justice as their competitive experience increases."

In economics the Duchess' Game is euphemistically called a "free market." But as Dwayne Andreas, former CEO of Archer Daniels Midland, an international agribusiness, points out, "There is not one grain of anything in the world that is sold in the free market. Not one. The only place you see a free market is in the speeches of politicians." Joel Bakan points out, for example, that the corporation, "is deliberately designed to be a psychopath; self-interested, incapable of concern for others, amoral and without conscience..." Our new markets without borders is a recipe for the injustices of contest to be magnified. Bauman points out that, "ninety per cent of the total wealth of the planet remains in the hands of just one per cent of the planet's inhabitants."

The thought that life *is to be won* has always been a shibboleth, interfering with our ability to correctly think about our relationship with life. Under its guise we are absolutely, irrevocably, morally certain of the righteousness of the wrongs that we commit. In his Nobel acceptance speech, for example, President Obama cautions that, "The United States must uphold moral standards when waging wars that are necessary and justified."

Our dependence on conflict to solve problems creates an intervention dilemma: we want the game to continue, but we don't want it to get out of hand. The problem is that although everyone talks about some imagined line in contest behavior that isn't to be crossed, no one knows where such a line is to be drawn. The importance of winning obscures such a line. We want our violence to be controlled. Of course, to accomplish our goal of controlled aggression we must at some point intervene to stop the escalation inherent in the game. The question is when?

In his critique of America's development of the hydrogen bomb Albert Einstein expressed the essence of the process of escalation saying that, "'In the end there beckons more and more clearly general annihilation.'"

We just don't know when and where that point is. We equivocate accepting borderline violence that violates the rules but is enjoyed as a legitimate and necessary part of the game. For example, is waterboarding torture or a necessary practice for national defense? The question is not whether violence is appropriate, but is the degree of force excessive.

Does spanking help redirect a child's misdemeanor? The same question is raised in state bills regarding spanking as in national legislation regarding torture. When does spanking cross the line and become abuse. Many adults, parents and professionals would not use the word abuse because they think most parents who spank have a very good goal, which is setting limits and trying to get their children to have good ideas. The problem is that as soon as one affirms the right of aggression the line disappears—no one knows where it is. Also, in the midst of an aggressive act it is virtually impossible for the aggressor to de-escalate their attack. Whether it is done to a young child by an adult, by a man to a woman, by football teams, gangs, or nations the desired outcome of hitting is "Shock and Awe."

Then the ends justify the means.

In the 1980's I experienced how tenuous the line between fairness and winning can be. I was asked by a political consultant from Washington,D.C. to run for the San Diego school board. Initially I found the idea both appealing and crazy. I didn't know anything about politics. He said I didn't need to. That was his job. He asked me to think about it and we would meet again in a week to discuss my decision. At our second meeting I said that I was interested enough to pursue the possibility. So we discussed more serious matters. First, he told me that I would have to move my residence. I needed to live in an area where I could win. That didn't seem fair to me. I would be representing myself as if I really lived in a neighborhood, when, in fact, I moved there just to win an election. I told him that I thought such a move would look suspicious to the people in my new neighborhood. He smiled and said that I shouldn't worry about that. He would take care of it. What he was going to do he didn't say. Then he asked me about my views on education and children. After I spoke for a while he stopped me and said that if I wanted to run I couldn't tell anyone what I really believed. He would write my speeches and I would read them. He emphasized that this was about my winning, not about my ideas. I began to feel more like a product, a brand name, than a human being. He said that there would be time after I won to try out my ideas. Then the seduction came. This school board position would be my first step to more powerful positions in San Diego and then perhaps in California state politics. What he didn't say was that this was a Faustian bargain. When, not if, I won I would become an insider. I could not win just once. Once I played the game I could never say what I really believed about children and education. This sounded like the ultimate proof that Darwin was right—only the fittest, and the meanest to survive, to get to be a politician, you first had to play the game. I decided not to play.

Referees, courts, governments, and organizations like The United Nations are designed to protect us from the excesses of the Duchess' Game. They are supposed to provide the illusion that the ideal of fair play and the reality of winning are kept in balance, that basically we are fair, and that it is only the perverse obstinate individual who crosses the line. We are supposed to forget that these cultural roles and rules are designed not to promote fairness but to maintain the illusion of the game itself. We really don't want the Game to end, just to be "played" within acceptable bounds. Consequently, we seek only to resolve conflict not to end it.

Too often it is the violence itself that changes men into half-men wired together with stunted needs, feelings, and responses. It is as if they are to live even their diminished lives the violence must continue. Conflict becomes the soul's nourishment.

## Us and Them

*Who sees the variety and not the unity must wander on from*
*death to death.*
—Katha Upanishad

*"Every war and every conflict between human beings has*
*happened because of some disagreement about names."*
—Rumi

Greek poet Constantine Cavafy in his poem, "Waiting for the Barbarians," describes a country where all public life is determined by the focus on an enemy. Normal laws are suspended. Parliamentary debates are canceled during the crisis.

*"...the barbarians have not come.*
*And some who have just returned from the border say there are no*
*barbarians any longer.*
*...what's going to happen to us without barbarians?"*

Then the worst happens. There is no "them." If there isn't a them, there can't be an us. And if there isn't an us and a them there can't be a Game. The Duchess' Game is a form of fission, a centrifugal force that scatters and atomizes people causing a loss of our innate humanity and our sense of belonging. In the Duchess' Game people become fictional selves invented to "play" our parts in each others contests. The price we pay for a perpetual state of adversarial relationship is the necessity to defend it and ourselves endlessly from all assaults, real and imagined. In the gap between the us and them lies the whole misery of humanity. An enemy provides us with our sense of self-esteem because our own sense of self has been up-rooted by the Game's delusions. Our pathological logic demands that as Robert McAfee Brown paraphrasing Uruguayan Jesuit Juan Segundo puts it, "the world that is satisfying to us is the same world that is utterly devastating to them."

A fearful psychosis takes hold of people when they distance themselves from one another which allows us to maintain the illusion of being human while doing inhuman acts. The contestant becomes defined as the normal well-adjusted person. People who make the coldly realistic decisions that have devastating effects on others are for the most part considered to be good people. The effects of our addiction to contest so disintegrate our personality that out of fear we firmly believe what we would know to be false if our fear permitted us to know it. In order to carry out the inhumanity asked of us by the game we must literally become "beside ourselves." Such a mind must create enemies and defend its boundaries. Paul Nitze, after he was named deputy secretary of defense, said that "It's us against the Soviets. Either we get them first, or they get us." Such a contest created self must constantly defend itself, in order to keep from being undervalued. Deprived of our own center of self-esteem we can inflate ourselves with the glory, glamour, honor, and revenge of the group. We rely on the game's fabrication that the game meets our innermost needs of belonging and self-esteem, things which it cannot do. We are, consequently, in a constant state of disequilibrium. This allows us to hold on to the delusion that we are reasonable, sane, and normal people even in the midst of our barbarity. Ingrid Betancourt, a former hostage of the FARC rebels in Columbia, was asked , "What was the worst thing you experienced while a prisoner?" She replied, "I think the worst thing is realizing that... human beings can be so horrible to other human beings."

## In the Duchess' Game we then know the price of everything but the value of nothing.

For the Duchess' Game to proceed everyone must know their place in the scheme of things. Not knowing one's category causes great confusion in the Duchess' game. Which team are you on? How can you be an enemy if I don't know who you are? Not knowing one's category spoils the game. Indeed such a person is a spoilsport. Immaculee Ilibagiza was such a spoilsport. She describes a day in her school in Rwanda when the teacher took ethnic roll call. He asked all Tutsis to stand up. Then he asked all Hutus to stand. Ten-year-old Immaculee didn't stand up either time. "Why is that?' in his hard mean voice the teacher demanded.

"I don't know, Teacher.'
'What tribe do you belong to?'
'I don't know, Teacher.'
'Are you Hutu or Tutsi?'
'I-I don't know.'

'Get out! Get out of this class and don't come back until you know what you are.'

The spoilsport is a subversive who performs an act of insurrection in the dehumanized, delusional world of the Duchess' game. The spoilsport does the one thing not allowed in the Game, he or she tells the truth and in so doing robs the game of its illusions, thus threatening its very existence. Consequently, the Duchess' game is harsh on spoilsports. No one wants to be told that the game they have devoted themselves to is a lie. As Vaclav Havel points out "when a single person breaks the rules of the game, thus exposing it as a game—everything suddenly appears in another light." The spoilsport obstinately refuses to honor the lies created by the Game, thus shattering the play-as-contest world.

Truth telling in the Duchess' Game cannot be forgiven. Huizinga points out that from the perspective of the game a spoilsport is "a coward and must be ejected." As children we call them tattletales or squealers. Adults change the pejorative term to stool pigeon or whistle blower. Spoilsports are branded as soft, emotional, irrational, and unpatriotic. Miller writes that during the Iraq war, for example, whistle blowers in the Pentagon were "dismissed as ignorant or ill-informed." Such people also lose their jobs, or are isolated and made to be irrelevant. In 2002 three women, Cynthia Cooper, Coleen Rowley and Sherron Watkins were *Time* magazine's person of the year because they spoiled the game for Worldcom, the FBI, and Enron respectively. Army Reservist Joe Darby is a recent military spoilsport who reported the atrocities of Abu Ghraib prison in Iraq. According to Zimbardo, Joe Darby made a very tough decision. As he puts it, "You have to understand: I'm not the kind of guy to rat somebody out. But this crossed the line to me. I had the choice between what I knew was morally right and my loyalty to other soldiers. I couldn't have it both ways."

A more well known example of the spoilsport process described by Weintrab occurred during World War I on Christmas of 1914. An outbreak of peace occurred during the Holiday Season. As early as December 4th neither side was firing across the trenches at meal times. For a brief time the extended families that soldiers recognize extended right across the lines to include the "enemy." On Christmas eve the rituals of the holidays, carols, trees, sweets, replaced the shells and bullets of war. During Christmas day there were gifts of food shared, souvenirs bartered, and football games played in the mud of "no-man's" land. The "live and let live" events of this Christmas, for example, were dismissed as unofficial histories. By threats and orders the high commands on both sides brought a stop to the lesser game so that the "real game" could continue. "For the rival governments, for which war was politics conducted by persuasive force, it was imperative to make even temporary peace unappealing and unworkable, only an impulsive interval in a necessarily hostile and competitive world." But still some soldiers resisted, making the routine acts of conflict impossible. As Herr Lange put it, "We spent that day and the next wasting ammunition in trying to shoot the stars down from the sky."

# Pro Deo

*"Beware the House of War when understood as the House of God."*
—James Carroll

*A certain conqueror said to Nasrudin: 'Mulla, all the great rulers of the past had honorific titles with the name of God in them: there was, for instance, God-Gifted, and God-Accepted, and so on. How about some such name for me?'*
*'God-Forbid,' said Nasrudin*
—Sufi story

"So help me God." Everyone assumes God to be on their side. Our individual rampages, our games and our wars are carried out Pro Deo meaning "for God." The hallmark of the Duchess' Game is that we confuse the secular with the sacred. Instead of humans being made in the image of God we fashion God in our image of fear and violence. War, for example, is a human activity pretending to be divine. In doing so play undergoes a profound shift from a life saving process to an act in service to culture. Our prayers are described in Mark Twain's classic *War Prayer* in which patriotic worshipers ask God to "tear their soldiers to bloody shreds... lay waste their humble homes... blast their hopes... and blight their lives. We ask it, in the spirit of love, of Him Who is the Source of Love... Amen." Tolstoy comments on the Napoleonic Wars, "the Spaniards, through their Catholic clergy, return thanks to God for their victory over the French on the 14th of June, while the French, through the same Catholic Church, offer praise because on that same 14th. of June they defeated the Spaniards." Killing is, of course, easier to do when the victims are not seen as human or even creatures of God. For centuries, Christians and Muslims alike have waged war with God against each other—the infidels. A Hutu killer expresses the issue honestly to Hatzfeld—"In truth, we thought that from then on we could manage for ourselves without God. The proof—we killed even on Sunday without ever noticing it." Another of the Hutu killers, said that, "We no longer considered the Tutsis as humans or even as creatures of God."

# Revenge: The Game's Escalation Clause

*"Wars never end warfare, they lay the groundwork for the next."*
—Kurlansky

*Vengeance is a brilliant moment.*
—Carl von Clausewitz

*An eye for an eye is a terrible way to blind the world.*
—Gandhi

*"Blood cannot restore blood, and government should not act for revenge."*
—Abraham Lincoln

Revenge is a beast that devours its own. The proverb goes, if you start out on a journey of revenge begin by digging two graves, one for your enemy and one for your child. A justified reprisal is not an end but a continuation creating a terrible lineage of conflict, like a pyramid scheme of indebtedness. The Crusades, for example, created such a powerful spiral of revenge and retaliatory violence among both Muslims and Christians that we still feel its effects today.

Turnabout is fair play. Except that the game isn't fair. An eye for an eye" is reflected in the Code of Hammurabi and in the Bible, Torah, and Koran. Recall the principle of retributive justice in the quotation from Exodus 21:23-27 in which a person who has taken the eye of another in a fight is instructed to give his own eye in compensation. This injunction neglects the law of escalation inherent in contest behavior. Indeed, the dictum that contests can stop contests is one of those falsehoods which, contrary to our experience, we repeat until it passes for common knowledge. The language of contest escalation is ethically illiterate and contemptuous of life because it masquerades equality as a pretense for retaliation. The perverse logic is that atrocity is supposed to cancel out atrocity—which of course it doesn't. The law of escalation actually is "two eyes for an eye." Writing of the "Dirty War" around Jerusalem Simon Sebag Montefiore points out that, "Each atrocity had to be avenged twofold." An eye for an eye would make for a vicious circle, but that is not how the game

81

works. We engage, instead, in a vicious spiral of ever increasing violence which we deem to be too important to be short-circuited by peace.

We live in a world of escalation in which revenge is often called justice. In such a game no one seems to know how to deescalate. Freeman Dyson, a nuclear physicist, describes his own heart hardening process of escalation. He was a young statistician working for the RAF Bomber Command in England in World War II. "At the beginning of the war, I believed fiercely in the brotherhood of man, called myself a follower of Gandhi, and was morally opposed to all violence. After a year of war, I retreated and said, Unfortunately nonviolent resistance against Hitler is impracticable, but I am still morally opposed to bombing. A couple of years later I said, Unfortunately it seems that bombing is necessary to win the war, and so I am willing to work for Bomber Command, but I am still morally opposed to bombing cities indiscriminately. After I arrived at Bomber Command, I said unfortunately it turns out that we are after all, bombing cities indiscriminately, but this is morally justified, as it is helping to win the war. A year later I said unfortunately it seems that our bombing is not really helping to win the war, but at least I am morally justified in working to save the lives of the bomber crews. In the last spring of the war I could no longer find any excuse."

The unwritten escalation clause is an inherent part of contests, but it is absent from original play. In its initial stages contest behavior appears to be play; it, however, easily escalates from minor altercations into fighting, and perhaps into killing. I'm often asked by mothers why their husband's play with their son turns into anger and crying. One wife, for example, described an interaction in which her husband and son seemed at first to be having fun. But before long her son is crying and her husband is angry. She doesn't understand that what they thought was "play" isn't play at all. While the interaction between father and son seemed to be mutually satisfying it was a contest from the beginning. It didn't take long however for their play to escalate until the father's force was excessive and too much for his son.

Such contest disguised as play can be much more serious. For example, two stepbrothers, as reported by Chenone, 14 the other 17 were engaged in "horseplay... chasing each other with blow guns and darts. But it escalated when one of the boys grabbed a knife." Now Michael is dead and Quantel is serving a life sentence in prison. Carcaterra describes growing up in the Bronx, "We were well schooled in revenge." Simon &

Burns point out that on the corner of West Fayette and Monroe streets in Baltimore the game escalates from snatching each other's ice creams, to stashes of drugs, to beating, and maybe killings.

This escalation process is, of course, not limited to kids on street corners. Carl von Clausewitz in his classic nineteenth century text *On War* warned that war "theoretically can have no limits." General and President Eisenhower echoed these sentiments in 1955, saying that "once you start you get deeper and deeper until the only limitation is "force itself." Thomas Jefferson put this trait of contest behavior starkly saying, "In war they will kill some of us; we shall destroy all of them."

Revenge is thought by many to be instinctive and inevitable, a normal, natural, and necessary aspect of human nature. Consequently, revenge becomes an integral part of adult activities and institutions including sports, business, politics and, of course, war. The result is a moral slide in which the scarcity of satisfaction requires an infinite progression of revenge, each step promising more satisfaction than the previous ones. We also see this progression of revenge in sports. In fact, it is often considered necessary for the promotion of a sport. Cain describes NASCAR officials telling its competitors "Boys have at it" hoping to market aggression and crashes into increased ticket sales and higher television ratings. For the players, revenge is the price worth paying for respect. For the spectators the promise of escalating violence is what we pay for.

Payback is also a common feature of business and politics. Kenneth N. Siegel, a psychologist and executive coach says that revenge is a significant motivator for success among business executives. Recently, in 2005 Brazil won a World Trade Organization ruling that US cotton subsidies distort world trade. Under WTO rules Brazil has the right to "retaliate" saying it no longer would honor US patents and copyrights on US movies and other items. The US did what contestants do—escalate the contest with their own threat.

Revenge is often raised to a code of honor, or moral requirement, in the Duchess' Game in which backing down is not an option. Even the smallest slight can justify an escalation. For example, On Sunday, September 28, 2012 Sirmone McCaulla just got off a bus and happened to bump shoulders with Christopher Gutierrez. They exchanged words, then fighting postures. Then McCaulla stabbed Gutierrez who died from the wound. McCalla went home and committed suicide. He wrote in his suicide note that he wasn't looking for a fight.

I am often called upon to intervene in fights that occur in schools. I intervened in one such fight between two high school girls in California. I did this not by approaching them as an authority figure, but rather as someone they didn't know how to deal with. So, instead of walking up to them and commanding that they stop, I crawled on my hands and knees between them and pushed against their legs. They had no idea who I was nor what I was doing. My role and position was so strange to them that they stopped fighting to try to figure out what was happening. They laughed at me. The fight stopped. I gave them a way out. The surrounding crowd dispersed because there was no more action. I sat with the two girls afterwards. One girl said that backing down was not an option. The other one replied that, "she didn't want to fight but she had to uphold the honor of her gang." They both agreed that fighting one person is much easier than fighting your own group.

The girls found themselves in the same predicament described by George Orwell in his essay, *Shooting An Elephant*. He was a police officer in Burma. One day he was asked to deal with an elephant who was ravaging the bazaar. He took a gun and searched for the elephant in the village. He discovered that the elephant had killed one man. Eventually he found the elephant, knowing that, "as soon as I saw the elephant I knew with perfect certainty that I ought not to shoot him." He shot and killed the elephant. Afterwards he, "wondered whether any of the others grasped that I had done it solely to avoid looking a fool."

Escalation can reach apocalyptic dimensions. In the Cold War, for example, the United States and the Soviet Union were "even." Our nuclear stand-off was even thought to be beneficial. In practice, however, there is no getting "even." For example, Dobbs, explains, "the unwritten rule of cold war diplomacy—never concede anything—made it very difficult for either side to back down." For two years President John F. Kennedy and Khrushchev played a game of nuclear oneupmanship. Then in October, 1962, this escalation, called the doctrine of Mutual Assured Destruction (MAD) was alive, well, and proceeded toward a nuclear climax in Cuba. On just one of the ships, the Aeksandrovsk, sent by Khrushchev to Cuba there was more than three times the explosive power than "all the bombs dropped in the history of warfare." Victor Yesin, chief of staff of the Soviet Union's Strategic Rocket Forces, reflecting on his experiences during the Cuban missile crisis said, "You have to understand the psychology of the military person. If you are being attacked, why shouldn't you reciprocate?"

Whether in a family, sporting event, business transaction, or warfare escalation is addictive. Just as drug and alcohol addicts must increase their dosage to retain the highs they seek, the game's addicts must always increase what they get from the game. What the game hides in its addiction is that the satisfaction that is marketed, bought and paid for can never be delivered. The resulting dissatisfaction is not merely a byproduct of the game it is the necessary force behind the game. Each party to this game is hooked by and dependent upon the violence of the other side. In a contest, each side is entirely dependent upon and consumed by the aggression of the other. Each side requires the violence perpetuated against them as their energy source to keep them going. Stalin's war-making, for example, was described as driven as much by revenge as by strategy. According to Carroll the dropping of the Atomic bombs on Nagasaki and Hiroshima, was seen as a fitting vengeance by Truman and others for the deep psychological and terrible loss of life suffered resulting from the Japanese attack on Pearl Harbor.

Each one in turn, willingly propagates the system of revenge which holds them in bondage. Since everyone engages in the same contest, no one is able to see through the farce. A system that relies on the use of force as the ultimate guarantor of safety and the threat of its use as the basis for social and political order is a fool's game. This fool's game of revenge has been updated and modernized into what Gordon & Trainor call the "preemptive doctrine" which says that a first strike or "preemptive" revenge is legitimate. This is called the Hobbesian trap. Where two groups are a potential threat to each other, the resulting mutual fear gives each a reason for striking first. And as Glover asserts, "since each can see that the other has this reason, the circle of fear is reinforced."

Like fire devours oxygen, revenge sucks the life out of living. We do not know how to extricate ourselves from the obvious insanity of this position. Shakespeare warns us of the insatiable spiral of destruction inherent in our contests.

> *"Everything includes itself in power,*
> *Power into will, will into appetite,*
> *And appetite, an universal wolf...*
> *Must make perforce an universal prey,*
> *And last eat up himself."*
> —Shakespeare, Troilus and Cressida

# CHAPTER 3:

# Adulterated Play

*Man has created the ultimate cheap, expendable, yet sophisticated human weapon, at the expense of humanity's own future: its children.*
—Romeo Dallaire

*Whatever its form competition is always play.*
—Johan Huizinga

*"Men love games and war is a brutal, deadly game, but a game, the best there is."*
—William Broyles

*"The soul of man, in all its majesty and mystery, has been dwarfed by the war game."*
—John Connell

When I was young on my uncle's farm, I went out to play with the horses in the fields, climb in the caboose hidden in the woods, and eat blueberries at the edge of the pond. I was away from adults all day playing with the world. I wasn't preparing myself for the adult world I was living in the world near at hand. This was unadulterated play before their theories and good intentions gave it purpose.

What began as spontaneous and full of wonder on the farm was slowly and pervasively adulterated into cultural play. At an early age I was kidnapped into the adult world of play as contest. I was told who I could and couldn't play with. My sense of all-belonging was narrowed to "us" and "them."

The adulteration of play is a fundamental shift from play as a life sustaining process into an act in service to culture. This change in consciousness has tragic consequences for childhood and children.

On the farm I was not in a contest with life. I never thought of playing war. When my family moved from the farm to Detroit it didn't take long until war was part of my daily play. On some days I wore my army surplus helmet, backpack, canteen, and toy gun. On other days I was a cavalry officer with gun and sword and blue hat with gold braid. On still other days I switched sides and became a Native American. What character I played often depended on what movie hero I had just seen at the local Saturday matinée. When I wasn't playing war outside I was planning and carrying out battles with toy soldiers on the floor of my room.

Every Saturday on the way to the theatre I heard the wailing of the air raid sirens. These sirens were a reminder that the war games I enacted were old-fashioned compared to the Game being played with ICBM's, Sputnik, and SAC bombers in the larger world of adults. My part in this larger war game was to "duck and cover" under my desk (my foxhole) in school air raid drills. Of course, we were lied to and told that we would be all right as long as we did not look up at the light.

Adulteration of child's play is a transformation in which children grow up with no cultural supports to lean on, no collective myth that makes their original sense of play seem real because it is lived by the adults with whom they share their worlds. In time our abduction into cultural play is so complete that we not only lose contact with our original sense of belonging but we discredit the immense enchanted world to which we belonged. Having been orphaned themselves adults don't have access to the way of being and belonging that they have banished.

This adulteration process is a profound forgetting. The tragedy is that in our distortion of kindness into fear and confusing man-made strategies with Creation we ignore both the wholeness and holiness of our world. Consequently, play is demeaned in language, form, and spirit. This demeaning of our original sense of play fundamentally alters childhood and children. Original play is creation's way of making another child. Cultural play, on the other hand, is culture's way of making another adult.

This is an important and little understood distinction. Original play is often mistaken for its cultural imitations, rough and tumble play and play-fighting. For those unfamiliar with original play the latter may appear to be the same as original play. The differences are in source and in function as well as in behavior. The source of original play is Creation; its purpose is the communication of a universal and inherent code of kindness. On the other hand, play fighting and rough and tumble play are cultural processes to promote and teach the standards, mores, and behaviors of the cultures within which the play occurs. There is confusion, for example, in cultural play regarding the line between play and fighting. No such confusion exists in original play. The Upanishads referred to this as the descent from *lila* or divine play to the shallow realm of vain frivolity.

## The Faustian Bargain

*Little children,*
*watch out for the simulacra!*

*"You're not here to play."*
—a parent to a child

*It is useless to attempt to reason a man out of a thing*
*he was never reasoned into.*
—Jonathan Swift

Dr. Otto Wolken, an Auschwitz prisoner, spoke of hearing an SS man talking with a ten-year-old boy through a barbed wire barrier described by Friedrich. The SS man said, "Well my boy you know a lot for your age." The boy responded, "I know that I know a lot, and I also know that I won't learn any more." This ten-year-old boy knows something that the adult guard didn't know. What is it that the boy knows? He knows that his childhood has expired like a long forgotten prescription. Childhood is adulterated when playing for real becomes playing for keeps. This is the *Faustian Bargain* to which each generation unknowingly and willingly injects the next with no inkling that they are complicit in a process that is self-destructive and severely life-eroding.

Creation outsourced children to parents because we are supposed to know how to finish the job. The human failure to protect children is a massive "breach of contract" with God. The plight of children around the world is difficult to understand. In the conclusion to his book, *Children At War,* P.W. Singer notes that in terms of recovering lost childhoods we simply do not yet have a bedrock of established learning on which to rest." How can that be? One would think that if adults could do one thing well it would be to care for their children. After all, isn't that what biological survival is about? How tragic that human beings do not have a "bedrock of established learning" on which to keep our children safe. Instead, we tend to both sentimentalize and denigrate children. The result is an unacknowledged contract that I call the "Faustian bargain." As Thomas Merton has pointed out, "There is nothing more tragic in the modern world than the misuse of power and action to which men are driven by their own Faustian misunderstandings and misapprehensions."

Goethe's *Faust* legend is an example of the belief that individuals will receive a life-sustaining gift but it must be paid for by adhering to an agreement with the devil. Cut off from his fellow humans by his life of abstract speculation in compensation for his weakness, Faustus desires limitless knowledge and power in order to assert himself against the world. There is no sign in him of the desire for real connection. Into this void steps Mephistopheles to offer him the treacherous bargain, a fantasy of omnipotence and omniscience in return for his soul. Soon it becomes clear that the powers Faustus has been given are nothing more than empty illusions. In his desire to make love to Helen of Troy, he is lured by the terrible temptress who lured others to war. It is not until Faust seeks a higher challenge in benefiting humankind that he says, "Oh, Moment stop!" But it is too late. In this instant the devil shows up to collect on their bargain.

*"All children are flotsam driven by the ebb and flow of adult lives."*
—Bryce Courtnay

Like Faustus we pay a price for our fear and greed. This profound negation of so many generations turns childhood, potentially our most creative period, into a neglected pastime or martyrdom. Children are conscripted into an adulterated world not made for them. Adults pretend that it is a fair exchange. Like land that is overused and undernourished, children are burned up before they have time to develop the gifts they bring with them. Adulteration takes the wonder and joy out of climbing trees, jumping in mud puddles, getting dirty. In so doing, we leach children of kindness, wonder, and love; dull their senses; arrest their development; and deprive them of their original sense of belonging. For example, M. is ten years old, near the top of her fourth-grade class. She dreams of being a doctor. But like so many children in India and other countries it looks as if her dream will be destroyed into a nightmare of childhood prostitution India is the center of the 21st century slave trade. M.'s parents have pulled her out of school and returned her to her native village. The worry is that her family will sell her to traffickers to be sent to a red-light district anywhere in India. Kristof, reports that M. is one of an estimated 1.8 million children who enter the sex trade a year. This is a world in which it is permissible to knowingly destroy children and their childhoods. Are such children victims of a terrorist act, an atrocity, a gang drive-by, a bloodbath, a massacre, an ethnic cleansing, a genocide, a holocaust, collateral damage, or merely benign neglect? God, enchantment, and the inherent sanctity of life are absent from such a world. Too often children such as M. are faces on the covers of Time and UNESCO publications where they remain remote and without substance.

The United Nations estimates that by 2010 there were between 25 and 50 million orphans in Africa alone. The *2006 United Nations State of the Children* report says that *one of every two children* in the world suffers in poverty. The World Bank recently reported that malnutrition is stunting the development of more than one hundred million poor children around the world. How do we cope with such numbers? We organize commissions and write reports. Children become statistics by putting them in studies, tables, charts, and graphs. Our clever words and numbers allow children to disappear between the lines. This is a world in which war is a culture and peace is an individual idiosyncrasy. It is a world whose diplomats are profoundly reluctant to breach state sovereignty and would rather quarrel about the definition of children's conditions than change them.

We teach children what we know, and what we know is conflict. We believe in the efficacy and inevitability of conflict as the basis for human life. As Archbishop Tutu of South Africa put it, "we seem almost to be programmed to have our identity defined by our againstness." We assume, in fact, that in terms of evolution humans have gone as far as we can go. We can, in such a view, only affirm our humanity against another. Not knowing what else to do we pass this inheritance on to our children. The successful child made to feel happy in his or her grasping, made content in its membership, and made complacent in the face of inner terror nourishes an environment that thrives on the ruin of childhood.

The *Faustian Bargain* predates the ideas of childhood joy and of child safety. In a world populated mostly by contestants there is little if any room left for children; and not many people would treat them seriously were someone to offer them for consideration. And so even when they know how to make the world better, the question remains: who would take them seriously. Society pulls this trick on every child, some more devastatingly than others. Abducted by culture children abdicate their ecstasy and are exiled from this awareness so as to be educated by those who have been reduced to orphans themselves with faint recall. Like orphans who are not told about our biological parents, our original feelings and memories of play are replaced with contests in such a way that the original is rendered very difficult to access. Drafted into the Duchess' Game children may be called upon to give their lives as martyrs in adult contests.

Our original play is degraded and counterfeited in the Faustian bargain in which children are deceived and coerced into accepting membership in a society in return for giving up their sense of belonging to all life. This bargain is a gradual process. At each step along the way, children are coerced into making the bargain because it appears that they have no other choice. Like flakes of colored glass in a kaleidoscope children are tossed about at the whim and fancy of adults' tunnel vision who cannot or will not see children for who they are. In this ruse, in order for children to be what they might become, they will have to cease to be who they are created to be. This phantom contractual agreement becomes the normative reference of reality and value for childhood. Often it is such negative memberships that keep people alive in the deadly game. For example, Robertson describes Adam, a Sudanese soldier conscripted by force admitted that if he didn't kill and rape he would himself be killed. The same kind of story was told to Mydans by Him Huy a Khmer Rouge soldier who killed five people to show his loyalty. He says that "whatever he did there he did on the pain of death. Philip Zambardo describes growing up on the streets of the Bronx, New York, "As part of the gang initiation process we all had to steal, fight against another kid, do some daring deeds, and intimidate girls and Jewish kids going to synagogue."

When play becomes contest, we are stripped of our natural armament and become utterly ashamed of childhood's gifts—the life giving riches that are meant to sustain us in terrible moments of attack and rejection. By trading away our sense of belonging to all life we later become the unquestioning adults necessary for culture's contests to function—contests built and sustained on greed. Incapacitated as we adults are, we misperceive childhood's gifts as threats. Our diminished consciousness reveals a terrible and frightening insecurity, a disconnection, suspicion, and sense of irrevocable exile unrelieved by any hint of trust.

In such a world one can trust nothing but one's own cunning and deviousness. There is no discernible center of integrity around which one can weave a pattern of trust and belonging. Not only is a sense of belonging and safety absent but these are replaced by hyper-vigilance, a feeling of being constantly under attack even though no hostility is shown requiring attention. Feeling abandoned and alone, our only obligation is to survive; everyone and everything else becomes dispensable and potential prey.

The parent generation drafts its children into their own special sense of discord, a discord with roots in lives long since gone. Garbarino shares that when asked what it would take for a child to be safe instead of answering "a parent" a nine-year-old says "A gun of my own." The child has no way of resisting this indoctrination. It is reinforced with rewards and punishments. An irresistible pressure is applied to make the child feel that membership is identical to belonging.

Of course the adults in the child's world are befuddled having themselves long ago accepted the switch. Each generation willingly propagates the game and its rules that hold them in bondage; and, since everyone participates, no one is able to see through the farce. Everyone is caught up in the unremitting fog of self deception. This is a vicious spiral of adults, shortening childhood and pressing adulthood on to younger and younger children acting out adult contests, followed by cries of frightened adults for adult punishments for younger and younger children.

With the truth of the Faustian Bargain obscured, children are enticed to be like the fir tree in the fairy tale that wants to be cut down and dressed up with colored lights, bangles, and silvery tinsel, only to be abandoned after the holidays. We "harvest" children too early, grafting onto them the expectations and responsibilities of later years long before their bodies, minds, and spirits are designed to carry them. Memberships and trinkets tell the child that he or she is somebody, a somebody in contest with other somebody's so as not be become a nobody. The binding power of the bribes maintains the delusion that trinkets are the stuff that satisfies the soul. This is especially macabre when membership in a killing organization like a gang or an army is deceptively camouflaged as belonging and an AK-47 is an enticement of machismo. Fisk reports that a fourteen-year-old Iranian cried when his petition to fight with two of his friends in the Iran-Iraq war was denied. A boy cries not because he can't go out to play, but because he can't go out to kill!

*It is immoral that adults should want children to fight*
*their wars for them. There is simply no excuse, no acceptable*
*argument for arming children.*
—Archbishop Desmond Tutu

Implicit in the Faustian Bargain is a kind of absurd retaliatory pact—in return for the membership, adults convey on them children are required to carry on our wars. The dangerous assumption is that we can consider war apart from children. In fact children are no longer considered collateral damage in adult conflicts. During a firefight between US soldiers and Iraqis in Karbala, Iraq, Lieutenant Colonel Chris Holden says, "We shot and killed children. But I accept full responsibility for that. That's the kind of fight it was." Increasingly the kind of fighting adults are doing around the world not only kills children because they are around, but because they are actively recruited to do our fighting for us. As a grandfather put it to Radwan in Yemeni, If the Americans land on Yemeni soil, "I will give my grandchild a weapon to kick them out." Forero adds, for example, that just after he turned twelve, a rebel group in Columbia offered Juan a life of adventure he would never get in his village. "They said they give a me a gun and that they'd pay me. I thought this is good I wanted to earn some money."

Children are increasingly bullied into becoming war's soldiers and victims. In his study of peace and war, William Shawcross points out that children are the world's fastest growing army. Lederer quotes U.N. reports that children are used as soldiers "on a massive scale." It is not a coincidence then that more children were killed in war from 1990 to 2000 than soldiers.

Singer declares that more than 40 percent of the total armed organizations around the world use child soldiers and in over three-fourths of the armed conflicts in the world in there are now significant numbers of children participating as active combatants. In 1998 Olara Otunnu, Kofi Annan's appointed UN special representative for children in conflict, reported to the Security Council that two million children had been killed and another six million wounded in wars and civil wars during the nineties. The young soldiers are found in 36 countries. In the Democratic Republic of Congo, Allen reports that, for example, the number of child soldiers in 2006 is estimated to be 30,000. Despite this knowledge, the numerous reports, commissions and declarations hardly advance this tragic condition. According to Singer from 1924 to 2001 there have been twenty-one international conventions on the use of child soldiers. The axiom "talk is cheap" is never more true than when it comes to the use of child soldiers. He adds that the United Nations, for example, has not yet taken one formal action apart from condemnation against known users of child soldiers.

Adults often make excuses for recruiting children to fight their wars. Singer cites a number of these. A Russian regimental commander said that, "Here they learn to be manly." In Sri Lanka the Tamil excuse for recruiting girls is that its a way of "assisting women's liberation and counteracting the oppressive traditionalism of the present system.'" For some other adults their children dying in our conflicts becomes a point of pride. Mothers in Palestine dance with joy at the martyred deaths of their children. A father in Kashmir adds, "Everyone treats me with more respect now that I have a martyred son." Other parents say that they are fighting for their children when in reality they fight for a country. Robinson quotes a forty-year-old father of five saying that, "he fights for his country first and his children second." Until each father can put his children first, before his country both are doomed to be accessories before the fact to the murder of their own children as they pass on their war to the next generation.

The Faustian bargain has taken on the stature and force of a species orthodoxy. Anguish grips us, but we don't seem to know what is right. One begins to expect the most awful things to happen, because they do. In a world with huge amounts of disposable income children remain disposable. In a world of tremendous hubris they are merely leftovers for liberal causes. We would rather speculate on oil and stock futures than invest in children's futures. This is a world whose knowledge is said to double every two years. In contrast, our wisdom and conscience are deadened, and our will is spent. We become willfully blind to what we know in our hearts we cannot tolerate. We are in a kind of hibernation of the spirit; we are again at the point that E.L. Doctorow described for the American Civil War, "It is life when it can no longer tolerate itself." We must keep up the charade because if we stop to acknowledge our deception, we will be forced to feel our belonging, and then not be able to let children perish. So we close our eyes and try to push them out of our minds. If we don't see them our pretense of innocence will be fortified.

Something in us shrivels. The fact that we all were children doesn't help us solve this problem. We may all have been children, but not all of us had a childhood. With our lack of compassion we shrink the world to the limits of our fears, and in so doing we deny who we are meant to be and become less than who we can be. Here's the Bargain—a child "freely" chooses to be a member and then is "allowed" to do what adults want him or her to do. A childhood cannot be lived in fear.

## Childhood—Null and Void

*"I've had enough of these grown-up quarrels that make children suffer. Stop!"*
—Nujood Ali

*"The death of a man is only the death of a man, but the death of a child is the death of innocence, the death of God in the heart of man."*
—Elie Wiesel

An abandoned child, innocence torn from her, sits among the archaeological rubble that was once a playground. She crouches like a piece of human detritus surrounded by twisted metal bars, scattered scraps of corrugated tin, curved fragments of brown and green glass, and pieces of cardboard scuttering over the hard-scrabble earth. Small clouds of brown dust swirl about her. Her arms and legs are like wire coat hangers on which what passes for clothes limply hang. It is as if she is more of a skeletal plan of a girl than a girl. The color in her dress has long since faded into dingy gray—not a gray with color in it, but a gray from which, like late winter snow, all color has been washed out. Shards of sunlight pierce the dusty space around her like rays of hope once bright, now faded and dim.

She is huddled, shivering, and coughing in the shadows scrutinizing passersby as if she were searching for someone who would end her unasked-for hurt. She could have been an orphan in Stalin's Moscow, Dicken's London, or Sherman's Atlanta. She could be alone now in Haifa, Darfor, Soweto, Dublin, Sarajevo, Calcutta, Bogota, Mexico City, Manila, East Los Angeles, Harlem or your city. We've seen her so often that her loss of childhood seems like some kind of career. She is living something that is alien to her; as if her childhood came stamped with a long passed expiration date, like a carton of sour milk.

A ragged patch of silence, a ventriloquism of pain, is sewn between us as if in an attempt to tie us together. Her body is like an "S" curve, leaning toward us with anticipation and simultaneously falling away with fear. And for our part we mirror her, wanting to reach out to her, but unable to because any smidgen of courage would crack our mask of control and leave us in emotional limbo. We act as if what she has is catching, like chicken-pox. And like the pox, it would mark us forever. So we move away, like dust motes skittering to the corners. Or, we see her as an unfortunate kind of lightening rod which prevents the cumulative electricity of misfortune from being discharged to us.

Her dirty face, furrowed as if her very childhood has been plowed under, is devoid of anger, but there is bewilderment and sadness. Her dark eyes reach out and touch us pleading with infinite dignity. We are gifted at subterfuge and denial, yet strangely disquieted by the simple truth in her eyes. "Why?" We open our mouths to respond and we are voiceless. That's our bland, meager answer and like a stone in place of bread, it doesn't satisfy.

This young girl's life is shortened and endured by a system that fails to protect her. No child should have to wonder: They love me; they love me not. We have moved away from childhood in such a manner that its memories have been lost to us and us to them. The hopes, loves, and aspirations we embed in our children too often disappear, swallowed up in the swamps of Vietnam, the droughts of Somalia, the shanty towns of Johannesburg, the bush of Rwanda, the streets of East Los Angeles, the alleys of Belfast and a thousand other similar places, only to be followed by similar disappearance in the political nuances of governmental reports. The bodies and hearts of children are thus tattered in the long nightfall of the human spirit we call maturity.

There can be no justification for our neglect of childhood and destruction of children. However, to pacify liberals we write laws and regulations, then to pacify conservatives we refuse to enforce them. As UNICEF states: The real extent of violence against children is impossible to measure.

Made hostage to the Faustian Bargain, children are cheap and childhood expendable. This is not surprising since "rights" in the Duchess' Game are based on the necessity of survival. Children are viewed as having little if any value in the world of adult contests. Politicians like to describe children as an "investment in the future," but we treat them as if they are a bad debt upon which we have heavily mortgaged. We invest in stocks and hedge funds but children are not deemed good investments.

The cultural infrastructure of contest is totally inadequate for the meaning and possibility inherent in childrens' spirit. The contest mind has succeeded spectacularly in developing weapons, computers, and communication technology, but it fails utterly when it tries to deal with the lives of children. Our traditional methods are not going to solve these problems, because it is our very "reasonable" methods which have created the problems in the first place.

The tragedy of human life is that when we adulterate childhood, we destroy what we cannot make. In destroying children we are like people finding themselves in a desert without water because they had abandoned it as unnecessary in a moment of plenty. Consequently, a child who once glided in play from assurance to assurance, now gropes through contests, from fear to fear. We might want to make our children into the people we lack the courage to be, but because there is no model for this, they grow up to be just like us.

Adults are good at studying children. UNESCO, Save The Children and other non-governmental organizations (NGO) and government agencies publish reports, as if it is information that we lack. We write reports and have conferences, but these are exhortatory and largely unenforceable. Some say it is inescapable. Others say it has always been and will always be so. We must be practical, they say. For example, Jeanne Kirkpatrick, U.S. ambassador to the United Nations called the Universal Declaration of Human Rights, "a letter to Santa Claus."

There's a difference between not knowing and choosing not to know what one knows and would rather not face up to, which becomes an excuse for paralysis and postponement. We have all the documentation we need. Saving children is so muddled by indifference, rationalization, institutional constraints and a lack of imagination that it cannot secure sustained top-level attention on its own merits. We continue to write prescriptions, as if writing solves the problem. As Janusz Korczak, asks, "When the devil will we stop prescribing aspirin for poverty, exploitation, lawlessness, and crime?" What we lack is will, not information.

Throughout the world in large cities, small towns, and rural areas "null and void" is stamped across the face of childhood as children are deprived of the safety and nurturance they need. The figures that confirm this tragic state are mind numbing. Theirs is a twilight world in which the longing for love and safety founders in a dangerous web of frustration, futility, and despair. More than two children die every minute of every day and most of these deaths are preventable. What the world's military establishments spent in one day is roughly equal to the sum that would have saved the lives of 50 million children during the decade from 1990-2000.

*There is no childhood when children are forced to abandon living in order simply to stay alive.*

Edmond Burke wrote that he did "not know the means for drawing up the indictment of an entire nation." And what of an indictment of a entire species. Here is our devastating report card.

# A Report Card for Humanity

## Subject: Childcare: Grade: F

- 29,000 children under the age of five die each day, and most of these deaths are preventable
- 1 of every 2 children in the world lives in poverty
- 1 of every 3 children in the world suffer from some type of malnutrition[1]
- 1 in every 5 children has no access to safe water
- 1 in 7 children has no access to health care
- 1/4 of the world's youth survive on less than $1.00 per day.
- 1.6 million children killed in conflicts since 1990
- 1.2 million children trafficked each year
- 25 million uprooted children in world
- 15 million children in world are AIDS orphans[7]
- 1 out of every 200 children in world suffers from a war related psychological malady
- 211 million children must work to feed themselves and their families
- 115 million children have never been to school
- 49 million Sub-Saharan children underage of 14 are laborers in 2004
- 25 to 50 million children in Africa will be orphans by 2010[3]
- 12 million African children by 2006 had lost at least one parent to AIDS[4]
- 2 million children were killed in armed conflict in the decade 1986-96[5]
- 6 million children have been forced into labor, 2006 the UN reports[6]

- 40,000 children die each day from malnutrition and disease, or as causalities of war and violence[8]

- 100 million poor children malnourished around the world[9]

- 1 billion children under the age of 18 were living in areas in conflict or emerging from war according to 2006 estimates. Of these an estimated 300 million were under age five. 18 million children were refugees or internally displaced.[10]

- About 1 in 10 girls under the age of 20 worldwide have been subjected to some form of forced sexual acts. [11]

---

Sources

[1] *The Hidden Costs of Malnutrition* Cynthia K. Buccini. Bostonia. Winter, 2006-2007,18-20.

[2] Michael Wines, *In Africa, hard labor and stolen youth,* International Herald Tribune, August 24,2006, 1,2

[3] *UNAIDS prediction of the United Nations Program on HIV/ AIDS* Melissa Fay Greene. *There Is No Me Without You.* London: Bloomsbury, 2006.

[4] Helen Epstein. *The Invisible Cure.* London: Viking, Penguin Books,2007. 213.

[5] The U.N. 1996 report *The Impact of Armed Conflict on Children*

[6] BBC News,2006.

[7] Dow, Unity and Max Essex. *Saturday Is For Funerals.* Cambridge, MA.: Harvard University Press, 2010, 178.

[8] UNICEF and National Children's Rights Committee, Alberts, 1997.

[9] The World Bank, (Greene,2006, p.389)

[10] Veneman, 2009, iv).

[11] Hidden in Plain Sight. Summary. UNICEF, New York. September, 2014, 6.

---

Such statistics are both shocking and numbing. It is important to acknowledge two facts: first these statistics represent a massive dysfunction of not just individual human beings, not merely political policy and cultural practice, but of species care. We are witnessing a massive failure, not of a particular policy or program, not merely of teachers and parents, not of a culture but of the genus *homo sapiens*. It is as if we are using Monsanto's "terminator technology" which causes plants to kill their own embryos. Humans are a disgrace to the race. We have abdicated our responsibility. The destruction of childhood is not random, nor is it accidental, but rather effects of a deep structural pathology based on our choice to contest with life.

Our contest minds retreat into the moral shadows and quibble over trade-offs, cost-benefit analysis, or market share. We have lived by a system that undermines our children—and we've called this survival. For example Singer reports that to stay alive, O. aged fifteen is told by his FARC (Revolutionary Armed Forces of Columbia) commander that he has to learn how to kill. Sadako Ogata the UN High Commissioner for Refugees has pointed out that, "for many children today thou shalt not kill is no longer the norm; it is not even a pious wish." War creates a world "unhinged" where child soldiers act like broken robots into which human hearts had been transplanted by mistake. In the use of child soldiers we witness tormented souls in a profound disaster in which they are driven away from their necessary childhoods into the world's tragic and horrifying default of humanity.

Secondly, and more importantly these figures represent individual lives. Boo describes Sunil, a scavenger in Annawadi, the makeshift settlement adjacent to the Mumbai airport, who said of his life, ""I don't like myself doing this work. It's like being an insult." It should be obvious to us by now that facts themselves do not and cannot assure their humane use. Such math masks individual experiences of hurt, humiliation, and death, moments of dread at not knowing how to be safe, who one can trust, and sorrow and emptiness at the loss of the cherished and familiar. Naomi is 15 but looks 10. A horrible burn scar shrivels the skin across her chest and shoulder. She had a broken leg, now reset. But her face is calm; she speaks clearly. The physical scars are nothing compared with the trauma she has been through. Dowden describes her as one of the so-called child witches of Kinshasa, rejected by her family and community at six-years-old and left to survive on the streets. As one boy told James Garbarino, "If I join a gang I'm fifty-percent safe. If I don't join a gang I'm zero-percent safe." Another thirteen-year-old boy mentioned by Allen, Ndungutsa saw his seventeen-year-old brother killed for refusing to join the militia. "Then they asked me if I was ready to sign, so what could I do—I didn't want to die." Stargardt presents seven-year-old Dawid Wulf on the run from the Nazis, who when asked by his mother to draw a picture of their home and garden with the sky and sun, confessed to her that he "had forgotten what the sky and the sun looked like." Such anguished cries from the depths of childhood precisely express a kind of knowledge. But the knowledge they convey cannot be proved or explained. It cannot be taught. These exclamations are not information. One either does or does not know what they mean. The induction of child soldiers in Rwanda and Sri Lanka, the death of AIDS orphans in Cape Town, the hunger of street children in Manila become distal events in a long and complicated dying world story. But, to the parent who no longer holds her child, this is not the death of a child, but of *her* child.

Targeting children is as much a part of the Duchess' Game in boardrooms and factories as it is on battlefields. Well-dressed men and women can explain in coldly professional terms how they negate children. The children enduring slavery in carpet factories of Pakistan, for example, must rely on themselves. Iqbal Masih, a Pakistani boy was sold into slavery and murdered at age thirteen as a result of his efforts to free children from violence and slavery. Lucy Hughes, director of strategy and insight for Initiative Media, the world's largest communication management company in discussing her company's advertising says that young children are "fair game." She described how they employed psychologists to help them manipulate young children and their parents. When asked her if it was ethical to target young children she replied, "I don't know." She quickly adds that her company's role is simply "to move products." Ms. Hughes has lost her sense of human affinity on the basis of a pure judgment of utility. It was her everyday duty, her job. She is described as successful. We know then that our language lacks words to express her offense, the demolition of a human being. In a more lethal, macabre example this means that toys for tots are "child-portable" AK-47's which weigh only 10-1/2 pounds and have only nine moving parts and can be stripped, reassembled and fired by a child less than ten years old. T. Singer reports that this weapon costs $12.00 in South Africa and $5.00 in Kenya. Unfortunately the question for both groups of adults in business suits and camouflage uniforms is not whether what they do is right, but whether it is profitable for them to destroy children. Such people think in costs, in winning and losing. Atrocities against children are awful, but they are not high priorities in corporate, national and international interests and too often do not measure up to the criteria for necessary intervention. *Save The Children*, for example, estimated that 100 million children died during the decade 1990-2000 because of adult-inflicted living conditions. As Philip Gourevitch points out two years after the genocide in Rwanda, "more than one hundred thousand children were looking after one another in homes that lacked an adult presence."

The war on childhood is essentially one of negation; of generations of a planned, closely argued, well-reasoned, and determined "no-ness." It's as if no one has jurisdiction nor responsibility. That children are cyphers is now recognized in pediatric psychology under the heading the "Destruction of Childhood.' Paulo Sergio Pinheiro the author of a recent United Nation's report on violence against children wrote that, "This is the moment to recognize children as being protected by rights, as full citizens." Graca Machel, for example, has pointed out that, "More and more of the world is being sucked into a desolate moral vacuum. This is a space devoid of the most basic human values: a space in which children are slaughtered, raped, and maimed: a space in which children are exploited as soldiers: a space in which children are starved and exposed to extreme brutality." Gracia Machel is not alone in speaking out against the destruction of childhood and the death of children. Elie Wiesel has written that, " society is often the enemy of the children." It is hard to imagine such a war, much less understand it. In fact UNESCO has pointed to a "Global aggressive culture" that is destroying our children. Wendell Berry writes that we are "unprecedentedly inhumane toward humans—and especially, I think, toward human children." UNICEF has characterized the postwar era as the 'age of neglect,' a time when governments have sacrificed children to the military.

Haunted by a vacuum, we may look back in a moment of wistfulness on the innocence of childhood, but having passed through a sort of one-way boundary euphemistically called maturity, we are caught like Hamlet between love that beckons us and an archaic sense of cultural duty in which we despair for who we might have been had we been loved. Having long since abandoned our original play, we try to protect ourselves from the wisps of childhood as if they bring contagions like winter drafts springing up in an old house, or like abandoned hulks of rusty cars left by the roadside.

Childhood is in a general state of neglect, condemned not because of anything children do but rather because they have no market value or winning potential in a contest world; they are not venture capital except as soldiers, laborers, and prostitutes.

Nelson Mandela laments the destruction of children saying that, "I know that Qameta (God) is all-seeing and never sleeps, but I have a suspicion that Qameta may in fact be dozing. If this is the case, the sooner I die the better, because then I can meet him and shake him awake and tell him that the children of Ngubengcuku, the flower of the Xhosa nation, are dying." But it is not just Xhosa children who are dying. We must, indeed, shake the God within ourselves awake and tell him that the children of the world are dying. We must make our peace not only with God. It is not enough not to kill children, we must act to save them. God must wonder how he created a being that could develop computers, create an atomic bomb, travel to the moon and not be able to care for its children! Consequently God must be considering a class action suit against humanity or at least appointing a guardian *ad litem* to serve as an advocate for children. Like the canaries that used to be carried into mines as warnings of the dangerous accumulations of toxic gases children are harbingers of the human ability to thrive. Childhood is a gift not a commodity. If we are not loved as children for who we are but for fulfilling the expectations of others the foundation is laid for our inhumanity. All children are our responsibility; soon enough we will be their responsibility.

# Part II:
# World As One,
# Childhood's Dream

*The world we have made, as a result of the thinking we have done thus far, creates problems we cannot solve at the same level of thinking at which we created them.*
—Albert Einstein

*"Nobody can think and hit someone at the same time."*
—Susan Sontag

*How wonderful it is that nobody need wait a single moment before starting to improve the world.'*
—Anne Frank

*This Sane Idea*

*Let your intelligence begin to rule*

*Whenever you sit with others*

*Using this sane idea:*

*Leave all of your cocked guns in a field*

*Far from us,*

*One of those damned things might go Off.*
—Hafiz

# CHAPTER 4

# Playing for Real

*The world is the playground of God...*
—Gandhi

## A Living World Story

*Our future as a species will be forged within
this new story of the world."*
—Brian Swimme

A child asks us, "Tell me a story," she says, 'One where nobody gets dead.' " Can we meet her request? Or will we tell her the same old story?

Will we be like Calvin in a recent Calvin and Hobbes cartoon strip? Calvin's father begins to read him a bedtime story. Calvin asks his father a series of questions that lead him to question whether there is, "Any violence at all in the story." His father answers, "No." Calvin replies, '"What makes you think I'll like this?" I've been asked the same question by adults who cannot imagine a world without conflict. They tell me that such a world would be boring. Christopher Booker points out, without some measure of conflict there can be no story. For most people a story without conflict is impossible.

We are like Calvin unsure of a new story. Maybe we won't like it. We're comfortable with the story we have.

Is there something we can do that re-frames life from our struggle for survival into something for which we have no precedent? Sharon Begley wonders, "whether it is possible to cultivate virtue through the way we construct a society, raise children or even train our own brains." "Newberg and Waldman ask the question differently: "So is there something more definitive that we can do to tame our selfish brain." Anne Harrington poses the matter this way: "Is there some way of thinking about life being precious that could go beyond thinking about survival?" Another scientist, Richard Davidson asks, "Are there strategies that may influence a person's affective style and transform the neural circuitry of emotion, and of emotional regulation, into a more positive direction?"

I say "Yes!" to the scientists, to the little girl and to Calvin. I'm suggesting that our old story is not predetermined, inevitable, or inescapable. I'm also suggesting that our intelligence has gotten us into trouble that it cannot get us out of. A new story is mandated. But it is not enough to tell a story; it has to be lived, not merely recited. Our new story must provoke and inspire.

As children we are taught the reality accepted by adults. But the social and cultural world in which we live does not exist in some absolute sense, but is simply one model of reality—a consequence of a set of spiritual, behavioral, and intellectual choices. What we believe about the world, the story we carry around in our minds affects how we feel about and experience the world. Our story tells us what is real and what is not. We've been told, for example, that conflict is normal, natural, and necessary, and peace isn't possible. This world-view isn't whole. This is especially troublesome when the voices of authority, parents, leaders, and scientists, claim that the part they leave out is *really* not there. Although it may seem far-fetched and absurd there is a story different from the contest one we have lived for so long.

How then do we use cultural processes to disengage from our contests? Do we even know the nature of the gifts Creation has given us? We don't. The answer doesn't lie within the cognitive boundaries where we have searched. I have become convinced that the only real wild card in human affairs may well be children. What the children are demonstrating is that the consciousness that truly knows original play is different from the consciousness of the person who is contesting with the world. Children's original play opens us to a wider reality requiring a profound shift in human mindfulness, unlike any that has come before. Nothing less will do. This is not a temporary shift into some new mental stance. It means being reprogrammed and transformed by basic and enduring psycho-physiological postures.

Humans need a new operating system—a collection of vision, values, mores, ideas and behaviors. We have up to now lived a dying world story. One which is both the basis for and derived from an operating system based on fear. I call this the contest operating system or COS. It is played for keeps and is based on the law of win-lose. Its activation releases the "dogs of war."

I am suggesting an alternative operating system for human beings. The implication of this suggestion is that there is a way to view and participate in the world based not on merely surviving but on thriving. I call this new operating system original play or OPOS. This is based on a living world story whose foundation is love. This system is played for real and is based on the law of give and receive. Its activation releases the doves of peace.

*Figure 5: Contest & Play Operating Systems*

As we have seen contest is the product of a particular way of thinking that enshrines fear and encourages self-defense as the basic identity of individuals, communities, and nations. Throughout history, the invincible warrior with raised sword has been the archetypal hero of the human race.

Our cities are full of such monuments to war. We have become accustomed to being less than we can be. We have been content to see the deadening process of a dying world story as the consensual form that gives meaning to human life, setting the values, bestowing meaning, determining morals, ethics, aims, and the purpose of life. The tragedy of our dying world story is that it is written with an infinite proliferation of language which reveals nothing other than its own fear, its destructive labels of violence, and its abject spiritual void.

We live in a world of escalating contests, which no one seems to know how to deescalate, much less abolish. Whether it is Sung Tzu some 350 years B.C. or the United Nations in 2012 the best we seem to be able to do is obstinately persist in lecturing each other with words of war. Chris Hedges points out that in 3,500 years of human life we have had only 268 years of peace. James Hillman adds that, "During the five thousand six hundred years of written history, fourteen thousand six hundred wars have been recorded. Two or three wars each year of human history." We cannot assume as Thomas Merton put it that because we are "sane" we are in our "right" minds. If peace were a poker hand we wouldn't bet on it.

Peace in such a world is really no peace at all. To continue to live as if contest with the world is our only choice is a delusion of the most dangerous kind. We should know by now that contests do not stop contests, they *metastasize* them. To kill an enemy is to make him immortal; his memory survives infecting like a deadly virus his children to be spread to our children and back to his grandchildren, back and forth unending generation after generation. But what our shortsightedness does not reveal is that in such a deadening process eventually there will be no children. We never understand that in this predatory game there is only prey.

While our dying world story may be true it is not the truth. What if, asks Albert Camus " these forces wind up in a dead end, what if that logic of history on which so many now rely turns out to be a will o' the wisp?" Then perhaps it can be, as military historian John Keegan writes, "possible to glimpse the emerging outlines of a world without war."

Our new story must contain a central plot bringing with it new knowledge, attitudes, actions, and institutions. and a sense of meaning that sees life as a whole. This new story must as Dr. Martin Luther King suggested "meet physical force with soul force." Is it just common sense or an absurd idea? When Copernicus and Einstein, for example, made their conceptual leaps they changed our understanding of the way the universe works. Galileo's seemingly harmless *Discourse on Floating Bodies* was thought to be attacking the very fabric of seventeenth century Catholic society. *Peace as Child's Play* is both common sense and an absurd idea overturning hundreds of years of conflict. This new story, encodes a way of being upon which we have repeatedly turned our backs, and in so doing, misplaced the key to the cipher. Our new story has been tucked away like a seed in the earth. It is time for it to blossom and take root. Our new story is a love story. But not just any love story will do.

*And if you love,*
*If you really love,*
*Our guns will wilt.*
—St. John of the Cross

We are born Holy. Our birthright is original play not original sin. The innocence is dismissed as we tell children to grow up, stop dreaming and playing around, and face the realities of life. Robert Johnson writes that, "In childhood we have innocent wholeness, which then is transformed into informed separateness. If one is lucky, a second transformation occurs later in life, a transformation into informed wholeness. A proverb puts it this way; in life our task is to go from unconscious perfection to conscious imperfection and then to conscious perfection.

When I went to children I wasn't looking to be transformed. I wasn't ready to have my world expanded. At first I was bewildered; the children's play provided no obvious firm foundation. I was being taken out of my normal structure, but it wasn't clear to me that I was being put into another framework. I was caught up in a seemingly strange world for which I was utterly unprepared. The children taught me to poke through the veils of culture and knead the substance of life. I was being introduced to a different kind of real that was much larger, grander, and more enchanted than I had been trained to accept. The children and their play were working every conceivable permutation on my sense of what is real, even in the most basic sense of my identity as a human being. I was becoming aware that I'd discovered a reality that inspired my whole life.

I couldn't go back to the way things were before. There were no "do-overs" as we used to say when I was a kid. Original play is a "Humpty-Dumpty" experience in which "all the kings horses and all the king's men" couldn't put my old world back together again. Behind it all is surely a love so simple, so beautiful, so compelling that once experienced I wonder how it could have been otherwise. This kind of real has to be experienced before it produces a fallout in the heart and mind that passes for understanding of sorts. After all the years leading up to and receiving my Ph.D. my education was finally posing fundamental questions and in doing so it was giving meaning to my life.

When I began to *play* I was experiencing a kind of real that I read about in Margery William's wonderful book *The Velveteen Rabbit*. I had read this book to my own children and to children in my kindergarten class, but at the time it was merely a nice children's story. The more I *played* the more important Ms. William's book became.

"What is REAL the Rabbit asked the Skin Horse one day."

"Does it mean having things that buzz inside you and a stick-out handle?"

"Real isn't how you are made," said the Skin Horse. "It's a thing that happens to you. When a child loves you for a long, long time, you become Real."

I felt like the Skin Horse in the story was talking to me as well as to the Rabbit. This is what was happening to me. I was beginning to understand that I become real through *original play's* loving and being loved. I was to discover that so much loving and becoming real went far beyond anything I imagined.

One summer day living in a small mountain community in Southern California, I was reading a book on my porch and enjoying the dappled sunlight coming through the tall pines and redwoods. A neighbor boy rode by on his bike, stopped, and looked up at me asking, "Would you like to go to the troll tree?"

I thought for a moment. I hadn't heard that word since I was a child in Michigan. I recalled from my childhood that I had heard people from Michigan's Upper Penisula called those of us who lived in the Lower Peninsula, trolls. I snapped back to the present and returned my attention to the boy.

"Yes!" I'd never been to a troll tree, I thought to myself.

I put down my book and jumped down from the porch to join the boy. As we walked he said, "I don't know whether they will be home. But they told me that I could bring special people into their house even if they weren't home."

We walked a few blocks. We stopped near a very large redwood with a burned-out center. He put his finger to his lips and whispered "Shh! I'll go first and see if they're home."

He disappeared into the center of the tree. From inside he motioned for me to join him. It was harder for me to fit my 6 foot 4 inch body through the slit but I was able to squeeze in sideways. We stood quietly in the burned out darkness. After a few minutes he whispered, " They're not home, but it's OK for us to be here." A few minutes later he added, " I think it's time for us to go."

We were quiet as we walked back. Then suddenly he asked me, "Do you know where shooting stars come from?"

He didn't seem to mind my silent surprise. I had a feeling that he wasn't asking an astronomical question. I replied, "No."

He said, "When you are far away from someone you love you think of them and throw them a kiss into the sky. Your kiss hits a star and bounces off in the direction of the person you love. Adults call that a shooting star but what you really see is a kiss sent from one loved one to another. This is what the trolls told me."

The little boy changed forever the way I look at the night sky. I know that what we call shooting stars aren't stars at all but rocks that catch fire due to friction as they enter the atmosphere. But I prefer to think of what I wish on not as a trail of debris but a kiss thrown from one loved one to another. I'm happy to see kisses go flying across the heavens. And when my friends ask me, "Fred you don't believe in trolls do you?" I do not take *them* to the troll tree.

Here is another story that strained my ideas of real. During one of my visits to South Africa I stayed with a mother and her five-year-old daughter. Their home was in the countryside, what they called the bush. One night at dinner I noticed that the little girl was stuffing some of her dinner into her pockets. Her mother noticed too. But neither of us said anything. When she finished the girl asked her mother if she could be excused to go out and play. Her mother nodded yes and off she scampered. When she had left the room her mother asked if I would go with her to see who the pocketed food was for. I agreed. We stayed behind so as not to be seen by the girl. The little girl did not go very far away before she sat in the grass. She reached into her pocket and took out small pieces of her dinner. She reached out and placed her food in the mouth of a cape cobra. Both girl and cobra seemed quite at ease. Which is more than I can say for her mother. I put my hand on her leg and my finger to my mouth to tell her to be quiet. I pointed back toward the house. We quietly moved back into the house. Not long after us the girl walked in. Her mother could hardly contain herself in asking, "Where were you?"

"I was sharing with my friend." Her daughter replied.

Here are two forms of real. For the mother cobras are fearful enemies, for the daughter a cobra is a dinner partner. I'm not asking you to choose which is real, but to allow for the possibility of both realities. Only then can play enchant, inform, teach, astound, revealing the most ingenious relationships. The world is transformed not by deception or sleight of hand but by our unknowing; when the doors are opened, the wonder of life can pour through. Some things can be explained. Some things can't. Sometimes I like the latter best. The opening of a mind—my mind— is accompanied by a learned anxiousness that is disquieting, sublime, and often frightening. Children help to remind me that I must always keep an open mind, but not so open that my brains would fall out. It is necessary to in Robert Johnson's words, "balance heaven and earth." Anything less could not include the grace and vastness of life's play.

A young boy in Poland also pushed my sense of real. Following a play session he and his father went to see a therapist. The therapist knew me and about original play. Knowing that the boy had just played with me and that he was having trouble with a bully at school she asked ,"Do you want Fred to show you how to use play to help with the bully?" "No, that's not what I want." "What then?" He replied, "When Fred plays he has an angel on his right shoulder and he is surrounded by white light. That is what I want." Where do angels live? Do they have an address? I don't know, but I learned years ago that some children can see things I cannot. The word angel originally meant messenger or courier. This boy was a courier whose message changed my life. Now I know I never play alone.

*Every blade of grass has its angel that bends over it*
*and whispers, "Grow, grow."* —Talmud

Here are three children whose sense of real transformed my life. Is there really an angel clinging to my right shoulder? Are cobras friends? Are trolls real? Are shooting stars really thrown kisses? My play with children re-awakened in me a sense of a larger real than I had become used to. It was as if they lamented among themselves that my sense of real was too limited. They conspired to help me widen my senses of love and of real. I didn't realize it at the time but playing for real was their gift to me.

## A New Story

Our new story begins with a dream. Not just any dream, but childhood's dream. Childhood's dream is a new vision of the real world and our place in it. This dream is in stark contrast to thousands of years of belief that contest and war are sufficient to sustain life. If we are to realize our humanity wisdom demands not only a new story and a new dream, but a new person. A radical reassessment is necessary. Do we know what and who we will create? Of course not. How wonderful! We dream together and create a new narrative that will heal, educate, and guide us. Who shall guide us? "And a little child shall lead them." Isaiah 11:6

Polish educator and pediatrician, Janus Korczak emphasized the importance of this prophecy when he wrote that children can be the "salvation of the world."

It takes two for this new story to catch hold and light a fire in the hearts of people. The ideas and stories in this book are the steel to be struck against the flint of your spirit. In this process the flint (spirit) is held gently with its dry tinder (mind); then the steel (this book) is struck with a glancing blow across the edge of the flint. If there is no spark, one tries again. When a spark lands on the tinder and it begins to smolder, you carefully blow on it—not too hard and not too soft—until it glows. As with all things in the matter of the spirit we are in constant danger of destroying the fragile substance into which one wishes to breathe new life. This storytelling process is like the lighting of tinder, do not subject it to outside criticism, or skepticism, or even constructive suggestion. It must be cherished inwardly. When it catches then no amount of wind will put out the flame, but only increase its energy.

## Childhood's Dream

*Hold fast to dreams, for if dreams die,*
*life is a broken-winged bird that cannot fly."*
—E.B. White

> *But most important of all, a sense of oneness is at the core*
> *of every system of belief, every view of the world,*
> *held by every child everywhere.*
> —Lyall Watson

Children bring a deeply encoded, urgent message, desperately trying to tell us that the world has to be set to playing again. But their hints are not taken up and their warning notices are ignored. We seem as ill-prepared as we can be to receive their message. How lost and unheard children must feel, but they persevere as if pushed by a still, but insistent voice from beyond the furthest star whispering: "Go and give, again and again, until they receive." Fortunately, Creation is undeterred by our arrogance and blind ignorance. An unread message from an unacknowledged source awaits us, as raw material, a lurking extravagant potential in every child.

It takes unusual vision to see the obvious; all children bear the signature of unfathomable Creation within a context of sanctity in which their worth is absolute and incalculable. Mere self-interest obliges us to realize that caring for our children is not a commandment but a necessary condition of life. To treat children as anything less is to give up on them and abort the mission Creation instilled in us. We must love our children enough not to leave them our wars to fight.

> *We give children life.*
> *It is our duty to act in such a way*
> *that they do not ask why?*

*Childhood's Dream* is how children are initiated, not into a culture, but into the universe. Creation's play bursts forth in a mind-boggling diversity of life, sending out a myriad of invitations. These invitations can be difficult to receive, but if you pay attention with your heart you will find one amidst the busyness of your life. By all rights, this dream is meant for life to thrive as one. It should be obvious that child conservation is a basic condition of elemental human ecological well-being. *Childhood's Dream* is a divine ecology in which we share the rapture of being alive, an ineffable experience where reality is the same in oneself as in everyone else, and where action emerges out of the present moment without reflection, where one sort of knows how one should relate spontaneously, without thinking, to every moment of life. We are meant to have a knack for such living.

I began life as part of Creation's dream. My mother continued this dream by putting a dream catcher over my crib. She told me it was an artifact that was passed down to her along with some porcupine-quilled birch bark boxes and a reed quiver with two arrows from my great grandmother who was Pottawatomie, a tribe in the Algonquian family. My mother called this artifact a *dream catcher*. It wasn't like the large New Age versions. It was a small willow circle about three inches in diameter. There was a smaller willow circle in the center. Holding these two circles together was a web of sinew. My mother told me that it was hung on the cradle-board of new babies. When the baby was asleep bad dreams would get caught in the web and not reach the baby. Good dreams, however, would navigate through the small open center circle to the baby. In the morning the bad dreams caught in the web were dissolved by the sun's first light. Perhaps this story is my great grandmother's way of expressing Creation's dream for me. Like my great grandmother's artifact each of us can be a dream catcher, allowing only Creation's dream to reach children. Then, as R. Carlos Nakai, the Dine flutist, reminds us in a CD liner, "Thus I should carefully choose that which will afford me the best dream possible so that I may 'walk in beauty, harmony and peace' into tomorrow. I shall be a child until I pass from this reality."

Dreams are the ships upon which humans voyage. T.S. Eliot reminds us that, "Only those who will risk going too far can possibly find out how far one can go." Former NASA chief Dan Goldin warned that, "If we don't dare to dream, we won't find anything."

Childhood is the irrefragable dream upon which Creation risks the voyage of life.—life is to be lived as one. Jesus, Buddha, Gandhi, Thomas Merton, Ramakrishna, Lao-tzu among others understood this. Jesus, for example, thanks God for revealing life's secrets to children: "I bless you Father, Lord of Heaven and Earth, for hiding these things from the learned and the clever and revealing them to little children" Hanh tells that while sitting under the pippala tree Siddhartha "was happy to see how unschooled children from the countryside could easily understand his discoveries." Meister Eckhart adds that, "If I was alone in the desert and feeling afraid, I would like to have a child with me, for then my fear would disappear and I would be strengthened—so noble, so full of pleasure, and so powerful is life itself." There is something about children that is admired even by presidents. In the tension of the conflicts preceding his presidency

Thomas Jefferson, as Jon Meacham describes, was exhausted. He wrote his daughter Patsy, "I long to be in the midst of the children, and have more pleasure in their little follies than in the wisdom of the wise."

To realize childhood's dream one must play with life. Perhaps this is why Nelson Mandela wrote that, "In South Africa, children must be able to play again." Why? Because in their original play children enact life's dream, which is the mechanism through which we can create a sustainable childhood for all children. With such a new understanding dismissing children to "go out and play" takes on a profoundly new meaning—a meaning for which humans have been searching all along.

To go out and play is a powerful acknowledgment that we belong. Hokusai captures my meaning: "At seventy-three I learned a little about the real structure of animals, plants, birds, fishes and insects. Consequently when I am eighty I'll have made more progress. At ninety I'll have penetrated the mystery of things. At a hundred I have reached something marvelous, but when I am a hundred and then everything I do, the smallest dot, will be alive." He speaks of our consecration, the sentient kind-fullness of original play, which animates all life. Here we have literally at our fingertips the basis for universal kindness. In living this dream we fulfill our humanity and discover our *Universal Kindness* wherein we recognize that we are each a face of God.

> *All things perish but the face of God...*
> —Rumi

Childhood's compact with creation radically alters the context of life on earth. Imagine, for example, a world with no winning or losing, no sides, no fault, no blame, no revenge, no self-defense, and no enemies. For some adults a world without contest seems downright boring; to many others this would be a fairy tale world. It was to me too. Such a world may seem unbelievable, but children have shown me that it is not unlivable. We can reinvent the compassionate human presence by sustaining childhood's dream. But, this will not be easy because to live this dream is a subversive activity that runs counter to the plot of our dying world story.

Childhood's dream is an auspicious beginning. It is like "spring fever," a flesh and blood experience, and a summons to belong to something grander, allowing one to bridge life's deepest divide. Like Spring winds the experience of living a new story blows open the shutters of an adult Winter and brings fresh, fragrant air to a stuffy mind, closed heart, and creaky body.

*That which is far off, and deep, very deep: who can find it out?*
—Ecclesiastes 7:24

*"If the human brain was so simple that we could understand it,
we would be so simple that we couldn't."*
—Emerson Pugh

# The Godsend Conspiracy

*We shall take upon ourselves the mystery of things
and be God's spies."*
—William Shakespeare, King Lear

*"I will lead thee by a way thou knowest not
to the secret chamber of love."*
—St. John of the Cross

*All has been consecrated.
The creatures in the forest know this,
The earth does, the seas do, the clouds know,
As does the heart full of love.*
—St Catherine of Siena.

Children know consecration too. Each birth is a revelatory experience so profound that it can only come as a contract with the divine. Every child is born Holy and belongs to all life. As St. Teresa of Avila understood, every bird knows that God's will is for a wing and every rose knows that God's will is for a fragrance. And every child knows that God's will is for loving-kindness. And in their sharing of this secret children become God's co-conspirators and in so doing realize that compassion is what life is all about. I am preprogrammed for this in body and brain.

The *Godsend Conspiracy* is a kind of contract in the human spirit for the purpose of reinstating the original meaning of childhood into the direction and growth of human life and thereby fulfills childhood's promise of peace. In this compact Creation and children conspire through their original play to see around the corners of life and to engage us in a model of peace accessible but hidden, suggested, but ignored. Creation's compact with childhood is described in Psalm 104, verse 2, 3, 4. A child says:

*I am His messenger sent to tell you the way to Him...*
*If you respect me, and leave me as I am,*
*And do not seek to seize me with a full and selfish possession*
*Then I will bring you joy:*
*For I will remain what I am.*

The Godsend conspiracy is one of life's best-kept secrets. H. H. The Dalai Lama is correct in wondering, "Whether in childhood we have a keener appreciation of such noble qualities but let them languish in ourselves as we grow older." None of my playmates talk to me about it, but the impact of this Conspiracy is unmistakable. I know that some will think that any conspiracy theory is the first sign of dementia. Well, maybe so, but this is how I imagine the Conspiracy works. God brings together children and animals and says to them, " There is this person on earth named Fred. He needs help. His concept of the world is too small. Who wants to help him?" Then there is a rush of hands, paws, wings, and flippers as everyone volunteers to help me realize the wonders of life. Some volunteer to continue crafting my body, others mold my mind, and still others open my heart. Creation whispers to the volunteers, "Awaken him." Tell him that his mind is too small. He doesn't know what he is missing. I have made a world whose safety is uncertain, a world the perfection of which shall be conditional, the condition being that each person does his and her best to love. And whisper to him that, I offer him the chance to take part in such a world. He must remember that his safety is not guaranteed. It will be a real adventure, with real dangers, yet he will always have the choice to do his best to love. Will he choose to be born and join the adventure? Will he trust enough to take the risk? Or would he rather than be part of such an uncertain world, choose to relapse into the sleep of nonentity from which he has been momentarily aroused by my voice? By agreeing to take the risk he will become a co-conspirator and in so doing realize that compassion is what life is all about. I am preprogrammed for this in body and brain.

This compact with the Divine is the genesis of original play. It is not an abstract moral system. It is a living peace process from the ground up designed to blur if not dissolve the lines between self and other.

God has sent out millions of messengers. Katie is one of these volunteer co-conspirators. Katie is a special needs playmate of mine in Southern California. One day when I arrive in the classroom Katie is wandering about, stopping momentarily to jump lightly up and down. She vigorously shakes her hand in front of her face. She walks a few steps toward me and repeats her self-stimulating motions. She seems disconnected from the other children and staff in the room. I say her name, get down on my hands and knees, and crawl towards her. She smiles, cocks her head, and sends me a delicate blue-eyed play-look which darts in like a hummingbird sucking nectar from a flower, hovers and darts away. Three-year-old Katie unselfconsciously opens her arms to embrace me as I crawl closer. We roll over onto a blue and yellow mat. She sits on my tummy and bounces up and down. As I turn over she slides off and laughs. We laid next to each other on our sides, our faces are just a few inches apart, and our eyes gaze into each other. I quickly turn away with tears in my eyes. I think to myself, I've just seen a face of God. I can't help but look back at Katie. Like an arrow, a thought impales my mind, I say to myself, "You know don't you." She giggles a tiny bubble of laughter. It seems as though she sent the arrow. "You know don't you." I repeat in my mind. Another bubble of laughter erupts from her. We roll over and continue our play.

After we finish playing I walk her to her chair for a snack. Before I leave she smiles at me and we hug. I feel like something very special has passed between us. Katie not only knew the questions that had been rummaging about in my mind like marbles in a tin can; she also knew how to share the answers with me.

What happened? What does Katie know? She knows that she's God's playmate. Should I tell her teacher? No, that doesn't seem like a good idea. I decide to write a letter to Katie's parents and share my experience. I sit down in my car and handwrite the note. I wait and give it to her mother as she arrives to pick up Katie. The next day when Katie's mother comes to drop off her daughter, she walks up to me and gives me a hug. With tears in her eyes she tells me that I am the first person, other than herself and her husband, to really see Katie. This is the quality of seeing "two looks away" that the Native American elders would one day share with me.

Katie's giggle is an inkling of something deeper that cracks my ordinary world, something within that cannot be expressed in ordinary language. Her giggle is a hint, a spontaneous response, a dynamic, childlike, and immutable principle of playful experience. It is a wholehearted "Yes!" to a moment that reverberates through all existence. The consciousness of life shimmers in Katie's giggle. Her giggle is like the little spark described by St. Teresa of Avila. "This little spark is the sign or the pledge God gives to this soul that He now chooses it for great things if it will prepare itself to receive them. This spark is a great gift, much more so than I can express." It's not that Katie knows more; it's that she is more. Katie does not make herself one with God, she is a face of God. She has never been anything else.

Our moment is not available to scientific investigation, educational pedagogy, religious condemnation, or psychological reasoning. Katie's bubble of laughter is like a hot spring in my heart that bubbles out of my eyes as tears on the drive home through the green fields of early spring in Southern California. As I drive I am reminded that when I was a young boy my Godmother used to tell me that I was a Godsend. At the time I didn't understand what the word meant but the feeling I had when she said it was wonderful. I felt cared for—that feeling of kindness is the Godsend Conspiracy and life's promise of kindness brought by children, who are indeed *god sent* or God's message of love to the world.

If Katie is God's playmate, who does that make me? I then felt like Alan Watts who found that when waking up in India and telling people that, "My goodness, I've just discovered that I'm God" they all laugh and say, "Oh, congratulations, at last you found out." This is a kind of GPS (God's Positioning System) the pattern recognition system or life's common sense Conspiracy that allows us to see beyond all of our categories and experience Creation's pattern of belonging.

Katie's giggle is the sound of the first child in each of us who profanes sacred belonging in order that the sacredness of the profane world might be revealed. Katie expresses a love affair with life that is indelibly imprinted in the human heart. What makes Katie so ordinary and special at the same time is that she is willing to come out to play and love, rather than retreat in fear and desperation. She does the one thing that most of us seek to avoid at all costs: to act wholeheartedly and put our entire bodies into a situation, and to refuse numbness and protection in favor of love and immediacy.

Sometimes the clearest signs are the simplest acts. She doesn't give me any instructions or discussions. We play; that's it, nothing more is necessary. Katie does not allow me to relapse into my sleep. Like a whack on the back from a Zen master's rod, Katie's giggle is a swift, living response to my inner questions, touching my body, tickling my spirit, and jarring my mind. Katie shares with me in a direct and unequivocal way an experience of the "Ah! Of life," before I think of saying "Ah!" I smile at my appreciation of Creation's gift, bubbling up through me, implying an advance to the farthest boundary, where only the sole fact of love has meaning, but this is an afterthought, coming after I experience the unspoken meaning of our belonging. This simple, direct experience of play, like a shaft of sunlight searing through expansive gray clouds of adult life leaving bright the ground around, dissolves my doubt and provides a glimpse of human possibility. Our play points to a world order based on love. Through Katie this divine play is made real. How delightful Katie is Sophia, God's Wisdom personified, who at all times plays with delight before God (Proverbs 8; 22-31). This is what I call the Godsend Conspiracy, our secret plan in which you, I and God can play more often.

## Bearers of Promise

*"Children know in their minds that all children are the same, all human beings are the same."*
—H.H. The Dalai Lama

*If you want one year of prosperity, grow grain.*
*If you want ten years of prosperity, grow trees.*
*If you want one hundred years of prosperity, grow people.*
—Chinese proverb

Children bring with them profound potential, but what is it? Heaven only knows, because we've forgotten. Children are messengers, Creation's co-creators; who Elie Wiesel calls "bearer[s] of promise." They bring a promise of forgiveness and peace created in a different state of consciousness than that which violates their humanity. Everyone has seen children play. But as Erwin Schrödinger correctly points out, "The task is... not so much to see what no one has yet seen; but to think what nobody has yet thought, about which everybody sees."

Like butterflies encased in cocoons too many children spend their childhood living in the shadow of this promise. But childhood's dream is nothing if not resilient. Here are children from different parts of the world who have lived with neglect and violence. These children, however, refused to give in to their suffering. I felt from them no blame, no anger, fear, or revenge. They had not lost their reason for loving. Their willingness to embrace difference and not retreat in fear takes great courage. They ask nothing more from me than the courage to return their love. They were able to transcend their victimization not by revenge but by the sheer force of their loving. To them peace is neither an idea nor an ideal, but a living relationship expressed in their original play.

One morning in the midst of a lecture to educators and social workers in Manila, The Philippines I heard the sounds of laughing and running children approaching the room. Eight street children from a nearby squatter camp hurried into the room. The six young boys and girls and two teenage girls were brought to play with me as a demonstration for the childcare professionals who observed our play from the safety of their chairs.

As the children entered the room I stopped talking and quickly put mats down on the tile floor. The children gathered around the edge of the mats. Their anxious smiles and excited bodies anticipated what was coming. The fact that we did not speak each other's language wasn't important.

I began to crawl toward the children. They squealed and ran around the mats. Some snuck around behind me, touched my back, and scampered away laughing as I lunged toward them. Before long their tentative touch evolved into jumping on my back and running into my arms. Soon all of the younger children and one of the teenagers were on the mats playing with me. One of the teenage girls smiled shyly, but stood back away from our playground. The older girl who was playing reached out to her hesitant friend with the invitation, "Come it's OK. He's human too."

Some months later I sat in the playground of a school in Athlone, a township near Cape Town, South Africa. Curious and excited the young children ran up and surrounded me. The teachers had told me that the children were not accustomed to a white person coming to their school and sitting down on the playground. They gathered around me talking, laughing, and touching me. They especially liked to press their fingers on the top of my head and giggle. I soon realized that their fingers pressing on my sunburned bald spot changed my skin from red to white, which delighted them.

From the back of the group the smallest boy squirmed through the others until he crawled into my lap. He seemed to be three or four years old. He reached out and wrapped his tiny arms around me as far as they would go and held me tightly. We didn't talk. He just snuggled in close in the midst of the crowding, jostling, and laughing children. I encircled him with my arms so the excited rush of other children wouldn't hurt him. The bell signaled the children to line up and return into school, but the little boy continued hugging me. After a few moments he got up, waved, and walked toward the school.

When I went inside a teacher who had observed us through a window asked if I knew anything about the little boy in my lap. I replied that I knew nothing about him. She said that he has been at the school for only a week. He was brought to the school after he was found tied up in a black plastic bag and thrown away in a pile of trash. I turned away and looked through tears back out onto the playground. This little boy's sense of courageous kindness as Hafiz puts it "reache[d] down and grab[ed] [my] spirit by its private parts." His lesson is simple, but very demanding. He demonstrates, in a way plain enough for any adult to see, the secret of turning the other cheek. Like all children, he is a messenger.

## Encoded For Kindness

"When one tugs at a single thing in nature,
he finds it hitched to the rest of the universe."
—John Muir

When I was young, I admired clever people.
Now that I an old, I admire kind people.
—Abraham Heschel

> *The game of "I" is up, no longer do I*
> *play against you, fellow beings.*
> —Frederick Franck

Whenever she was frustrated with me my Mother used to say, "Fred, you don't have the sense you were born with!" She wasn't talking about a kind of reasonableness or conventional knowledge. She was speaking of a deeper common sense, a deep awareness of what all life has in common with Creation. And of course, she was right, I had lost my common sense. What happened? How did I lose my common sense? And what is this common sense?

The hallmark of my acquired consciousness was that I thought of the world as a series of contests to be won. With this foundation play was contest, children didn't offer me anything of importance, and peace was merely an ideal. I was wrong on all counts. Yann Martel was describing me when he pointed out that, "it's only with a child's imagination that grown-ups can begin to conceive a better world." The *peace* that for me was an ideal, for children is a practice. Peace is already in the child, who takes nothing more seriously than what I dismissed as sentimental and childish.

When the children tugged me to the ground they yanked on my imagination as they tugged on my pants. Children's original play demonstrates that unity lies at the heart of our world and that it can be experienced and shared. This kind-fullness is life's common sense. The children were bringing me back home to my common sense of kindness. Over and over again children and animals *actualize* what is one of the most important discoveries in the *Kindness Sutra* from centuries ago and more recently in neuroscience; we are hardwired to connect. Austin tells us that centuries ago the "sutra on kindness" in India suggested that, "even as a mother watches over and protects her only child, so with a boundless mind should one cherish all living things, radiating friendliness over the entire world, above, below, and all around without limit." This kind-fullness is as compelling a force of nature as the migration of salmon and Canada geese.

If in the normal course of growing up I lost my common sense of kindness, could I regain it? Could I replace the very brain chemistry of contest that I had learned? Could I exercise a choice to contest or play with the world? Could I change my mind and in so doing rewire my brain? The children were initiating me into a sense of expansive belonging in which I was becoming a co-conspirator. This is an act of insurrection in a contest world. Having accepted that responsibility I am never again absolved from the responsibility of seeing God in all life.

Original play's common sense kindness is more than a one-to-one morality. It is also a very radical step up in that it also refers to not only the recognition but the behavior reflecting that all life is of only one kind. I have mentioned elsewhere in this book about the role I take in breaking up fights. This role has been recognized by de Waal among chimpanzees. Such altruism is also present in whales. Candace Calloway Whiting writes about humpback whales appearing to try to intervene when a pod of orcas attacked a baby gray whale off the California coast.

Suppose such a realm of experience is open to everyone. This is being alive while I'm alive!

This common sense can be felt as well as lost. Here are two stories that illustrate both what happens when we lose this common sense of belonging and what happens when we are in coherence with our surroundings. In Darfor there's a joke that made the rounds among the military and aid officials. The most important peacekeeper in the Darfur region right now is the rain. The rain turns the dusty, arid plains into impassable bogs and rivers. But when the rains ended the killing resumed. Since people didn't know how to bring peace to Darfur they relied on the rain to keep the peace.

Here is another much older story about rain, told by Richard Wilhelm from his stay in China that illustrates the sense of belonging to all life that was absent in Darfur. A tiny man with a gray beard lived in the mountains. Following a disastrous drought in the land below he was brought down to a town to help. He asked to be left alone outside the town in a small hut. After three days it rained and even snowed. Richard was allowed to interview the old man and asked him how he was able to make it rain. The old man answered, "I haven't made the rain, of course not. You see it was like this—throughout the drought the whole of nature and all the men and women here were deeply disturbed. They were no longer in *Tao*. When I arrived here I became also disturbed. It was so bad that it took me three days to bring myself again into order, then naturally, it rained."

The old man in China symbolizes a kind of relationship with the world that has coherence and creative power far beyond our cultural processes to support and sustain the human energies necessary for life to thrive not merely survive. Our emphasis on survival is based on our assumption that fight-flight-freeze is not only our best but our only viable response to life-challenging crises. This is "zoomorphism," that is, anthropomorphism in reverse. This is not merely an abstract ideal, but a felt reality. Instead of reaching out, it compels a person to find his safety within the confines of the self. In this process life is degraded.

The elderly Chinese man, on the other hand, doesn't try to manipulate the outside world to fit his desires, hopes, or fears. He knows that never works. He realizes that genuine flourishing comes about by his being in tune with his surroundings. The old man feels his belonging through and through—body, mind and spirit. This is the common sense that my Mother was referring to.

This sense of one-kindness has been felt and described by many others with a rich variety of linguistic, scientific, and spiritual descriptions. Poet and farmer Wendell Berry describes this belonging as a "commonwealth" one in which, "every thing that exists is a divine gift, which places us in a position of extreme danger, solvable only by love for everything that exists, including our enemies." To Archbishop Desmond Tutu this belonging is called *ubuntu*, "to have what it takes to be a human being... one whose humanity is caught up in your humanity." For the Dalai Lama it is a feeling of interdependence, in which he is connected in such a way that his personal boundaries dissolve. Another term for this sense of being consecrated is *ipseity*—our essential way of being beneath the layers of culture, thought and reaction, identity and adaptation. It is the essential self prior to the autobiographical self. This individual self is described by Siegel as universal. Jung called it "all-belonging." This is a special kind of knowing called in Greek *gnosis*, knowledge of God. Much earlier in China Lao-tse spoke of this way of being as Tao. Zen speaks of *kensho*.

> *When the heart is right*
> *'For' and 'against' are forgotten.*
> —Chuang-tzu

Life has buried in our genes a code of peace whose wisdom is at once biological and spiritual, ecological, and ecumenical. I believe that this code of peace is activated in original play during which all of our natural emotional and behavioral potentials are realized. The brain is our original playground where all categories disappear.

Plant biologist, Barbara McClintock for decades was virtually alone in her view that "basically everything is one." Physicist David Bohm agrees saying, "Deep down the consciousness of mankind is one." Nobel winning chemist Ilya Prigogine's stresses life's interdependence and interconnection. Physicist Erwin Schroedinger points out that the most popular name for this great Unity is God. Neuroscientist Donald W. Pfaff found an ethical command that "seems to be true of all religions, across continents and across centuries"—the Golden Rule. Biologist Bruce Lipton asserts, "Survival of the Most Loving is the only ethic that will ensure not only a healthy personal life but also a healthy planet." The Dalai Lama argues that the basic human nature is compassionate, loving-kindness and that its importance and effectiveness have now been established from the scientific standpoint. This sense of unity is written in code, a code so deviously simple that it does not need to be hidden in numbers, series, or symbols. It is in plain, simple language that everyone can read, yet few are able to decipher.

While many scientists and sages acknowledge that a sustaining pattern of unity exists in life, they haven't known how to develop it. Nor do they know where to look to find it. H.H. the Dalai Lama, for example, writes that he doesn't have any particular ideas as to what specific techniques might be used to bring about this pattern in children. Psychologist Paul Ekman also does not have any suggestions as to what practices can shorten the refractory period in fear. Father Bede Griffith has encountered life's sacred simplicity as a philosophy but only rarely has he seen it embodied. Biologist, Francisco Varela adds that the question of increasing compassion has not only not arisen in biology it has not been imagined. Scientist Steven Strogatz points out that "we still know almost nothing about the laws governing the interactions between genes, or proteins, or people." We are like a rider who leaps from one of the four horses of the apocalypse to another without realizing that he must get off of *all* of the horses.

"Kind-fullness" is life's first principle. Behind the apparent diversity of life lies a hidden symmetry, life's common sense of kindness. Dag Hammarskjöld found this code within himself. As he put it, "our inmost creative will intuits its counterpart in others, experiences its own universality—and thus opens the way to knowledge of that power of which it is itself a spark within us."

Creation has provided us with a sacred endowment, a core neuro-pattern recognition system that allows us to access life's kindness. Siegel asserts that, "Kindness is to our relationships, on this precious and precarious planet, what breath is to life." We know that gravitation keeps us connected to earth. Now imagine that we have a built-in neuro-GPS, a (God Positioning System) system that uses kindness rather than latitude and longitude to position oneself on earth. Original play is our GPS, a kindness positioning system allowing us to *feel* life's code of internal kindness among people and other living beings. This is what five-year-old David was describing when he declared to me, "Fred, play is when we don't know that we are different from each other."

Original play's breathtakingly ingenious neural pattern recognition system is an innate ecological intelligence or pattern of kind-fullness that not only recognizes that all life is only one kind, but embodies an emergent pattern of behavior that sustains this sense of life's deepest belonging. Play's ecological wisdom serves as a defibrillator to contest's deadly arrhythmia in the pattern of human life. This is an ecological relationship in which egocentricity is replaced by eco-centricity. In this ecology one's gentle touch is local and particular while one's reach is global and universal.

*Original play frees us from the illusion of separateness and simultaneously widens our circle of compassion.*

I had to be hit in the heart to rediscover this pattern of kind-fullness. The transformation is far more fundamental than I imagined. Children changed more than my mind, they changed my brain. The more I played, the more my brain replaced the contest patterns with new patterns of play. As my friend and mentor Dr. Björn Wrangsjo told me one morning at breakfast in his home in Stockholm, Sweden, "Fred you've played for so long that you've changed your brain." Björn's statement was profound. Is it really possible to change one's brain by playing? Yes, it seems that the life I was living in play with children was reshaping my brain. Goleman adds that, "In effect, being chronically hurt and angered, or being emotionally nourished, by someone we spend time with daily over the course of years can refashion our brain." It is difficult to imagine the implications of such a process.

*The most important and profound message of this book is that we can change our minds and our brains; we can choose to love instead of fear. In so doing we can change the game and truly play with life.*

This is a radical notion. Fortunately this pattern can be discovered and experienced by us. We have a choice; we can re-play the game of life. Original play taps into implicit, hard-wired capacities of our native kind-fullness. The recent findings of neuro-plasticity suggest that we can remodel our neuro networks and indeed can train ourselves to be more kind, more compassionate beings. Research also indicates that as Siegel puts it, "the resonance circuits have been shown to not only encode intention, but also to be fundamentally involved in human empathy, and also in emotional resonance, the outcome of attunement of minds." Iacobini has called mirror neurons the cells in our brains that make our experience of others deeply meaningful. He continues, "They show that we are not alone, but are biologically-wired and evolutionarily-designed to be deeply connected. Wiring connects us all at our common human core." "We are, as Desmond Tutu put it, "programmed—hard-wired—for goodness." This means that at a neural level our brains can encode not only what we physically see, but the intention that we imagine. Daniel Siegel suggests that, "In the next now, what happens actually matches what our mirror neuron system anticipated and the coherence between that anticipation and the map of what interconnected with one another." Daniel Goleman adds that, "The social brain actually creates a profound state of coherence." When he was a soldier in Mongolia Morihei Ueshiba, the founder of aikido, describes such a moment of coherence during which he "could intuitively see the thoughts, including the violent intentions, of the other." This state of kind-fullness is life's common sense.

To use the language of computers, creation's kindness code is a different operating system from contest.

Original play is the software application that activates this code throughout life. The salient property of original play's coherence is that it transforms the context within which we live our lives. It transforms time and space, drops out the categories of the psychic and social, and even species self, and in the process disrupts our automatic fear response and transforms what constitutes our self-defense relationship with reality. Original play functions like a sort of circuit breaker shutting down the brains flight, fight, freeze circuit and re-establishes an inherent sense of kind-fullness. Original play is a coherent state in which our fight or flight mechanism of the sympathetic nervous system is reduced while simultaneously promoting the healthier, growth potential of the parasympathetic nervous system. Accordingly, original play reflects not only the covert ways our normal brains' attention networks have been wired by fear but more importantly how these networks can be rewired to process that vast other reality beyond the grasp of our fearful egocentric selves. Bruce Lipton describes the brain functioning as a light switch—off and on, fear and love. Newberg & Waldman say the same thing in different words: "Love goes up, and fear goes down. Anger goes up and compassion goes down." H.H. The Dalai Lama points out that "the brain cannot develop properly and people cannot be healthy in the absence of human affection."

Within original play's sense of kind-fullness we can feel the boundaries of self and other disappear. This is the pattern that I believe Gregory Bateson was seeking when he asked, "What pattern connects the crab to the lobster and the orchid to the primrose and all four of them to me." This pattern is a first cause and a consequence of a certain *kind* of knowing. Neuropsychologist Jaak Panksepp argues that the brain contains distinct neuro systems devoted to the generation of rough and tumble play in organisms from rats to humans." This pattern is not an idea, but an experience. It is not a mystery to be solved, but one to be lived.

I have experienced, for example, this synchrony of kind-fullness or coherence with children and animals whom we don't usually imagine capable of such connections. A number of years ago I took a Tai Ji workshop from Chungliang Al Huang. The workshop was at Esalen on the northern California coast during the annual migration of Monarch butterflies from Canada to Mexico. Thousands of Monarch butterflies hung from the trees like orange and black Christmas bulbs. Al said that if we were to do our Tai Ji outside and move like the trees the butterflies might land on us. Although I could imagine Al doing Tai Ji with the grace required to attract butterflies, I couldn't imagine me doing it. Nevertheless, I was very excited about the possibility. I spent as much time outside practicing Tai Ji and aikido sword movements as I could. At first I watched and tried to imitate the trees. I was very awkward. In order to imitate the trees I had to wait for them to move first. Then I would try to imitate the tree's movements. This meant that I was always hesitating to see how the trees would move so I could follow. My motions weren't fluid. I'm sure the butterflies could tell the difference between a tree and Fred pretending to be a tree. I was giving up one category, Fred, for another, tree.

Before too long I realized that such pretense wasn't what Al was suggesting. He was pointing to something else entirely. But what was it? I was not to imitate the tree but to give myself to the wind so that I could receive it with the same touch and presence as the trees. Then I would resonate, and in that harmony Fred would disappear. I dropped my efforts to be a tree. I was now mirroring not imitating trees and butterflies. Before long a butterfly landed on the tip of my bokken (wooden sword). The butterfly stayed with me the entire afternoon. During the afternoon Al came out and the butterfly flew to him to share in his Tai Ji. The butterfly would walk up and down the length of my sword, then flit back and forth from sword to my shoulder, to my hand and back again. We moved together on the Esalen lawn. As evening approached I put the butterfly on a bush and said good-bye. The next morning as soon as I awoke I ran to the bush. I was hoping to continue our play. I was disappointed to see that the butterfly was not where I had placed it. Then I glanced down to the ground. There below the bush were four butterfly wings. This is what the Japanese call *"ichi-go, ichi-e"* one encounter, one opportunity. Two neurons mirroring, one called Fred the other Monarch butterfly. Here in a flash an ephemeral moment between human and butterfly in which living is now or not at all.

Another example of playing beyond our accepted categories involves a boy with autism. He was eight-years-old. We had just finished a session of original play in his school in Seattle. Contrary to the expectations of research his play was indistinguishable from that of other children. He did no stimming and no echolalia. He played with me, not at me or next to me, but *with* me. No parallel play. No autism. This was not merely a lack of ego, but a dynamic blending of two people beyond the categories of their everyday lives. Following the play session we were sitting on the edge of the mats waiting for his teacher to come and walk him back to class. As he sat there he exclaimed, "I wish I had a normal life. I wish I had a normal life. This play is my reminder of a normal life." Not only did he play, but he also commented on his experience of play as a world outside of autism. Often professionals encourage parents to focus their autistic child on the real world. Which "real' world" is that; the one that excludes him or the one that includes him.

It is this inclusive world outside of the categories of Fred, butterfly, and autism in which original play takes place. Such a playground only arises when we abandon our categories and our emotional attachment to them. Original play is life encoded for kindness—immediate, nonverbal, and without category. Such play with butterflies and autistic children remains outside the accepted categories of social and natural science. Autistic children and butterflies aren't supposed to be able to play. For example, it is often said by natural scientists that, "Only mammals play."

Since autism was discovered in the 1940's by Leo Kanner in Baltimore and Hans Asperger in Vienna there have been 100's of case studies in the medical literature documenting in detail the symptoms of autism, which fall into two main groups: social-cognitive and sensorimotor. The first group is thought to be the single most important diagnostic symptom: mental aloneness and a lack of contact with the social world coupled with an inability to have empathy with others. Psychologists and educators often explain that, "Children with autism cannot participate in social play. They cannot demonstrate empathy." It is still a commonly held belief, for example, among parents, educators, and scientists that humans with autism do not engage in social play, because they "are almost blind to the feelings of others" Neuroscientist V.S. Ramachandran adds, "Autistic children express no outward sense of play." It is common for parents to add that their autistic child may play *beside* another child, but not *with* another child. He adds that, "How sad it must be for parents to see their sons and daughters impervious to the enchantment of childhood." As the boy above demonstrated autistic children engage in play, but not the cultural variety that adults imagine. We can turn around Dr. Ramachandran's statement to say, how sad it must be for autistic sons and daughters to see their parents, teachers, and therapists impervious to *their* play.

When parents and social scientists talk about the limitations of children with autism they say that they are just being realistic. Their realism, however, carries with it an implicit and unrecognized assumption, coming as it does from being an observer or analyzer who makes cognitive judgments about children's play from the perspective of a believer and a participant in a contest world of cultural play. As useful as such categories as autism and Asperger's may be to get families much needed educational and medical help they are not helpful in original play. During the past forty years I have played with thousands of children and adults with autism around the world. They participate in original play, making eye contact and engaging in social touch just like other human beings.

## The "Real-Life" Experience

When we let go of our hold on our assumptions, models, and theories of culture we enter into a state of "no categories" allowing us to be increasingly open to life. I cannot grab life and grasp the universe at the same time, but I can play on the razor's edge between heaven and earth. Original play then becomes a divine reverberation through time, space, matter, and form. Original play's kindness opens us to a range of choice simply unavailable to the contesting mind. In fact as Lipton points out a sustained self-defense response inhibits the creation of life-sustaining energy. When we undergo a threat, we experience an "amygdala hijack" which triggers a flood of stress hormones with a range of negative consequences including lowering the effectiveness of our immune response." Paradoxically, when given infinite choice I do not make a deliberate, conscious choice to perform a specific action. What happens? I believe that the inhibitory circuits of my left prefrontal cortex are very active resulting in a decision moment that is more open and creative. Original play increases the range of options but does not increase the time needed to make a choice. This is in contrast to the research cited by Hall indicating that when the range of choice increases so does the time needed to make a choice. Original play's access to a wide range of choice is below the level of consciousness and does not result in what is clinically called decision paralysis. In fact, the opposite is true. The time available matches the task. This happens so quickly that I do not feel like a decision is being made at all. I call it a moment of "no-choice." This being in the present is the only way to play for real. It is as if the right option was present all along. What is required of me is not decision-making but being present. With time and practice this becomes my default brain response to potentially dangerous events. I have experienced this "no-choice" moment in experiences with rhinos, wolves, an African lion, a Doberman Pinscher, and a grizzly bear as well as with people. These "nearest-to-life" moments have a number of things in common: the paradox that infinite choice is "no-choice;" time is both real and eternal; my awareness is both wide open and directed; there is no sense that "I" do anything; there is an all-embracing sense of peace-fullness; there is no option but to proceed and enter into the event; the experience is one of relationship without categories; after the event is finished my sense of "I" returns and cannot explain what had happened. The action happened "of itself" spontaneously, reflexively. It is as if I am operating outside the constraints of culture. Language, logic, emotion were not present. I am a kinetic learner, that is, I learn by carrying out an activity. I was unsure, however, of what it was I was learning, or even if it was "I" who was doing the learning.

We can see how this moment of "no-choice" happens by comparing two dog attack incidents, one imaginary, one real. Dr. Austin describes a pretend situation involving a Doberman Pinscher. In his scenario, there is a high chained fence between you and the snarling dog. You're safe. He goes on to say, "Otherwise, had this Doberman actually been right *behind* you and ready to bite, the signals from your pulvinar and limbic system to the central gray area in your midbrain would have caused you to be intensely frightened."

Now let's take a similar, but real situation. One day while walking home in Hemet, California. A snarling Doberman Pinsher crashed through the front door screen of a house and charged across the lawn toward me. There was no time to think. I stopped, stood still, slightly tilted my head and extended my arms down at my sides in the unbendable arm motion that I use in both aikido and play. The dog charged at me until it got to about two feet away. Suddenly he skidded to a stop, leaped toward me, and yelped, as if he had hit an invisible wall. He circled around me looking for a way to get at me. He would jump up as if to attack but fall back onto his feet unable to penetrate closer than the two feet. There was no opening through which the dog could enter. After a while his owner came out on the porch and gruffly called to the dog and walked down, grabbed his collar and returned to the house. I walked away.

What happened? Were there no signals from the pulvinar and limbic systems to the central gray area in my midbrain? I felt no sense of fear, not because I'm tough or fearless.

Here is what I think happened. Original play's "remapping" enables the brain to process information much differently than in contest consciousness. Original play's kindness destructures, deprograms and deconditions fear making whole new orientations possible. Original play promotes neural plasticity and strengthens specific neurological circuits that generate peacefulness, awareness, and compassion.

With practice, seconds of kindness can be stabilized into temperaments becoming familiar and effortless. The result of such training is a sense of ecological coherence that can be instantaneously activated and communicated to others. Perhaps my play over the years had as Austin describes"deconditioned my limbic system and frontal regions of their more maladaptive responses while liberating some of the most highly evolved associative functions represented farther forward in the frontal pole and temporal pole." It was as if at subcortical levels my preattentive system scanned my experience for safe, appropriate options. There was no self-defense. In fact there was no sense of "I" at all. After listening to my experience,  a neurosciences friend said that he thought my brain knew that I was safe before the dog attacked, but he couldn't tell me how my brain knew that. Such a brain becomes as Dr. James Austin points out, "a resource which could serve as the basis both for our long range biological survival and for our cultural advancement."

Contrary to adult first impressions original play is not easy. It's tough to be kind. To step into the magic circle of play is to step beyond culture and all of its categories. But there's more, we must also not give our allegiance to our fears. As Albert Schweitzer put it, "Until he extends the circle of compassion to all living things, man will not himself find peace." Original play's kind-fullness is a blend of heightened awareness, emotional sensitivity, grace, and a great deal of physical practice. I had to learn the movements of original play through painstaking practice.

In the beginning I thought I must defend myself and consequently I made some unfortunate choices. One day in a park with the children from MOBOC (Mobile Open Classrooms)I was on my hands and knees and a large boy ran at my side. My immediate response was to "hold my ground." I became rigid and strong thinking that this was the best way to handle his playful rush. His knees hit me squarely in the ribs with a thud. The problem was "squarely." I went down quickly unable to breathe. As a result of my rigid unforgiving stance of self-defense I had cracked ribs. I learned painfully as Bruce Lipton points out, "The simple truth is that when you're frightened you're dumber." Fear undermines intelligent decision-making. In time I would be smarter and learn to make my body rounder and more resilient.

There are times in our lives when we are immersed in an emotional turning point from which it seems that we may not recover. At such times being kind can be extremely difficult, even seemingly beyond our capabilities. On a late winter Sunday I had an extremely difficult and painful personal experience. I spent the night crying and could not imagine how I was going to survive. It seemed easy to lose hope and just forget about playing. I could not imagine how I was going to play with children the next day. I was exhausted from no sleep, crying, and feeling devastated. Thankfully I went to school and played and I got help from an unexpected source.

My helper was A.J., a young boy with Downs syndrome. A.J. was a special needs child in a Moreno Valley classroom.

When it was his turn A.J. ran and jumped on me with his usual joyful exuberance. In our previous play his only verbal response to me had been to say "Hi" and "Bye." On this particular day he hugged me and whispered in my ear, "I love you." I was so startled that I looked around to see who was speaking. A.J. kept right on playing as if nothing out of the ordinary had occurred. How did he know that was exactly what I needed to hear? I don't know. I left his classroom with no understanding, but with tears and a smile of surprise at life's mystery. I recalled Zen Master Yun-men's saying, "When a great act presents itself, it does so without rules." For the next month everyday I came to play in his room A.J. would hug me and whisper "I love you." in my ear. A.J. was able somehow to feel my unbearable pain and react with compassion.

Considerable courage is required to let go of our categories of self-defense and make oneself accessible in life threatening situations. Jack Kornfield describes two kinds of people; Those who are unafraid to kill and those who are unafraid to love. Even in situations of great danger, true strength chooses love. We have met some people in this book who have chosen this path of mastery. They do not ignore life as it is, rather they plunge into life's terrible and wonderful midst but choose to respond from outside culture's expected responses, so far outside, in fact, that their responses are unrecognizable.

One either feels it or does not feel it. Whenever we dare to penetrate the surface of the life around us that aliveness can be felt. Like a master magician who wisely conceals an impenetrable secret—it is the nature of life's kind-fullness to reside in the ordinary mysteries of life. Nothing changes and everything changes. I no longer belong to myself, but to all life. This original play is the starting point that relocates the center of gravity in an individual from fear to love and from self to God.

> *And, while with silent, lifting mind I've trod*
> *The high untrepassed sanctity of space,*
> *Put out my hand, and touched the face of God.*
> —John Gillespie Magee, Jr.

As Ken Wilber points out the directions to finding God are printed on the box your heart came in. Only it's in code.

## CHAPTER 5:

# An Initiation in Original Play

*"The child must teach the man."*
—John Greenleaf Whittier


*I tried to teach my child with books,*
*He gave me only puzzled looks.*
*I tried to teach my child with words,*
*They passed him by often unheard.*
*Despairingly I turned aside,*
*"How shall I teach this child," I cried.*
*Into my hands he put the key,*
*"Come, he said, Play with me!"*
—Anonymous


*Every child comes with the message that*
*God is not yet discouraged of man.*
—Rabindranath Tagore


*It is easy to find lots of reasons why God is something we cannot do*
*without. But this much is certain: the grown-ups aren't bothering*
*about him, so we children must do it.*
—Rainer Maria Rilke


*And if you would know God he is not therefore a solver of riddles.*
*Rather look about you and you will see Him playing with your*
*children."*
—Kahlil Gibran

*"Grown-ups never understand anything by themselves, and it is exhausting for children to have to provide explanations over and over again."*
—Antoine de Saint-Exupery

# No School

"I was excited, and thought of becoming a Master of Play. I don't even know what that is, but I thought, wouldn't it be wonderful if there were schools somewhere that taught humans how to become true masters at the art of play?" I would say to the youth in Brian Swimme's book, that I, too, do not know what it means to be a "Master of Play." But I do know where to go to learn the art and practice of our original sense of play. We must go to the masters. Yes! There are true masters of play. But they aren't who we expect them to be. Play's masters are children. To be an apprentice to children in play is not a regression to childishness. It is, on the other hand, a recovery of the lost characteristics of childhood.

There is no school for original play. Original play's "no-school" is not a cultural institution of any kind. The "no-school" school of original play is not a specific place; it has no buildings, no staff, no curriculum, no credentials, no degrees. There are no colored belts and no diplomas. This is not a place jealously guarded by scholars, mystics, or hermetic groups. There is no exclusive store of knowledge that opens a secret, hidden gate. The idea that there is a teacher and a learner is never articulated. Unlike didactic teaching play's skills aren't acquired by listening or memorization. There is no homework. There are no tests. There's no failure.

Children do not practice play; they play. Mystics used the mind as a pathway to God. Children were already playing on this path with their bodies. In original play nothing is acquired theoretically; everything is experienced. In original play determined practice achieves that which cannot be practiced. Do you practice taking a bath? No, it sounds silly. You simply take a bath. Most things we do everyday we don't practice, we just do them. What is required is an action done with one's whole being, anything less is half-hearted. But after years away we approach what once came so easily with the effort of one who hums because he or she has forgotten the words to the song. Practice itself is simple, but it is not easy to become one who practices. I must play wholeheartedly. Learning to play takes a lifetime of practice. There are no short cuts. Fortunately, children are always ready to help me learn more. As the Sufi story shared by Feldman & Kornfield, puts it: "

'Mulla, Mulla my son has written from the Abode of Learning to say that he has completely finished his studies."

"Console yourself madam, with the thought that God will no doubt send him more."

## To Be A Beginner

*"In the beginner's mind there are many possibilities, but in the expert's mind there are few."*
—Suzuki Roshi

*What the caterpillar calls the end of the world, the master calls a butterfly.*
—Richard Bach

*Our destiny is to go beyond everything, to leave everything, to press forward to the End and find in the End our Beginning, the ever-new Beginning that has no End*
—Thomas Merton

Normally as adults we enter into apprenticeships with some idea of what we are getting ourselves into. My apprenticeship was different. I didn't consciously choose to be an apprentice. I never imagined I would be an apprentice to children. Not only were the lessons difficult the manner of teaching was new to me. My masters didn't talk to me. My learning wasn't theoretical. I was learning by experience.

I was a beginner. After thirty years of contest behavior, there was so much I had to let go. My old ideas and opinions about teaching, children, and play as contest were no longer appropriate. I had no idea what I was doing. I was being re-introduced to the child's full-of-wonder view of the world. I was, so to speak, raw, like a piece of unbleached silk or uncarved stone. Zen master Shunryu Suzuki calls this open-mindedness "beginner's mind."

It wasn't so much that I was somehow creating a beginner's mind. It was more that beginner's mind was creating me. It is one thing to be a beginner and not know it, but it is another thing to be a beginner and know it. But the children never let me be complacent, so that I can say, "I've got it!" It was as if the children were asking of me, "What would you like to become? We will help you come to completion. They were happy to fulfill Creation's craft. In their crafting of me I was becoming real. But this was a different "I." It was an "I" that no longer would struggle in contest with the world, but an "I" that contains the world. This is not a cultural tradition, religious doctrine, nor a learned philosophy; it is a practical experience. Fortunately, I did not have to believe in something or other. The children provided no explanations, just guidance heart to heart, hand to hand in affirming life's living paradox: in original play when "I" am real there is no "I" who experiences this realness! `

I wondered, is this what Mother Teresa meant by being real?

I had no idea that loving and becoming "Real" would hurt so much. Mother Teresa commented that such, "love, to be real, must cost—it must hurt—it must empty us of self." In other words, becoming real. Mother Teresa is right.

The children leave their traces in me, pushing my mind beyond the limits set by me and culture. They guide me into mystery and in so doing are what Stephen Mitchell calls, "the fulcrum of the possible." It seems that Jiddu Krishnamurti understood about this sense of real when he wrote that, "So a man who is seeking to understand violence does not belong to any country, to any religion, to any political party or partial system; he is concerned with the total understanding of mankind." Gradually it was as if the children were redicting my moral compass from being centered on me to being God-centered. What truly mattered was not how to get the most out of life, but how to live so that life got the most out of me. Original play is for God's sake.

## Letting The World Tickle My Heart

*Education is an admirable thing, but it is well to remember from time to time that nothing that is worth knowing can be taught."*
—Oscar Wilde

*"Seek not what the old masters did; seek what they sought."*
—Basho

*"Childlikeness' has to be restored with long years of training in the art of self-forgetfulness.'*
—Herrigel

*Children know enough not to search for bird's eggs in a cuckoo clock.*

**"**Once upon a time" when I was a young child on my uncle's farm I was a master of play. To me the whole world was a playground and everything was a playmate. Like a daffodil's first push through the early spring earth I ran out the screen door into a world full of playmates. I was living a feeling of belonging as old as all life and as young as infancy. I knew and was known by every field, tree, and animal. The cornfield, apple orchard, barn, woods, pond, horses, and fox were my tutors. The farm had wandering places like the woods and "you'll hurt yourself" places like the trees in the apple orchard and the barn's hayloft, and rest places like the hilltop in the back pasture. Surrounded by the farm was like being tucked into a down comforter on a cold, frosty night. I was as much inhabited by the farm as I inhabited the farm. I played with an undivided mind, intent upon play's demands and pleasures, reconciled to its hardships, not complaining, never believing that I might be doing something better, and certainly not bored. The farm was a blessing place. As Laurens van der Post and an old Zulu oral historian put it, "The place where one goes to be known at last, as the first spirit has all along known one." Here I lived sacred moments in secular days when I knew and felt as all along Creation has known and felt me. To put it another way, I felt my place in the scheme of things. I was living childhood's dream, what cosmologists and saints take on faith; that we can

141

personally connect in a meaningful way with the larger world we live in. The farm needed not just the attention of the adults who lived on it; but, there was a coherence on the farm that required a childhood being lived within its provenance.

Then for years I forgot to remember. I was busy doing something else—becoming an adult. It was as if the existence of the children's world didn't concern me, so it didn't have any meaning. There was a caesura in my life. My spontaneous and wondrous play on the farm became a pastime, then, like a teddy bear stored in a trunk, a memory. Poet e.e. cummings had it right when he wrote, "As up I grew down I forgot." Mine was a profound forgetting. I agree with R. D. Laing, "We have forgotten most of our childhood, not only its contents but its flavor." My return to original play was a forward and backward learning process of learning and relearning, remembering and forgetting. It wasn't easy. I had to risk over and over again. At first it seemed like I was only risking my body. I was a cube trying to be a sphere. After years of misuse my corners needed rounding off. In order to play I had to learn to untie all of the knots in both my mind and my body. When I first began to play I came home each day and soaked in a hot bath with Epsom salts to sooth my sore joints and muscles. The bath helped my body but did nothing for the knots in my mind. When I lie in the bathtub after a bruising day of play and feel the merciless tenacity of my defects, weaknesses in my body and illusions in my mind I recall something from St. John of the Cross.

"Once I said to God, "How do you teach us?" and He replied,

"If you were playing chess with someone who had infinite power and infinite knowledge and wanted to make you master of the game, where would all the chess pieces be at every moment? Indeed not only where he wanted them, but where all were best for your development; and that is every situation of one's life."

Fortunately, the children knew all of this. But when I looked to them for answers, they would, if they looked at me at all, just smile. As if to say, "Just because." My questions then just die of natural causes. It is as if the children were "nightlights" in my life dispeling the unknowns hidden within the darkness of my fears. I must live original play's gifts for them to be realized. The paradox is that when they are realized my categories disappear. If "I" disappear who is learning? The answer comes from the Vedic saint Nisargadatta Majaraj.

*Wisdom tells me I am nothing,*
*Love tells me I am everything.*
*Between the two my life forms.*

The children's enthusiasm was an embodied command, 'We won't take no for an answer." "Come down to play and skin your knees and bruise your heart with us and God." This was the children's summons. Here was an invitation that no cross-examination by pure reason could shake. The children did not allow me a way out. Each day I came to play the children eyed me with an air of expectancy, as if they had given me a test and were waiting for me to discover the right answer. They knew there was more in play than I perceived. They knew I needed to take a second look. They set the implacable precondition that my new awareness had to be lived before it could be understood and known. To do so meant that I must learn to travel light and free, with as empty a mind, as flexible a body, and as open a heart as possible. To be a beginner requires that I let go of the psychological and social baggage I carry around with me. I cannot return to play carrying these burdens; instead of romping with a child I would then be fussing with my luggage.

The children invited me to join them and enter a mystery in which I was approaching the edges of my known world. I had read the children's stories of magical openings through which one disappeared into another world, like the wardrobe in C.S. Lewis's *The Lion, the Witch, And The Wardrobe*, or Dorothy clicking her heels, or Alice falling into the rabbit hole. I knew the writings of mystics and sages who remind us that to reclaim wisdom and peace we must become as little children. But what about me? I am neither a mystic nor a sage. How was I to become like a child again? I couldn't imagine learning anything valuable from children. It never occurred to me that they could teach me anything about play. After all, I had played sports throughout my childhood and into my college years. Nothing in my life prepared me for what I was to encounter.

Children became my most patient tutors. The children do not tell me how good I am; nor do they blame me for my mistakes. The children treat me as capable; they mentor me as if I have the capacity to actually learn what they know. They know a lot is going to be asked of me, but my intrinsic capacity and wisdom will handle whatever arises. But they are also the sternest judges of how well I carried out my sacred trust to love beyond fear, trust beyond knowing, and belong to all life. And yet, with all of my uncertainty I had a sense that children were smiling as they had been promising me this all along, waiting for the time when I would realize that a new world was being revealed to me. I was entering a life long training in being someone other than I had been, but who Creation had promised I could be.

One day I was playing with Linda who, because, of a severe sun sensitivity, cannot be in the sun for even a few minutes. Linda is four years old and blind. One day we were playing together in the shade and she asked, "Fred what does sun feel like?"

"Just a minute Linda." I ran out into the California sun and rubbed my hands together in the sun. I ran back to Linda.

"Here Linda I have some sun. Can I rub it on your face?"

"Yes. Please. Rub some sunlight on my face."

I rubbed my warm hands on her face. She smiled and giggled.

Then she reached out and put her hands on my face and rubbed. She gently moved her hands around my whole head as if she were molding it out of clay. She finished and exclaimed," Oh, Fred you have a head!"

Is this a question or an exclamation? I don't know what to think. Is she surprised that I have a head? Or is she saying that after her careful touch, I do indeed have a head? Do you recall in the living world story that we fell to earth unfinished? So, each of us is a work in progress with the potential to transform our behavior, consciousness and our spirits. Through her giving and receiving of loving touch Linda helps finish God's handiwork. It is one thing to appreciate a rose in full bloom. It is quite another to feel the same appreciation when the as yet to bloom rose is covered with snow. Linda knew this and it is both pleasing and reassuring to feel her touch as she crafts me.

Normally we think of adults giving shape and content to the lives and thoughts of children. But original play turns this relationship upside down. It's as if I had become lost and children were sent to find and guide me back home. Suddenly with no warning my body and spirit were yanked into a world I had long since departed. I was being initiated into original play. I had no idea that they were pulling on my spirit as much as my clothes. The children welcomed me warmly. They didn't ask, "Where have you been?"

I began to understand play by playing. Children knew that my heart has divine instincts; it just needed to be turned loose. It was clear that in moments of confusion I was not left simply with my own rational contrivances. I was supported by something beyond my levels of knowledge and awareness which made itself present to me through the spontaneous actions of the children. The children trusted that to my little knowledge greater wisdom will be revealed. As I went to the ground with the children it became clear to me that I could learn, but they weren't going to teach—at least not in the manner that I was used to. In fact, they didn't tell me what to do at all. For someone who had spent most of his life being in traditional educational relationships being mentored by children wasn't easy. My mentors are sometimes noisy with laughter and guttural sounds, but they are silent when it comes to teaching. I suppressed my constant urge to talk and ask questions; their responses were decisive and direct making it clear that my task is to get down, be quiet, and pay attention. They expected me to play if I wanted to learn what they know. If I try to approach play in a normal way in what passes for study, such as with a particular doctrinal stance or scholarly perspective, the real message will be lost. Life was at once more wondrous and more arduous. In his *Flute Blown Upside Down* Genro captures this difference:

> *The bellows blew high the flaming forge;*
> *The sword was hammered on the anvil.*
> *It was the same steel as in the beginning.*
> *But how different was its edge!*

To return to our original play is not merely a return to a capricious, childish life, but a recovery of Creation's gifts, which lie dormant within us. Do you remember when you first colored with crayons on blank pieces of paper. There were no lines to stay within. As we got older such playing with color bothered adults. We were supposed to draw horses that looked like horses. We were given ditto sheets and coloring books. Our coloring now had to fit between their lines. Children begin to see horses as adults see horses.

In original play we are being invited to go outside the lines and approach the world through a different lens. Children know that the world is a playground. They know, for example, that puddles are for jumping in, trees are for climbing on, and fields are for running through. Children are like dandelions; they grow almost anywhere, and that is their undoing. Adults might try to manage them, and that is our undoing. Like soils, childhood and play come in their own time; neither responds well to the rush of the adult world, refusing instant gratification and demanding a great degree of patience, intimacy, and deliberation.

It is not enough to read, theorize, observe, and analyze children's play; it has to be lived. The tacit knowledge necessary in original play requires hard, committed practice over a long period of time. When I let the world tickle my heart the meaning of original play is inscribed into my mind, heart, and body like etching. Etching is an old term referring to the process used to prepare a surface for printing. It implies that something has to be first removed, prior to the next step in the process. Initiation begins the process of effacing my ego and removing my categories so the new habits of original play can take hold. My apprenticeship process has three exacting dimensions—crafting the body, opening the heart/mind, and participating in grace. These come together not as abstract principles but as a living experience. Japanese sword master Ittokusai described this, "when mind and vital energy are united in emptiness, right action takes place of itself, independently. It is as if a god acted through you."

In each encouner I feel the preciousness of life in a single being, and in so doing let the world tickle my heart. J.D. was four years old in a California, Head Start program. His teacher asked me to come and play with him and seven other boys because they were aggressive. After playing, the boys laid down on the grass, holding their shoes. Of course they were capable of putting on their own shoes, but I put their shoes on each of them. Using the same play touch to put on their shoes helps to transition them from play back to classroom activities. When I got to J.D. he looked up at the sky and said, "Nothing can ever get better than this!" He reminded me that the ordinary world is already enchanted. Then it's as simple as letting the world tickle our hearts. Tickling of the heart is not a laughing matter; it is feeling the quickening or aliveness of life's reverberations. Eventually I am able to play not as I, but God in me.

## Two Looks Away

*Everything comes down to this: having sensations and reading nature ... To read nature is to see it beneath the veil of interpretation.*
—Cezanne

*Seeing begins when you forget the name of the thing you see.*
—Paul Valery

*Original play—that I let go of what I thought I knew in order to realize truths I had never dreamed of. What at first appears to be childish nonsense can instead when experienced make perfect sense.*
—Fred Donaldson

*"I always thought they were fabulous monsters!" said the Unicorn. Is it alive?"*
*"It can talk," said Haigha, solemnly.*
*The Unicorn looked dreamily at Alice, and said "Talk child."*
*Alice could not help her lips curling up into a smile as she began. "Do you know, I always thought Unicorns were fabulous monsters, too!" I never saw one alive before!"*
*"Well, now that we have seen each other," said the Unicorn, if you'll believe in me, I'll believe in you. Is that a bargain?"*
*"Yes, if you like." said Alice.*
—Lewis Carroll's *Through The Looking Glass.*

Believing is seeing. Alice and the Unicorn agreed to take a second look at each other. If we are to believe in childhood's dream we must, like Alice and the Unicorn, take a second look. Then perhaps we will believe in children. But this kind of seeing isn't easy. Appearances can be deceiving. Adults have always looked at children playing, for example. But what do we see? Nothing much, just children playing. When it comes to children's play we do a lot of looking, but unfortunately very little seeing.

147

Some years ago I was invited to join a research team from the University of Montana to look for wolves in the Northwest part of Glacier National Park. On my way there I stopped to visit some Native American elders. We were sitting in a small circle together on the grass facing the magnificent Rocky Mountains to the west. They asked me were I was going. I replied that I was going to join a university team on the other side of the mountains to try and find wolves. They silently smiled to each other. Then one began to speak softly. "White people try to see wolves by improving their eyesight. They buy expensive equipment to help them see wolves. But they will never see a real wolf that way." He stopped speaking and looked up toward the mountains. When he began again he was speaking even more softly. I leaned forward to hear. He said, "A real wolf lives two looks away. If you want to see him you must use two looks." As he whispered this his hand went first to his eyes then down to his heart and then straight out toward the mountains.

What is he talking about? What enables the elders to see further and deeper to a wolf that is "two looks" away? They didn't say. Not because they didn't know, but because they knew that telling wouldn't help. If I wanted to "see" I must learn how to look with my heart not just my eyes.

Contests and categories distort and block not only eyesight but also vision. Researchers see the wolf they are trained to observe.

The Native American elders were inviting me to take a second look. Taking a second look opens one's heart to possibilities that are never imagined and to surprising truths that could not have been predicted. Antoinette Lilly viewed this cosmic crack in the world through a whale's eye. The poet Kathleen Raine saw this connection as a flow of living light between herself and a hyacinth. Barbara McClintock for example, forgot herself through the microscope and found herself right down there with the chromosomes who were her friends. As Evelyn Fox Keller points out, "Good science cannot proceed without a deep emotional investment on the part of the scientist." Einstein adds that the effort required to discover nature's laws rests on sympathetic understanding; "the daily effort comes from no deliberate intention or program, but straight from the heart."

Humans are like words; our meaning is in our connections. Like words taken out of context when we lose our connections we lose the fullness of our meaning. As neuroscientist Gregory Berns points out, "Categories are death to imagination." There is a story of how Mother Teresa was able to see beyond categories to care for an elderly woman. This old woman who was dying on the streets of Calcutta said that she could not be touched by anyone other than a Brahmin. As Mother Teresa was about to touch her the woman asked if she was a Brahmin. Mother Teresa asked herself "Who is a Brahmin? I felt anyone who serves his people is a good Brahmin so I said, 'Yes, I'm a Brahmin.'" Mother Teresa brought her to the home.

During a cancer retreat a woman told me that her totem animal is a bear. The problem was that she was frightened of bears and couldn't see them as helping her with her cancer. Her fear was compounded by dreams of bears who were chasing her. In her mind they were trying to attack her. The animal that was to protect her she thought was trying to kill her. After listening to her, I suggested that there was another possibility. I told her that her ideas about bears weren't necessarily wrong, but just one possibility. Perhaps if you take a second look you can see another, different bear. I described my play experiences with black and grizzly bears.

I asked if she could imagine taking a second look at the bear in her dream.

"What would that be?" she asked.

"You can change your dream.," I suggested. "You can play with the bear in your dreams." Such an idea startled her. She looked at me as if I were crazy. But, she also smiled and agreed to try. Then I suggested that she, "Imagine that the bear is chasing you because it wants to play with you. So, instead of running away from it, you turn and embrace it with open arms in a big bear hug."

She said that facing the bear was frightening to her. I added that I'll be with you to encounter the bear. This seemed to reassure her. She said that she would try. We found a quiet room. She sat in a comfortable chair. I sat at her feet and was silent. She went into her dream state for some time, perhaps forty-five minutes. When she awoke she was smiling and related how she turned around in her dream to face the bear she thought was so menacing and he wasn't frightening at all. It was easy for her to hug the bear as it embraced her. She now has an ally she can believe in.

Sometimes even in the most violent circumstances the hardened crust of our categories cracks allowing our deeper humanity to seep through. When this happens the Duchess' game is momentarily destroyed. One such instance is shared by Glover; it occurred in Durban, South Africa in 1985 when police attacked demonstrators. "One policeman chased a black woman, obviously intending to beat her with his club. As she ran, her shoe slipped off. The brutal policeman was also a well-brought up young

Afrikaner, who knew that when a woman loses her shoe you pick it up for her. Their eyes met as he handed her the shoe. He then left her, since clubbing her was no longer an option." George Orwell describes a similar sharing of humanity during the Spanish Civil War. He describes a Fascist soldier running half-dressed at him holding up his pants ... I refrained from shooting at him ... I had come here to shoot at 'Fascists'; but a man who is holding up his trousers isn't a 'Fascist, he is visibly a fellow creature, similar to yourself, and you don't feel like shooting at him." These instances of humanity stand out starkly as exceptional when compared to the deceit and/or destruction that surrounds them. The fact that they are isolated incidents is grim testimony to the power of our categories to mask our humanity.

As these stories demonstrate we can meet life without categories. This playground of no categories is the field beyond right and wrong that Rumi wrote about. Such playgrounds are not found on any map; they are nowhere and everywhere. I recall playing in a home for special needs children and adults in South Africa. The children were brought in and placed on the mats. I noticed that there was an older special needs man who knelt down just off the mats. He focused his attention on his hands which he held in his lap. When I was playing with the children on the mat I noticed that he would give me a furtive glance and the quickest smile whenever one of the children pushed me over. I moved so that I could fall near him. At first when I did this he smiled, turned slightly away and pushed me away. I reacted to his touch by falling back toward the kids. When I did this he turned back toward the mats and pushed me each time I sat up. He smiled and seemed to delight in the effect his push had on me. The more we repeated this pushing the more he subtly edged closer, eventually sitting on the mat. In the staff discussion following our play session the staff were surprised that he played with me. They said that he did not allow anyone to touch him. In fact, he touched a *different* "me."

I told the staff that I had disappeared as a cultural category. The man didn't touch the "me" that is a therapist, teacher, or an adult. He touched a playmate. Our play allowed for a new relationship outside of cultural patterns. The special needs man and I had taken a second look at each other and in doing so conveyed a radical, straight forward message of loving kindness that erased our categories.

We do not play in the categories within which we live. In letting go of my categories I begin to develop a capacity to face uncertain and ambiguous situations with integrity, spontaneity, and compassion. Behind all of the forms of life there remains something subtle, intangible, and graceful. Once during a youth conference at St. John The Divine in New York City I was talking with a group of gang members and suddenly I was jumped from the back. My "attacker" and I rolled with each other on the cathedral's stone floor. When we got up I recognized a young man whom I had played with two years earlier in a Bronx high school. At that time he was in a gang. He shared with me and the startled bystanders that following that hour of play with me he decided to quit the gang and he was now in college.

Life's playgrounds are available anywhere on earth, even in an elephant reserve. When we see beyond our categories something beneficial is shared from one being to another. Some years ago I was invited to visit an elephant reserve in South Africa. The reserve had six orphaned baby elephants and an old matriarch. The owners of the reserve wanted to put the six babies with the matriarch back into the wild but they were worried that in doing so they would endanger both the babies and other animals as well as the local population, because male orphan elephants who do not get the touch they need as youngsters often become rogues. Young elephants are raised in a multi-tiered network of female caregivers. Female elephants are fiercely protective of the babies and these babies likely saw their parents killed by poachers. It's no wonder then that as Lyall Watson puts it, "It is becoming abundantly clear that young elephants from broken herds are as wayward and rootless and socially inept as human children from broken homes."

I went into the large enclosure with the babies. The idea was for me to demonstrate to the staff how I use touch with animals so that they could continue after I left. I don't recall how old the babies were but they were all over eight feet tall. They immediately crowded around me, nudging me with their heads and exploring me with their trunks. When I moved away they followed me. If I ran, they ran, quickly catching me. Their favorite activity was to surround me and reach out and wrap their trunks around my arms pulling my arms into their mouths and sucking on them. At first I thought, Oh! Yuk I'm being sucked on by elephants. Then I remembered that they are babies. I'm mom. I certainly had crossed the line between human and elephant and in doing so I became someone other than who I thought I was. Like a receding wave takes the sand from beneath my feet on a beach it is as if my normal categories upon which I had built my life was being pulled out from under me.

We live most of our lives trapped in categories which we believe to be the whole truth. But when we take a second look we see that there is more. We see that human existence is not merely the time/ space we take up on earth, but the sacrement we are meant to be. When we believe and see "two looks away" we let the world tickle our hearts. In such a second look there are no categories, no boundaries, no self-defenses, all melt away like ice in the sun.

Without the distractions of categories our minds are free, moment by moment to move not as a matter of effort but with the ease of no effort. Also when we present no opposition, there is no one who can oppose us. The play of the universe penetrates our bones, brains, and blood. This is not a matter of morality, but mental hygiene. Then we discover Creation's ultimate secret—we are all faces of God.

## Accessibility

"Do I have to get down to play?" I am often asked this question from worried adults.

"Yes. In more ways than you imagine." To "get down" is to give up the scaffolding of adulthood, letting go of the structures and roles we have spent years acquiring. Original play requires that we leave our categories outside. This may be the hardest part of playing because our habits of contesting are so strongly developed and resitent to being dismantled. The excuses of some adults seem trivial. A teacher in an American school for special needs children quipped, "I don't get down to play because I don't like snotty noses." For others their excuses simply reveal ignorance. A young man in a school for special needs children in Warsaw, Poland said that,"These children do not know what is good for them. We know." For still others it is a matter of status. In a South African school only one woman would get down to play with the children. She said to me, "Fred, you must understand that these women now have their first jobs. It is a very big step up for them. They have come up in the world." She laughs heartedly and adds, "And now you ask them to get down!"

We must make ourselves accessible and allow the world to tickle our hearts. Getting down to play is a movement of humility made with the spirit as much as with the body. This is not mere posturing, good manners, nor is it a subservient act. It is an outward expression of compassion, respect, and a centered state of mind. A colleague Steve Heitzer, an educator, theologian, father, and director of a private kindergarten near Innsbruck, Austria, describes what it means to be accessible to young children. "For five year old Tabetha the circumstances of her life and her slow development make us decide on an extra long time right from the beginning. With Tabetha we had to be very patient. I started out, sitting down at a little distance from her. We looked at each other a bit furtively out of the corner of our eyes. I realized that sometimes it is just better to be quiet. Words may be intimidating. Speaking sometimes is just too loud. Almost obtrusive. Insistent. Slowly we started playing with sounds and words, too. And we sometimes even looked in each other's eyes."

There are times when making myself accessible means entering into the midst of a conflict. My experience is that children don't really want to fight but, like their seniors, they don't know how to extricate themselves from the escalating ladder of contest's aggression. This is especially difficult when a crowd of bystanders gathers and exhorts them on. One day at a high school in Southern California I arrived on campus to find a crowd of teenagers surrounding two girls who were ready to fight. I got down on my knees and crawled through the crowd and between the two girls. I pushed against their legs. they had no idea who I was or what I was doing. Dumbfounded,they backed up. In doing so their attention went from each other to me. They began to push me and laugh. The crowd was confused. The fight connection was broken. It was over.

Placing my body between the fighters breaks the magnetism of the contest by redirecting their energy toward me and away from each other. I am like a sheet of newsprint put between two beehives. Robert Johnson describes what I mean by entering with the problem of merging of two bee hives. "Suppose that you have two beehives that you want to bring together. If you take the bottom of one and the top off another and try to force them together, the two colonies of bees will kill each other, as I have learned from experience. However, if you spread a sheet of newsprint between the two hives and then stack the two hives together, by the time they chew through the paper they will smell enough alike that they won't be able to tell one colony from the other. Then they will join into one hive."

My presence between the girls was disarming. When the crowd dispersed the two girls and I talked. One of them admitted that she didn't want to fight but it was easier to fight one girl than everyone in her gang. The other teenager nodded in agreement. Neither the girls nor the school system knew how to effectively stop the fight. Frans De Waal describes a similar process among both captive and wild chimpanzees. A chimpanzee takes a "control role" that decreases aggression and increases reconciliation. among the fighting chimps. De Waal asks an important question regarding this control role. Why do the chimps do it? I ask the same question of myself. It would be easy enough to disassociate myself from the fight as it has nothing to do with me. But this would be a delusion. I have experienced my intervention serve as a force multiplier for positive action. Or, perhaps, the reason is both simpler and more profound. As Steinbeck wrote in the *Log of the Sea of Cortez*, "all things are one thing and one thing is all things."

*"I knew it would not take me long to turn you back into God."*
—Hafiz

I think of getting down as a gesture of gratitude, a prayer, and a signal that I am ready to give and receive. Getting down is a matter of both mental and physical agility requiring an openness to life's mystery, a capacity for fearlessness to greet the unknown, and a willingness to steadfastly practice. It is also something more.

Getting down I must be open to possibilities. Which possibilities? Any possibilities. " I was like fledging birds to whom from the safety of their nests, flight seems downright dangerous. Food is not grown in their nests. They must go beyond what they know. Likewise, if I am to play I must go beyond what I know. This readiness to receive can be thought of as accessibility training. Accessibility to what? To children, to life, to God.

My initiation into children's play required me to get down and be accessible. As with mastering a foreign language, I had to learn not just the literal meanings of play's gestures, but also its connotations, and to grasp these I had to get my hands dirty, have scraped knees, and torn pants. Speaking of skinned knees, I didn't think twice about crawling on the ground. It may sound simple but it isn't easy. It never occurred to me that there was a correct and incorrect way to crawl. But my knees weren't used to crawling. It didn't take very long before I had red, sore knees. Why don't infants get rug burns like me? Then I began to watch infants crawl. They lifted their knees up as they move. I had been sliding mine along the floor.

Getting down was not only a fundamental paradigm shift in how I move but also in how I think. To illustrate this imagine a rope that goes smoothly through a pulley. In play my actions would be like the rope that moves with ease through the pulley. If, however, I begin to think, for example, about winning or losing, about being careful, about how I look such thoughts are like knots in the rope. Now the rope does not slide smoothly through the pulley. Each time a knot comes to the pulley the rope is stopped. Likewise such thoughts check my actions in play.

One day while playing with young children in a California private school the teacher brought a new girl, Samantha, into the classroom. At first I thought she was just shy as she held on to the teachers pants and moved around the room with her. As the morning progressed I realized that it wasn't her shyness that kept Samantha near the teacher. It was me. She seemed to always have her eyes on me. As I moved around playing with other children she would move to place herself in another part of the classroom. Each day I came to this classroom she would notice me and move away. I would place myself in the room as far as I could get from Samantha and place my back toward her. In a few days she wandered over and without touching me stepped over my feet. I didn't look at her. A few days later she stepped over my lower legs, again without touching me. This behavior went on for over a week. We had no touch and no eye contact. Then one day while I was sitting on the floor playing with the other children I could feel the slightest touch on my back, like a butterfly landing on me. It was very difficult not to turn around and look at her. Some days later I arrived in her classroom and the children were outside playing. I looked out the window to see where she was so I wouldn't surprise her when I went out. Samantha surprised me instead. As soon as I was outside she ran up and held her arms up to me. I knelt down and she put her arms around my neck and hugged me. I sat down and Samantha spent the playtime in my lap. Samantha provides me with what I need to know. My task was not to try to make something happen, but to be accessible to her needs.

I learned later from her teacher that Samantha's parents were drug dealers and she was given to a friend when they went to jail. Before arriving at the school she was put by this friend, also a drug dealer, in the trunk of his car for a number of months.

# Crafting

*When you learn a craft, practice it.*
*The learning comes through the hands.*
—Coleman Barks

155

Like other adults I had seen children play. And like other adults I never thought much about it. Children's play was nothing to take seriously. How mistaken I was. Although there are no specific lessons or classes given in a set order, my mentors always seem to know what I need to learn. Knowledge of original play is like snow flakes falling into a hot pool. It dissolves and becomes part of me. This growth pattern in play feels similar to the four degrees of prayer described by St. Teresa of Avila. She uses the metaphor of bringing water to a garden. At each succeeding stage more water is acquired with less effort as she moves from using a well and carrying water, to using a water wheel and aqueducts, to divertng a stream, and finally water is provided by rain. I remember, for example, in the beginning I was very clumsy and awkward. In time my motions became smoother and my body softer and more flexible. With more time and practice I became increasingly comfortable not interfering with my body's motion. What initially requires a great deal of effort eventually is accomplished by doing nothing at all.

*The child Jesus made clay birds just as the other children did, but he touched his and made them fly.*
—Lynda Sexson

*The craft is in the hand, but the effect is in the heart.*

There are no short cuts to the path of learning original play. I am continually put in situations in which my mental and physical habits are challenged. My apprenticeship in original play is like riding one of those childhood seesaws, up and down, learning and relearning, remembering and forgetting. Most lessons I learn repeatedly, over and over again for the first time. There are days when I'm discouraged, times I need a hug as first aid for a bloody nose. Fortunately, my mentors are always ready to help.

Many of my lessons were simple, but difficult. Early in my training one four-year-old girl, for example, caught me unawares with a punch in my right eye. Her small fist fit neatly into my eye socket, breaking my glasses, and giving me a black eye. I went home put ice on my eye and bought a new pair of glasses. I thought to myself that I had to learn to move faster. The next day I was playing with the same little girl. Again she was too quick for me. This time she punched me in my left eye. More ice and another new pair of glasses. On the third day I was learning how to gauge the time, distance, energy, and intent of her strike so that I wasn't hit. I felt proud; I was learning to blend. She smiled at me as if to say, "Well, it only took you two black eyes and two pair of glasses to figure out my lesson." And the lesson was? Enter. I must move into not away from her energy and do so without defending myself.

Some years later Gracie gave me an advanced lesson in spatial awareness. Gracie has autism. One day we were sitting on the lawn in front of her school in Fairfield, Connecticut. She was sitting with her legs crossed and I was about one foot away in front and to her right side. Suddenly she kicked out with her right leg. Her foot inside a Doc Marten "combat" boot whacked me on the right side of my face. The blow knocked my head to the side. Again I was at the wrong distance. Gracie just sat and smiled as if to say "Be Careful." I didn't sense any aggression in her kick. It was as if it was a reflex action. I recalled the little girl's punches and inched forward closer to Gracie. Now I put my arm along side her leg so before her next kick could gather momentum I deflected it to the side. My touch did not just parry her kick it nullified it in such a way that her entire body changed. She smiled again as if to say, "Good. You've figured it out." I was learning.

Black eyes, bruises, bloody noses, bites, and cracked ribs all are results of my learning how to judge spatial intervals between myself and others. Children were teaching me about correct spacing and like martial arts masters they played for real. They seemed to know instinctively exactly were the impact of their thrusts would be. Their strikes had focused energy exactly where they wanted it to be not two inches from my face and not enough to seriously hurt me, but precisely enough to gain my attention.

Another lesson was learning to fall down. When I began to play I didn't know how to fall down. I didn't even know that I didn't know how to fall. As a toddler I fell down and got up all the time. As an adult, however, falling and getting up unharmed has to be relearned. Robert gave me my first lessons in falling. I met him in a San Diego child development center. He was eight years old and diagnosed with autism. The staff commented about his awkwardness as he ran around the lawn. I saw something else. He knew how to fall. He melted to the ground as if he were a mound of ice cream on a hot plate. I saw that Robert didn't fall over; he fell down. It never had occurred to me that there was a difference. I wanted to be able to do what he did. So I run along after him and imitated his falling. But I didn't get it right. I kept falling over, not down. It was as if I had been taking falling lessons from trees. My shoulders, hips, elbows, knees hurt. I felt like I was a cube trying to be a sphere. He watched my clumsy falling over and quietly smiled. This went on for a few weeks until one day he took my hand and fell down with me. Holding Robert's hand he guided me down, not over. That's it! Fall down, not over! I was hanging on to my "upness." A tenet of jiujutsu expresses it well. Those who hang on will certainly fall; those who don't cling need have no fear of falling. With practice I'm learning to glide rather than crash to the ground.

Recall that the purpose of the Godsend conspiracy between children and Creation is to craft a fully human being. The children help me to come forth. Over forty years ago the children began their work on me to summon life from within through their playful touch re-orienting me to my wobbly, roly-poly orientation to life that had been flattened in order to make me more secure. They do not create a new me as much as they release a me that, though hidden, already exists. They were like Michangelo who claimed that he merely removed what needed removing from a block of marble, revealing the figure that he "saw" with his heart's eye. The children could see the roundness hiding within my angular movements.

I tell people that it will take a minimum of ten thousand hours to become a teacher of original play. Some are dismayed, others are angry, and all are astonished. The" ten-thousand hour/ten years rule" is a common touchstone for how long it takes to become very good in a discipline. Herbert Simon has claimed that acquiring real mastery of a skill may take up to ten thousand hours. Psychologist Daniel Levitin remarks that, "this number comes up again and again" in studies of basketball players, composers, fiction writers, and ice skaters. In his book *Outliers* Malcolm Gladwell points out that, "There's a magical number: ten thousand hours of diligent, intentional, informed practice." John Hayes studied five hundred masterworks of classical music. Only three were published with the first ten years of the composer's career. O'Sensei Ueshiba said that in aikido," 'Iriminage and shiho nage, ten years. Ikkyo is your whole life." He adds that to throw someone with a touch of a finger takes a minimum of ten years of serious training. And, Ueshiba adds, this is just to master the basics and reach the first rung. Kenji Tokitsu got the feeling that Zen requires twenty to thirty years to gain one's center. Shigeo Kamata says that "at least thirty years of training will be required to glimpse the essence of the Way." The craftsmen of Tibetan traditional painters and woodcarvers study as apprentices for ten years or more. The Dalai Lama has said that, "In some Buddhist texts there is the suggestion that it generally takes three innumerable eons to perfect compassion." Alan Wallace suggests that it would be "really important if we could find ways that are not bound up with Buddhism or any other tradition to develop these skills." The best advice I have is to forget about time, just play now—after all that is the only place you can play anyway!

In original play ten thousand hours refers not only to actual hours of play but to something more, which in Chinese philosophy is described as the "ten thousand things" of the universe which means everything that exists. Not only must I play for ten thousand hours but I must play with everything that exists! I'm exhausted just thinking about it. There is only one way to handle this. Forget the mind numbing and body tiring number, ten thousand. Let go. Just play. Then your mind and body are released to do what they do best without your interference.

Here is another story from Leggett that emphasizes this principle of play practice. A group of students invited their master to a house to give them instruction. He told them that the goal was to realize the divine. The process is like filling a sieve with water. Then he left. After he left the students argued about the meaning of "filling a sieve with water." One fumed that he was already doing that by meditating every day and helping people. But I'm just like I was before. Some agreed that he meant that only temporary upliftment was possible. Others thought he was laughing at them. Some thought he was telling them that they were wrong. And still others thought that he was referring to some point in the classics. In the end they all left. Except for one woman who went to see the master. He gave her a cup and a sieve and they walked to the seashore. He told her to fill the sieve with water. She bent down and scooped the water with the cup and poured it into the sieve, which immediately emptied. He took the sieve from her hand and threw it into the waves, where it floated momentarily and then sank. "Now its full of water. And it will remain so. That's also the way to practice. It's not ladling practice into the self, but throwing the self into the sea of practice."

I felt the consequence of not being fully immersed in my practice during an aikido class. I was thrown by a more senior student. When I hit the mat I could hear the crunch. I crawled away and sat in seiza holding my arm. Immediately sensei know something was wrong. As I sat there dazed I went over in my mind the sequence of my *ukemi*. Everything seemed fine with my attack and *nagi's* throw, until the very last second before hitting the mat when everything went black. I hit the mat, not with a roll, but with a crunch. I knelt and could feel the wave of heat and nausea roll over me. In my daze I recall Ace Sensei repeating over and over that aikido required 100 per cent attention. I realized that I blacked out just before hitting the mat. I had given it 99 per cent. It was during the last 1 per cent that I had lost my awareness.

To be fully human I must give myself up mentally and physically to be handmade by the master craftsmen of original play. I must literally put myself in their hands, paws, and flippers. Through their touch they pass on a literal body of knowledge which is largely invisible to the untrained hand and eye. Neurologist Frank Wilson points out that people who use their hands have a way of knowing about the world that is inaccessible to those who do not. This crafting process is unusual for adults, as we are used to being the makers not the raw material. Some children treat me as a block of marble, a chunk of wood, a slab of clay, a bush, or a piece of steel. They pound, chip, carve, prune, and forge me until all that is unnecessary is removed. I am keenly aware that I am the raw material to be worked. Sometimes the intensity of my apprenticeship makes me feel like I've come like Mother Teresa "from the furnace of a heart filled with love." Thousands of children and animals have crafted me into more than I was, more than I thought I could be, and certainly more than I can put into words. This is my initiation.

I am like a pot to be thrown, wood to be carved, iron to be forged. Sometimes when I finish a play session I feel as though I am a mound of clay upon which children rub, jump, pound as if they are trying to soften and make me more pliable. I feel a kind of all over rawness, as if my body has been touched, moved and stretched in every possible way all at once like what I imagine it feels like for a slab of clay to be initially worked. With their energies my impurities are burned away, getting me to be bare, polished, and essential. They do not embellish. Sustained in the fire, I am formed out of the intimacy that love molds. While part of me feels unable to move, another deeper part is springing to life in an extraordinary fashion.

Some days I am like wax waiting for a seal. I am melted in Creation's play so that I can easily receive the stamp of belonging, bearing the truth of who I am meant to be. In order to take this stamp I must be soft and pliable, because if I am hard, dry, and brittle I cannot take the stamp. In such a case the seal descending upon me grinds me to powder. If I spend my life trying to escape from the heat of the fire that is meant to soften me, I will be destroyed by the event that was meant to shape my true self.

Then there are times I feel I've been crafted as in the making of a fine Japanese sword as shared by Saotome sensei. I am continually stressed as if forged in flames, softened by the heat of aggression so that shaping and refinemernt can take place. I am beaten pounded, folded back upon myself, heated, pounded until all of my impurities are driven away. Then, as if plunged into water my temper is set, the fires are controlled, and wisdom prepares to sharpen my edge. My hidden layers number more than a million. But the finished product is simple and pure of line. I am strong, yet flexible, and my being reflects all that is around me.

Sometimes, it feels as though children are chiseling me into shape as if I were a piece of marble, at other times I felt as if I were being hammered like a piece of bronze, and still, at other times I felt as if I were being pruned and shaped like a Japanese garden to seem more natural than if I were left to myself. Then there were the times they let me be, as if I were growing like a wildflower. Sometimes I am treated like a teddy bear with bald patches and exposed seams, hugged intensely, then put down and allowed to be, or dragged around by the arm. And all the time it was as if the children were asking me, "Who do you want to become? We will help bring you to completion."

To be handmade is to feel a part of it all, to belong in the deepest way. Like the sword maker and the potter, children know that they make the outside of an inside, and it is the inside that is the key. There is a story from China told by M.C. Richards of a potter who is interrupted in his work by a passing nobleman who stops and inquires about his pottery. "How are you able to form these vessels so that they possess such convincing beauty" "Oh," answers the potter, "you are looking at the mere outward shape. What I am forming lies within. I am interested only in what remains after the pot has been broken."

Play's communication, as in any craft, is in its actions, simple, basic and direct. There is a sense of integrity embodied in play that expresses an inner psychological wholeness, a coherence between hand and heart, and an extension of this harmony into what is touched. After forty years of being touched I am burnished, inside and out, to a fine patina—a soft luster appears with a glow from within. This patina is the union of heart and hand in a task elegantly conceived and gracefully done. The process is very complicated and no part can be omitted.

The children craft my inner and outer selves. They add something uniquely themselves, some element of themselves unites with the material, me, between their hands. Something literally rubs off. I remain a work in progress. As with other crafts I am never finished to be put in a glass case and admired from afar. I am made to be used, not revered. Like a teddy bear I need to be comfortable and durable enough to withstand a lifetime of use.

But there's more. Something of Creation is rubbed into and onto me. The child's touch performs a sacred function that fulfills the fundamental promise of life. Clay that has been left out and untouched, like humans, becomes rigid, hard and brittle. But when played with clay is wonderfully pliable stuff. Through the touch of child's play we, too, can become delightfully pliable stuff. We become, like plain pots, well made, good to handle and live with, and above all, alive with use. There is a trace of life which lingers on after the touch. In me this trace lingers from all of my playmates, children, adults, wolves, dolphins, bears, butterflies and so many others. We may think of it as a haunting. A crafts person recognizes that she is in the presence of an inexhaustible wisdom that makes what she touches a dwelling place for a higher presence. Craft is thus a way of connecting human and divine energies. The poet Rilke said that, "When a poet rubs a piece of furniture, when he puts a little fragrant wax on his table with the woolen cloth, he registers this object officially as a member of the human household." In their play the children register me as belonging on earth.

All my mentors present me with learning through direct experience, personal discovery, and intuition. In the choreography of original play the entire I-me-mine field of categories disappear leaving the ecology of kindness within original play—"the peace that passeth all understanding." After playing with some special needs children in a center in Cape Town, South Africa I was taken on a tour of the facility. I briefly stepped into one room with a number of young adults and some staff. As we walked back into the hall one of the patients walked out with us and stood next to me holding my hand. A staff member asked him to come back into the room. He shook his head. She persisted. He merely kept holding my hand and shaking his head. Without thinking I walked back into the room and he walked with me. Once inside he let go. When I left the room I turned and we looked at each other. I'll never forget his face, so serene and full of grace that I felt like I was seeing a face of God. As I walked away I realized the profound grace of "one encounter one opportunity." He re-awakened

162

me to the essence of life; living is now or not at all. In our encounter we are like two cherry blossoms, whose vibrant color and beauty remain only briefly before we are scattered by the wind.

Children present me with unusual lessons. Robert, for example, leads me into the art of falling down. Gracie's swift kick, on the other hand, alerts me to always be aware. Katie introduces me to a face of God. Samantha presents me with the opportunity to learn patience. While Lindsay, helps to craft my face. Danny confronts me with a chance to give love at the point of attack. With their countless touches, punches, caresses, strokes, rubs, the children are crafting Fred: caressing and rounding off my edges, forging my strength, burnishing my body, cradling my hurts. This is like the difference between a wooden surface that is brought to a high gloss with the addition of a number of coats of paint compared to a wooden surface with a patina brought out by years of touch. In the first the desired effect is added on, while in the latter case an inner polish is brought out.

Their lessons prepare me not only for playing with children but also for playing with life. Playing means hundreds of thousands of repetitions, each done for the first time. Eventually these active principles take hold. But with all the action what I learn is the visible form of the invisible, never forgetting that it is the invisible that is the model. Their lessons are supremely personal and yet simultaneously universal and sacred, tangible and intangible. There is a wonderful economy of means here in which everything is pared down to its essence, without removing the poetry inherent in the invisible connective tissue that binds the elements into a visible meaningful whole. Play's perfection is a direct pointing to the human heart.

> *"Enlightenment is an accident, but practice*
> *makes you accident prone."*
> —Roshi Richard Baker

# Part III:

# Play in All Worlds

*"...nor will they train for war any more."*
—Isaiah2:4

# CHAPTER 6

# In The Provenance of Childhood: An Apprenticeship in Original Play

*Until he extends the circle of compassion to all living things,*
*man will not himself find peace.*
—Albert Schweitzer

*Born within the enso of the world,*
*The human heart must also become an enso.*
—Nantenbo

## Surprise! Life Comes Without Warning

*"I do not seek. I find."*
—Picasso

*"If you make a sincere search you will find nothing to say except*
*that The representation of the universal order in the {divine}*
*preknowledge together with its necessary and appropriate time is*
*the thing from which that order with its organization and details*
*flows in an intelligent manner. All this is providence."*
—Ibn Sina

Initially play came to me naturally as a birthright. Its rediscovery, however, is by no means easy. Playing with children was not what I intended to do with my life. I had planned a career as a university professor. I did not find universities to be the learning environments I had hoped them to be. I wanted to be with people who were really learning. I needed time to plan my next step. I spent a year living in a beach community in San Diego surfing and finishing my first book: *Blacks in the United States: A Geographic Perspective.*

One day the man from whom I rented my beach room suggested that I visit a school where a friend of his taught. At first I paid little attention to his suggestion because I had no experience with children. It was very hard to give up my career as a professor. Needing the money I decided to visit the school.

I met with Dave Ulrey, the director of The Children's School in San Diego. Since I had no experience with children, Dave suggested that I begin as a teacher's aide. It didn't work out because I was spending more time with the children than I was preparing the room for the teachers.

Dave suggested that we meet again. He said that everyone wanted me to stay but that he didn't know what to do with me. Suddenly, I blurted out, "I'll be a special teacher in play and exploration." Dave quickly responded, "Fine do that." We looked at each other realizing that we didn't understand what we had just agreed to. There was no such job at the school. I made it up. This agreement was to profoundly change my life.

On my first day at school I was excited and apprehensive. The teachers didn't know what I was supposed to do; they smiled and went about their routines. Fortunately, the children knew what to do with me. When I was on the ground, I was a giant teddy bear with cubs scrambling all over me. When I stood up I was a fruit tree with wiggly fruit hanging from me. I was discovering children's play all over again for the first time.

Their play was far from simple-minded childishness. Their play was carefree, but never careless. I felt there were patterns here. I just had to find them.

The children didn't talk or explain the lessons I was receiving. the lessons were presented physically because children don't talk about play... they play. It was as if they knew that there behavioral hints would become embodied wisdom when my own experience gave them meaning.

I took notes every day after playing. At the beginning this was more a left over habit from my university days than a dedicated search for information. While I was trained to look for patterns, I wasn't consciously looking for them. As I reread my notes I began to tease out three patterns in the children's play: eye contact, touch sequence, and no contest. First, the children used their eyes to give an invitation and an acknowledgment. I call this a play look. This look is very quick and conveys the message: "you're lovable. There's nothing to be afraid of." This look is not staring; it is neither aggressive nor submissive. It is independent of culture and species.

Secondly, the children's movements were not random or chaotic.

Their play touch is sequential beginning with either hands or feet, then moving up the body. The head is touched last. Notice how different this is from where adults first touch children they do not know. Too often with children adult's initial touch is on the face or head.

The third pattern was the hardest for me to understand. Their play had no contest in it. The fighting among children that I had thought to be so normal and natural simply wasn't present. The constant pickering and fighting for position in a pecking order wasn't there.

There was no winning or losing, no blame or fault, and no revenge. Their touch was also more gentle than I expected. This was an heretical idea. My experience contradicted the cherished views of ordinary people and scientists who accepted the inevitability and necessity of conflict as both common sense and scientific fact.

After some years playing, I wanted to find out if these patterns were limited to the kids in The Children's School. I decided to go to Tijuana, Mexico. I didn't speak Spanish, nor did I know anyone there. It was, however, easy to find kids in parks and on street corners. I approached them just as I did kids in The Children's School. I got down on my hands and knees and crawled toward them.

Two things surprised me. First, they played with me just like the kids back home. Unexpectedly, even though these were older street kids, from around ten to eighteen years old, there was no aggression in their play.

The pattern was getting bigger. Street kids in Tijuana played just like the kids in San Diego. That didn't make sense to me. I needed more experience with different kinds of children. I wanted to find out just how wide this pattern of play was.

I began to play with all kinds of kids: gang members, children with autism, schizophrenia, Downs syndrome, cerebral palsy. All of the children played the same. Cultural, social and medical conditions didn't make any difference.

After years of playing with children I wondered if the patterns I was experiencing were part of some larger design. I was curious to see if animals played in the same way. I didn't know anything about animals. But that was not a hindrance. After all, I hadn't known anything about children either. But I had a problem. I didn't know how I was I going to play with wild animals.

Some time later, I was visiting friends in Seattle. Vicki invited me to join her on a visit to Wolf Haven. I had never seen a wolf, so I was excited to go. When we arrived we sat in a small trailer and talked with Jack, the wolf biologist. I looked out through the rain streaked window at a group of wolves lying on a small hill. Suddenly I said, "I want to go in and play with the wolves."

I surprised all three of us. Jack smiled and said that, "These aren't pets." I briefly explained my reasoning. He asked me to write it up and he would take it to the owners and the board for approval.

I was excited on our drive back to Seattle. Maybe now I would get a chance to play with animals. I wrote a brief summary of my ideas, drove back to Wolf Haven and gave my proposal to Jack. In a few days Jack called and said that I had their permission to play with the wolves.

They agreed with two conditions: I could not hurt the wolves; and whatever happened to me was my own problem. Perfect. Steve, the owner and I shook hands, beginning a number of years of play with wolves.

So, I began my exploration of play in the realm of animals. Over the years, the scope of my play grew larger as I played with bear, coyote, fox, elk, moose, deer, mountain lion, lynx, lion, elephant, dolphin, whale, and butterfly. It was clear the this pattern of play was inherent in life. I was a part of it. I call this pattern "original play" because it is not an artifact of culture but a gift from Creation. Original play is a code of kind-fullness within all life. It is believed by Strogatz that a pattern of synchrony cannot form unless the population is homogeneous enough. Original play taps the largest possible homogeneous population—all life on earth.

After years of playing I realized that I had changed. My body was becoming rounder and more fluid and impacts from other bodies were absorbed more easily. Neither my body nor my mind held on to their hurts for as long. I was becoming more appreciative and welcoming of surprise, both in my play and everyday life. Being vulnerable no longer meant being weak, ineffectual, or powerless. My experience was far outstripping my modes of cultural explanation. How could I account for the reality of a pattern of play that was the same across medical, social, cultural and even species categories? How do prisoners in a South African prison, street kids in Manila, Sao Paulo, South Africa, and Namibia and gang members in Los Angeles, New York and Singapore know how to play without aggression? It seems that Creation's gift of original play is capable of liberating life from the limitations imposed by our cultural and species frames.

What was happening to me was not a minor temporary change, but rather a reprogramming by basic enduring psycho-physiological processes which consist of shedding archaic fears of self-preservation and substituting them with the wisdom of being fully alive. I was embarking upon a life long quest, one in which children and animals were to turn me back toward God.

I was mindful of Dag Hammarskjöld's words.

*The way chose you—*
*And you must be thankful.*

An apprenticeship in *original play* calls for discipline, practice, and heart. In making the love of our hearts into the play of our hands we are faced with a behavioral paradox: we are to acquire a way of being that we already have. Like other skills, original play is learned in the presence of masters. But unlike other skills the masters of original play are children. This presents us with two problems.

First, we don't think of children as being able to teach adults anything of value.

Second, we think play is childish. This thinking is the source of two common beginner mistakes made simultaneously. The adult newcomer underestimates the skill necessary to play, and at the same time overestimates their own skill.

The assumption is that what is required to play is merely a retreat into childishness is nothing but a prolongation of an adolescent attempt to prove that we are no longer children. This is like leaping into the sea with carefree abandon without first learning to swim. One drowns in one's own pretensions. This also confuses childhood spontaneity with a justification for doing one's own thing, impulsiveness for immediacy, indulgence for naturalness, and insensitivity for innocence.

There is another behavioral paradox that seems to reoccur in my play practice. There are often times that as St. John of the Cross declared, "If a person wishes to be sure of the road they tread upon, they must close their eyes and walk in the dark." There were many times that I was faced with situations for which I had no training.

One day while building fence at a friend's wolf reserve I heard some of the wolves growling and snapping at each other. I was used to them getting in short fights over meat or bones or turf so I didn't pay much attention. I glanced over and quickly returned to digging the post hole. The fighting did not let up as it usually did. I turned a second time and could see blood on the white wolf. I put my shovel down and walked to the gate of their enclosure.

I had no plan of what I would do. I opened the enclosure's double gates and walked in. The wolves were so focused on their attack that they didn't seem to notice me. I walked up and knelt down next to the three wolves.

Two wolves pinned the white wolf against the fence, biting her over and over. She was cowering and shaking violently.

I put my hands into the mouths of the two attacking wolves. Their mouths were now clamped on my hands. Without thinking I did *kokyu-ho* and the two wolves flew through the air in large circles attached to my hands by their teeth.

I had practiced one form of *kokyu-ho* at the end of every aikido class, but it was never like this. *Kokyu-ho* is a breath throw and basic to aikido. In class we would kneel, facing a partner who would grab both of our wrists. The idea was not to struggle against the grabs, but to receive, and join your partner's energy. Often as a beginner I would try to use my arms to throw my partner. Sometimes this worked, but it gave me a false sense of confidence which Ace sensei would quickly dispel when he grabbed me and I couldn't do anything.

I felt with the wolves what *kokyu-ho* is supposed to feel like. There was no contest. I wasn't trying to throw them. It was as if I was the center of a whirlwind. It felt like the energy was coming from deep inside me and flowing outward through my arms into my hands. I felt no pain from the wolves' teeth only firm pressure. My hands swung up and out in spirals lifting the wolves into the air and spinning them to the ground behind me.

When the wolves landed on the ground they let go of my hands and trotted away. I turned my back to the white wolf and extended my arms toward the other two as they circled me. They backed off. I turned and hugged the white wolf who was trembling and frightened.

She initially nipped at me, then sagged into my arms. Each time the other two tried to return I merely extended my arms toward them and they retreated. It was as if my arms created a barrier that the wolves wouldn't cross. In a half hour help came to take the white wolf to the veterinarian.

*If you would be a real seeker after truth, it is necessary that at least once in your life you doubt, as far as possible, all things.*
—Rene Descartes

What happened when my hands were in the mouths of the wolves? Why were there no teeth marks? I don't know. My experience reminded me of an experience years earlier with a wolf named Windsong. I described this experience in *Playing By Heart*. Windsong had bitten my hand with such force that her teeth went through my hand, but there were no puncture wounds and no blood.

What happened? I don't know. But perhaps something that biologist Bruce Lipton wrote provides a hint. He asks in his book why we can't put our hands through a brick wall if matter is non-material. His answer is, "As physicists have discovered, it isn't the density of matter that stops us, it's the density of energy." So, let's ask the question in reverse. Why can a wolf put her teeth through my hand with no injury to me. The answer, I believe, would be the same. It is a matter of energy. If we assume as most physicists do that the world is made up of atoms and void is the main reality of atoms. In fact, there are no objects at all only relationships of energy. As physicist Fabiola Gianotti describes, "we are nothing but quarks and electrons and a lot of empty space. Physicists call this the "zero-point field." This zero-point field is described by McTaggart as "an ocean of microscopic vibrations in the space between things—a state of pure potential and infinite possibility. Particles exist in all possible states until disturbed by us—by observing or measuring—at which point, they settle down, at long last into something real." As Lipton adds, "In other words, reality exists on a need-to-exist basis. I can ask then from my experience with wolves—what if reality changes on a need-to-change basis? This seems like nonsense. But suppose our worldly conventional idea of truth is merely a collectively agreed upon truth and not the ultimate truth. In the case of Windsong and myself, reality is a complicated tissue of event-space in which different perceptions overlap. In that case, what happens? Suppose I experienced a kind of fusion that Buddhist monk and scholar Matthieu Ricard speaks about at a particle level, "They fuse." They become one thing because they have no dimension. But if two particles fuse with each other, so do three particles, and then a mountain, and the whole universe could fuse into one particle." Windsong-Fred as one-particle.

There is a story about Zen master Shoju with wolves that is similar to my own experience.

Shoju heard of a pack of wolves that were harming villagers around Narasawa village. He decided to meditate where the wolves frequently gathered for seven consecutive nights. The wolves gathered around him, jumped over him, and nudged him with their muzzles. It is said that neither wolves nor the Venerable Shoju existed." Perhaps my experiences are what Morihei Ueshiba meant by the source of aiki being the creative interaction of universal energy. Again, I don't know. The common sense of my experiences left me in a cloud of unknowing in which the whole seemed greater than the sum of the parts. The trouble with trying to combine real world play with particle physics is that my experience defies my sense of order and reason, of cause and effect, of the very idea of me and you as separate beings. I'm left with a perplexing mixture of physics and faith, that I call grace.

I must learn to proceed with serenity and grace in a practice that cannot be practiced, realizing in due course that what I seek has been in me all along. This inner power is the ability to make choices unhindered by fear.

This gift means that my choices are not limited by self-defense and hostility, but rather by an emptiness filled with love. Only then are my choices optimal in any given moment. Relearning original play is re-programing my reflexes to acquire a new habit or way of being with the world. Original play demands that I keep its principles in mind and in practice, that is to stay centered between Heaven and Earth. This *centering process* has a number of active dimensions: self-disappearance, just right, nothin' special, and enthusiasm. All enfold and unfold, reverberating through one's body, mind, and spirit in original play.

Comprehending one means understanding them all.

*Figure 6: Dimensions of Apprenticeship*

# Self Disappearance: Open Heart Surgery

*The word 'I' remains the shibboleth of mankind.*
—Martin Buber

*There was a child made all of salt who very much wanted to know where he had come from. So he set out on a long journey and traveled to many lands in pursuit of this understanding. Finally he came to the shore of the great ocean. How marvelous, he cried, and stuck one foot in the ocean. The ocean beckoned him in further saying, "if you wish to know who you are do not be afraid." The salt child walked further and further into the water dissolving with each step, and at the end exclaimed, "Ah, now I know who I am."*

—Traditional story

Original play is an ongoing process of open heart surgery. Open-heart surgery should not be undertaken casually; it is not for the fainthearted. I am not talking about the kind of open heart surgery performed in a hospital operating room, by skilled surgeons, using the latest technology. What I am suggesting is an operation we have never imagined. This is surgery without anesthesia! Open-heart surgery is radical but simple; the purpose is to open your heart, making each act one of compassionate affirmation. Children are the surgeons. Earth is the recovery room. Love is the rehabilitation. The effectiveness of the operation lies not in demanding proof, but in simply loving that needs no evidence. Perhaps this doesn't sound like a promising operation. Then, perhaps, you need a second opinion.

Original play's open-heart surgery can be a rather grueling process which most people choose not to undertake. This surgery is a process of de-categorization in which the social roles and cultural categories of everyday life are removed. Naturally our selves don't appreciate the idea of such massive vulnerability as disappearance. Disappearance is viewed as a potential failure of disastrous proportions. The Duchess' Game has created a siege mentality in which the self is always on the defensive. In such cases the loss of identity is unacceptable. In the Duchess' game, one's honor must be asserted and protected at all costs.

Believe in the simple magic of life, in service in the universe, and the meaning of this surgery will dawn on you. The purpose of this operation is to heal the "cardio-sclerosis," or hardening of the heart that we have undergone for so many years. Once relieved of its hardened categories the heart is free to function as it was created, unhampered by fear. The training in original play captures an important truth stated by Armstrong, "we are at our most creative when we do not cling to our self-hood but are prepared to give ourselves away." This is what the Sufis call "the path of annihilation." But don't worry as Rumi says, "there is a way of passing away from the personal, a dying that makes one plural." How wonderful, when "I" disappear, "I" become we. As Meister Eckhart pointed out, "To find nature herself, all her forms must be shattered." Self-disappearance means nothing less than abdicating the sovereign I, abandoning all of the ramparts defending me, and abolishing attachments to mine. The I-me-mine triad has had long years of practice with which to entrench itself. It is expert at camouflage, sabotage and revenge. As Martin Buber has put it, ""without It [what I call categories] man cannot live. But he who lives with It alone is not a man." Self-disappearance is a realization of our deeper kinship. This self-disappearance is not suicide; it is rather sacrifice, that is to make sacred.

Children require that I leave my pretenses, expectations, and worries outside of the playground. We all have those areas of psychological or physical vulnerability where our internal and/or external balance can be upset. These are areas of our posture or personality where we can be blindsided, those places where I feel the need to defend myself.

Children are very good at zeroing in on such carefully defended aspects of self. Like skilled surgeons with scalpels, when children sense such a weakness in me they swiftly focus their efforts to remove it. For example, for years during my play I was embarrassed by showing my bald spot to adults. I tried to manipulate my movements so that adults would not see my baldness. One of the ways I would do this was by immediately standing up when parents came to pick up their children. As naïve as it seems I assumed that because I am tall no one could see that I had a bald spot when I was standing.

Often with surgical precision, children take care of something that we have been hiding for a long time. My surgery came at a school in Idaho. I was invited to give a talk on mountain men to a fifth grade class. While I was at the school I also took time to play with the children on the playground. During my visit there was a ceremonial Native American dance held outside on the playground. The entire school went outside for the ceremony. There was a hush as we were all gathered in a large circle waiting for the dancers to enter. I was sitting on the ground on the edge of the circle. Some of the little girls with whom I had played were behind me. They began to play with my hair. Suddenly one of the girls shattered the silence with, "Look Fred doesn't have any hair on top!" I could feel the eyes and smiles of every adult in the circle glance toward my bald spot—something that I was sure I had kept a secret. Of course everyone knew my secret; I just didn't know that they knew it. More children ran over to see, the adults smirked, and the dancers entered. As swift and sure as a surgeon's scalpel, the little girl excised the source of my embarrassment.

In a course for teachers at the University of Bridgeport I explained that the following day we would be going to play at a school for children with autism. None of the teachers had any experience with autistic children. I told them that we were there to learn not to teach. One woman came up to me after class and told me that she was undergoing "chemo" for her cancer treatment and as a result wore a wig. She was afraid that she would lose it during play and that would be very embarrassing for her as she didn't let others know that she was wearing a wig. I smiled at her and told her of my own experience of being afraid about my baldness being exposed to adults. I warned her that sensitive children have a way of reading such fears as if we advertised them with neon lights. My suggestion was to sit outside the play mats and then to play as she felt comfortable.

The next day the teachers all sat on the edge of the mats as the first group of children came in. One little boy in the group ran around the adults and like a lightning strike reached out and grabbed the woman's wig and ran away with it. Her first response was shock and to reach up to hold her wig. She was too late, her wig was gone. The boy quickly threw the wig down. I retrieved it and gave it to the woman who smiled at me. She went to the bathroom and returned with a scarf tied around her head. She joined the play. Neither the boy nor any other child pulled her scarf. "How did he know?" she asked. "Thanks to him I'm not afraid or embarrassed any more." She smiled.

Proper training in original play requires mastery of both the hand and the heart. The physical training and mastery of technique are essential, but are not enough. If you do not train the heart your intention will be unclear and your movements will be "heartless" no matter how much you have trained in technique. Playing by heart requires not being bound by forms or categories so that we are able to feel the spark of life in a given situation.

Bound by form, a mere posturing; we cannot respond with the spark of life to a new circumstance. It is often too easy to act on the basis of our categories and expectations. For example an elderly woman came to one of my workshops in Johannesburg, South Africa and asked to tell a story. She related how she had come to a workshop of mine two years previously.

She wanted to tell of an experience she had since that time. One night she was awakened by a noise. She sat up in bed looking at two men with masks over their faces and holding rifles pointed at her. She did not say a word. She threw off the covers and walked up to them. She reached out her arms with her hands pointing toward the two men. As she approached them she stuck her index fingers into the muzzles of the rifles. With her fingers in the gun barrels she turned the men and walked them to the bedroom door. She calmly said, "You don't want to be here." They left. This is an amazing example of clear intention.

> *I must decrease that He may increase.*
> —St. Paul

There is a story from India that reflects this disappearance of self and our underlying unity. There was once a zoo in India which had a lion and a tiger. They were the public's favorite animals. Everyone came to see the lion and tiger. One night the tiger died. The zoo keeper didn't know what to do. It was too expensive to buy a new tiger. So the keeper was instructed to hire a person to be the new "tiger." He hired a beggar to dress up in a tiger suit during the day and pretend to be the tiger. This worked well. People came as before and believed that their favorite lion and tiger were still there.

One day in front of the tiger's cage two visitors began arguing about who was stronger the lion or tiger.

"The tiger is the strongest," exclaimed one man.

"No, it is the lion," replied his friend.

Their argument continued all day. Finally they asked the zoo keeper which was strongest. He said that he didn't know.

"We must find out." Argued the first man.

"How are we to know?" asked the second man.

"I know." Yelled the first man, "We'll put the lion and tiger together and see which one wins."

The zoo keeper did not like this idea. But the visitors finally convinced him that there was no other way they could find out for sure.

Having heard this plan the tiger was terrified.

That night after all of the visitors went home, except for the two men the zoo keeper opened the lion's cage and let him in with the tiger. Before the tiger could say or do anything the cage door opened and the lion bounded in with him. The lion chased around the cage, and pounced on the tiger.

This is the end thought the poor tiger. I am about to be eaten by a lion.

But just then he heard soft whispering in his ear, "Not to worry I'm the same as you."

We all wear tiger suits. Like the lion and the tiger underneath all of our outer roles and categories we are the same kind, you and I. When we leave our categories we are cleared as if by customs and immigration to explore beyond culture's frontiers to discover who we truly are.

> *When the heart is right, "for" and "against" are forgotten.*
> —Nuowen

The categorical change may also transform one from enemy to human.

David Bohm spoke of this when he wrote that, "If someone is perceived as an enemy, matter is organized differently than if he is perceived as a friend." Such a change is the basis of a story told to me by a woman in Poland.

During World War II her family's home was invaded by a German officer and his men. The officer ordered the family to carry what they could and get in the waiting trucks. While everyone was hurrying to obey his order a little boy came out and stood on the shiny, black boots of the officer and hugged his legs. The officer looked down and said, "I have a son at home." He ordered his men to leave the house. He said to the distraught family, "Your little boy saved your life." He left.

There is a wonderful story told by psychologist Jerome Bruner about Niels Bohr and his children that illustrates this same principle. "Bohr told me," Bruner wrote, "that he had become aware of the psychological depths of the principle of complementarity when one of his children had done something inexcusable for which he found himself incapable of appropriate punishment. He said to me, 'You cannot know somebody at the same time in the light of love and in the light of justice.'"

Neurologist James Austin writes that, "it was becoming increasingly plausible to contemplate highly sophisticated 'mirror'-like nerve cell systems. Somehow these would enable us as individual human beings

178

not only to mimic other persons, but also to anticipate (perhaps even to share in) their belief systems, attitudes, positive and negative emotions, perceptions, and intended actions."

It is what Loren Eiseley refers to as "the capacity to love, not just his own species, but life in all its shapes and forms." We then discover that we are Schweitzer's "circle of compassion" whose circumference is infinite. We are then, ensos. An enso is Japanese for the calligraphic circle depicting completion and emptiness. In original play it symbolizes a circle of infinite compassion with no circumference. This is our original play before categories.

Toni Packer tells a story that she saw on TV that beautifully typifies this self-disappearance. It was a news program with Dan Rather in Somalia. He was far out in the desert with a few soldiers. They came upon a few tents with some *Doctors Without Borders* physicians were working. A small baby with bullet wounds in the head was brought to one of the doctors. The calm doctor began bandaging the baby's head and at one point asked Dan to steady the baby while she turned away. He held the baby and massaged a foot. He was visibly shaken and asked the doctor whether the baby would live. "Maybe another four weeks. It's hard to tell." In the middle of nowhere a courageous doctor was caring for an infant who might or might not live. "And so was Dan Rather: in tenderly massaging the baby's toes,the famous anchor had totally *disappeared.*"[italics mine].

*Man, if thou wishest to see God, there or here on Earth,*
*Thy heart must first become a pure mirror.*
—Angelus Silesius

*The universe is the mirror of God—the mirror in which*
*His majesty and perfection are reflected, the mirror in which*
*He sees Himself—and the heart of man is the mirror of the*
*Universe:*
*if the Traveler then would know God,*
*he must look into his own heart.*
—Aziz ibn Muhammad al-Nasafi

## Just Right: From Know How to No How

One day I was resting outside on the grass having lunch between sessions at a Head Start pre-school in Southern California. A teacher rushed out and yelled to me, "Come inside quickly. There is a hummingbird in the classroom. We've tried everything and can't get it to go out. We don't want it to be in the room when the kids arrive. You know about animals. You do something."

As I hurried into the classroom I was thinking to myself, "I don't know how to catch a hummingbird. What can I do that they already haven't tried?" I had no idea what to do. The teacher had turned off the lights to try and calm the bird. I could see it darting around one end of the room near the windows. Without thinking I simply raised my hand in the air. As soon as I did it, the hummingbird flew across the room directly into my hand, as if it were flying home to its nest. I cushioned it gently and moved quickly to the door and opened my hands into the air. It was still for a moment. I raised my hand in an upward motion somehow feeling the bird's readiness for flight that seemed to propel the bird up and it suddenly darted away soaring above the school. For a moment I stood stunned wondering what had happened. The teachers congratulated me and asked me how I did it. I shook my head. I knew that "I" didn't do it. This is not know how, but "no how," a shared living wisdom which expresses itself in a moment of instantaneous action. The hummingbird and I were brought together where the gentleness of giving and receiving are the same. And for a moment we, the hummingbird and I, lived in the midst of reciprocity. Did I catch the bird or did the bird place itself in a nest called my hand?

In this moment there was a direct exchange of energy with neither thought nor technique. I am reminded of the story told by John Stevens of two martial artists. "There were two master sparrow-catching samurai in old Japan: Teishun and Genban. Genban, however, admitted that Teishun's technique was far superior. Genban almost always killed or injured the birds he grabbed. Teishun, on the other hand, could catch and release a sparrow unharmed; not only that, he could do so without scaring the other birds away." These are moments I call "just right."

It is like the fairy tale of Goldilocks and the Three Bears. The little girl, Goldilocks, comes upon a house in the woods. No one is home. She tries three steaming bowls of porridge; she sits in three chairs and finally lies down in three beds. The father bear's porridge, chair and bed are all too much for Goldilocks. The mother bear's porridge, chair and bed are not right either. But the porridge, chair and bed of the baby bear are "just right."

Actions speak louder than words. Original play's skillful movements demonstrate brisk and fluid actions arising from sensorimotor pathways liberated from fear.

"Just right" responses are:

- expressed from a foundation of stillness

- spontaneous, fluid and round

- simple and efficient

- creative yet solve the immediate situation

- designed to heal not to defend

- touch that is gentle and strong

- liberated from categories and thoughts

- graceful

I have experienced this sense of "just right" with many children and animals. When I first began to play, I didn't know how to use touch in such a sensitive way. I was given a lesson in "just right" by my daughter, Etienne. One day she, her brother, Anthony, and I were playing on our front lawn. Suddenly, she ran crying into the house. I followed her thinking that I had hurt her. When I went to her she sobbed and said to me, "You don't play with me like you do Anthony." At first I didn't know what she meant. Did she want me to use the same amount of energy with her that I used with Anthony? No. That wasn't it. She wanted me to use the "right" amount of energy with her. I had backed off thinking of her as a girl. By treating her as a category I could not correctly sense her energy. I gave her less than she could handle. In feeling this she felt that I didn't trust her. This was difficult for me to hear. I told her that from now on I would be more aware of her energy. We went back out and I began to match her energy. I was getting the "knack" of playing with her not as a category called girl, but as Etienne.

Animals also give me lessons in "just right" touch. They use their weight, claws and teeth to teach me. For example, a wolf named Sybil is a master of the "just right" kind of touch. She re-calibrates her strength instantly feeling exactly how much energy to use in playing with me. Sybil demonstrated this "just right" touch in a kind of game we played. She liked to place her jaw firmly on my lower arm with just enough pressure to hold firmly but not hurt me. It was more of an embrace than a grab. Then I would swing my arm in a large arc into the air away from the ground. This would lift her off her feet and she would spin in the air with her jaws clamped onto my arm. She would land on the ground with a thud as if she were taking a high, hard fall in aikido. She would regain her footing, shake herself, and grab my arm again, as if to say, "Do it Again!" We then would repeat the activity. She would hold my arm with enough force to remain attached as she flew threw the air, but with never enough force for her teeth to break my skin.

I also recall playing with a grizzly. It occurred on one of my meanderings in the mountains north of Yellowstone Park. When I wander the mountains I go to be with animals, not to search for them. These are different processes. If they choose to be with me that is fine. If not that is also fine.

After some time a grizzly bear walked out of the trees. He slowly made his way over to me turning over logs, sniffing at plants along the way. There was no sign of aggression in his approach. His attitude was so calm that it was disarming. In fact he walked up and put his head on my shoulder next to my ear and nuzzled me. Immersed in soft fur and a musky, dusty bear smell I nuzzled him back. He put a paw on my shoulder and lightly touched down my arm. Then I did the same to him. He stood next to my shoulder and gave me a gentle shove, just enough to unbalance me, as he walked on his way.

One day I encountered a black bear in the same valley. At one point in our play, I was lying on my back underneath him. He stood over me with his front paws next to my head. He lowered himself, like an elevator, slowly until his head was next to mine. It was like lying under a living bearskin rug. He knew exactly how much of his weight I could handle. Later in our play session I was on my hands and knees. Just like a little child he climbed on my back. Again he gave me only the amount of weight I could handle. I moved with him on my back and with one smooth arching move of my arm up and over my body I threw him off to the side. Wow! I thought I threw a black bear! Well, I didn't really throw him. Neither did the bear give up. It was just right.

How do these animals know exactly how much pressure to use with there claws, teeth and weight? I don't know.

Such *just right* touch has been described as a prominent feature of Taoist craftsmanship. In the stories of the Chinese wheelwright, Bian, and the Chinese carpenter, Ch'ing, they had learned their crafts beyond expertise. Their minds were not caught by effort, success, or failure. This is the art of self-forgetfulness expressed by the Chinese carpenter, Bian:

"when I work on a wheel, if I hit too softly, pleasant as this is, it doesn't make for a good wheel. If I hit it furiously, I get tired and the thing doesn't work! So not too soft, not too vigorous. I grasp it in my hand and hold it to my heart. I cannot express this by word of mouth, I just know it."

Here is how woodworker Ch'ing describes his process. "My Lord,' Ch'ing said, 'I'm just a simple woodworker—I don't know anything about art. But here's what I can tell you. Whenever I begin to carve a bell stand, I concentrate my mind. After three days of mediating, I no longer have any thoughts of praise or blame. After five days I no longer have any thoughts of success or failure. After seven days, I'd identified with a body. All my power is focused on my task; there are no distractions. At that point, I enter the mountain forest. I examine the trees until exactly the right one appears. If I can see a bell stand inside it, the real work is done, and all I have to do is get started. Thus I harmonize inner and outer. That's why people think that my work must be superhuman." This is the process of moving from "know how" to "no how."

I first experienced this sense of *just right* as a child on a farm. My uncle had a farm that my parents often took me to visit during the summers of my youth. We even lived in the farm for some time. Those were wonderful times for me because I was let loose on the farm. There was a man who worked on the farm who my father and uncle called "a good hand." They were referring to Wes, a "handy man" who did virtually all of the outside chores in the barns and fields. I liked the phrase "handy man" and I liked Wes.

I could tell that there was something special about him. He fit. He had what my mother called common sense. He seemed to move within the boundaries of the farm with as much ease as he moved within his faded blue, baggy bib overalls. Wes was a good hand because it was in his character to be so. On the outside Wes could be a crusty old farmer who had always been on the farm. He had no fuss about him and in this he was different from the other adults who only lived on the farm. Wes belonged on the farm.

I was eager to follow Wes around, because I too wanted to be a "good hand." Sometimes I would ride on the hay wagon as he drove the team of horses down the lane, around the gentle rounded hills, and through the fields.

He belonged to the farm; he was fully present in the barn, fields, orchard, and pastures. He was at home there. He saw what needed to be done. I couldn't express it at the time, but I felt a kinship between my play and his work. It was as if we did different things in the same way. He reached out gracefully to serve the farm. He would "set the farm to rights" as he would put it. His wisdom was lived and so I was mentored. I could feel in Wes what I was to learn from the children years later—unless something is lived one does not have it. Wes didn't bother with what we call teaching.

His hands were hard-used and perhaps because of that I felt all the more comforted in them when he held my hand or put his hand on my shoulder to nudge my attention in a direction he wanted me to attend to. There was kinship expressed as kindness in Wes' touch; his hands knew the feel of the dirt in the cornfield, the bark on each apple tree, the fine coats of each horse. He knew the sweat that went into the corn and the potatoes.

The land and the animals of the farm, and I, soaked up his wisdom and were the better for it. Sometimes I would run after him giving my little hands to the chores. My Mother used to say that "many hands make light work," but I wasn't so sure in this case. I think now that I was more in the way than not, and that my help was negligible. But Wes always made me feel useful. Like the land, I responded well to Wes' good treatment. I was needed by Wes and the farm as much as I needed them. We belonged, Wes, me, and the farm. This was the time to be a kid. Wes always seemed to find time for me. Sometimes at the end of the work day we would sit on overturned feed buckets in the open double doors of the barn. Often we just sat quietly. At other times he shared mysteries of the farm and animals.

There was a peaceableness, ample and light, between us as we rambled around the farm. Rambling I learned, is an art of moving between here and there with neither hesitation nor hurry, not burdened by necessities or urgencies, and always being present. It is like wandering in the woods and rummaging in the barn. Wes freely gave me whatever he thought I needed or wanted. With a feeling eye, he saw what no one else saw and often gave it to me as a treasure to keep in my pocket until a better place could be found.

Wes sensed my wanting to know what he knew. Wes didn't talk much; he was silent most of the time, but he was a demanding mentor when he needed to be. When I asked him a question he answered quietly; he would sometimes respond with a story or often with just a smile and a touch. But most of the time Wes was silent. It was as if he was listening to everything around him and if he talked he might miss something important. He expected me to listen even when he wasn't talking.

With Wes I began to feel life's common sense. Wes did his handiwork as gestures of kindness—a kind of ecological intelligence, not just for the owners of the farm, but for the land, and for those who came before, and for those who would come after. The result was a sense of "just right" between man and place.

Wes's life was lived in what Martin Buber, called, "the currents of universal reciprocity." This is not an abstract or ideal virtue, but the practice of passing on the realization that one belongs to an order greater than one can know. Wes came from an older world. I didn't realize it at the time but Wes was handing on a way of life that was really passing on with his passing. I felt proud to receive his knowing and sad for its passing because I think that I am the last to feel his inheritance. Even as a child, I could see in Wes that the flowering of a man's kindness is as natural and as strict a process of nature as the opening of an apple blossom. Wes bestowed upon me and the farm a kind of propriety that I have come to cherish.

*"We know truth not only by reason, but also by the heart, and it is from this last that we know first principles."*
—Blaise Pascal

At any moment in original play there is no wrong move and only one right move. Japanese poet Basho expresses this invisible giving and receiving inherent in original play in his poem:

*To the path of the sun*
*Hollyhocks turn*
*In the rains of May.*

When the heart opens and the self disappears one's play is "just right" and there is "no how." This is what Suzuki refers to as the ultimate goal of all of the Japanese arts, "Where learning gained is learning lost." Original play invites you to enter into a transaction by presenting you with emptiness out of which to create forms, stillness out of which to create motion. Play's action proceeds with no residue to hold one's attention. This is what Seng-Ts'an was referring to when he told his students, "Don't keep searching for the truth: Just let go of your opinions." Rumi described this more succinctly, "Let the way itself arrive."

Both training and insight are necessary, but when one's conscious actions are guided by preconscious intuitions of one's whole being then one moves beyond practice—from know how to "no-how."

## Mastery; Nothin' Special

*When a man reaches highest perfection it is nothing special,*
*it is his normal condition.*
—T'sai Ken Ten

*"If you continue this simple practice every day, you will obtain some wonderful power. Before you obtain it, it is something wonderful, but after you attain it, it is nothing special.'*
—Shunryu Suzuki

When I was a child I knew about doing "nothin.'" I was good at it. In summer on a farm there was never enough time to do all of the nothing I wanted to do. It was as if "doing nothing" was the default activity of my brain. My daily comings and goings on the farm were expressed as doing "nothin.'" I remember bounding out the door of the farmhouse on the first day of summer, taking in un-deciphered, all that lay before me.

"Don't chase the horses!"

This is the warning that my Mother yelled at me as I ran out the mud room door to play on my uncle's farm. She would shout this because she was afraid I would get trampled by the horses. She had seen me running down the lane between the pastures after the six horses. Because I was always running behind them it looked to her like I was chasing the horses. Actually, I was running with the horses, only I was much slower then they were. What appeared to be Fred chasing horses to my mother was *really* me being a slow horse.

I disappeared quickly beyond the range of my mother's voice. I ran about greeting the horses in the barnyard. Buster, the Saint Bernard bounded along with me through the tall green rows of corn.

At times like this I encountered each day as an adventure, attempting to be everywhere at once. I played with the frogs in the farm pond, ran with the horses down the lane, explored the old caboose in the woods, rested on the top of the hill watching the clouds. I was being initiated into the world, where the earth gets ground into my skin and a sense of belonging gets under my skin. Here *no-thing-ness* became a sanctuary in which I felt safe out there in the fields and forests of the farm. My eyes were wide open. I was constantly surprised. It was a wonder-filled world.

When I heard the ringing of the large dinner bell that stood on a post outside the kitchen door I meandered home for dinner stopping along the way for just one more little visit, until finally I'm at the mud room door.

I ran past my mother as she yelled, "Stop right there!" I thought she was going to remind me to wash before dinner. Instead she looked down at my torn pants and the dried blood on my knee and asked, "What happened?" I looked down too.

"I don't know. How did that happen?" "I just asked you that," she reminded me.

"Well, hurry and get cleaned up for dinner. And put on another pair of pants.

She continues as I run through the kitchen,

"What were you doing?"

"Nothin.'"

*Nothin'* was just out playing. I had all day to do *nothin.'* It was as if my mother and I had a mutual, unspoken agreement acknowledging that *nothin'* was as an apt description of my day at play as she was going to get out of me. Her smile and my *nothin'* explains as best I can a conversation both essential and impossible. We understood each in our own way that sometimes what we don't say can bring us closer together.

We both knew that my ordinary, "nothin' special" day was special. John Keats put this idea well in one of his letters: "The only way to strengthen one's intellect is to make up one's mind about nothing."

The *nothin'* of original play is not to be confused with boredom. Doing nothing in play is neither complacency nor is it passivity. Original play is the doing nothing which encompasses everything. It is beginner's mind, a kind of *tabula rasa* of cosmic proportions.

As a child I was wired to receive the whole world. This is a wholeness that is experienced beyond our categories and sets us in a much wider constellation beyond our abstractions, categories, and pedagogies.

This *nothing* is the pregnant emptiness of Creation. Singer states that in astrophysics this is called a "singularity" is a state in which things become so radically different that the old rules break down and we know virtually nothing."

How is it that one goes about doing *nothing*. It's not as easy as it sounds. It isn't being lazy, passive, or doing one's own thing. Perhaps we can look for help from two unexpected sources, Winnie the Pooh and acting teacher Constantin Stanislavski.

"How do you do *Nothing*?" asked Pooh, after he had wondered for a long time.

"Well, it's when people call out at you just as you're going off to do it. What are you going to do, Christopher Robin, and you say, Oh, nothing, and then you go and do it.'"

*All human evil comes from this:*
*man's being unable to sit still in a room*
—Blaise Pascal

It's the first day of class with the director, Constantin Stanislavski who asks the first student to go up on the stage. She is nervous and Stanislavski says, "Calm yourself. and let us do a little play. This is the plot."

"The curtain goes up, and you are sitting on the stage. You are alone. You sit and sit and sit... At last the curtain comes down again. That is the whole play. Nothing simpler could be imagined, could it?"

He asked each of the students to go up on stage alone and do the same little play. Each student awkwardly squirms their way through it. After their first round, the director asks them to return to the exercise and this time they will learn how to simply sit on stage. The students declared that's what they had already done. "Oh, no" he replied. "You were not simply sitting." The director went on stage and sat. The students sensed the difference. When they sat, "their helplessness and desire to please were ridiculous." There was, on the other hand, an actual pleasure in seeing the director merely sit and not act anything. As the director pointed out the point was to sit. As Stanislavski points out, "You may sit without motion and at the same time be in full action." Here stillness, as in play, does not imply passiveness but focused intensity.

*With a wall all around, a clay bowl is molded; but the use of the bowl will depend on the part of the bowl that is void... So advantage is had from whatever is there; but usefulness rises from whatever is not.*

—Lao-tzu

This "time to do nothing" may be a certain kind of blessing. Leo Buscaglia (personal communication) once shared with me the following story. He was asked to judge a contest to find the most caring child. The winner was a four-year-old boy whose next door neighbor was an elderly man who had recently lost his wife. Upon seeing the man cry the little boy went into his yard, climbed into his lap and just sat there.

Later, when his mother asked him what he said to the man, the little boy said, "Nothing, I just helped him cry." Dr. Jung had a similar experience once with a young girl. When he was asked how he had achieved such positive results so quickly Jung wrote, "I did nothing much. I listened to her fairy tales, danced with her a little, sang with her a little, took her on my knee a little and the job was done."

*Nothing* can hurt as well as heal. Sometimes, for example, in the adult world of categories *nothing* can take on a sense of a profound negation. We may look back, for example, in a moment of wistfulness on the innocence of childhood, but we quickly reemerge into the world of function, value and status where childhood itself is a nothing. In this sense *nothing* describes a vacancy putting a child in a void where they don't count.

I recall a Mother who felt this emptiness at the heart of her being after taking her son to visit a neurologist. Erin, eighteen months old has severe cerebral palsy. She told me that Erin's doctor explained to her that, "Erin's brain is not growing. He has no intelligence." She was distraught because she interprets the doctor's words to mean that her son, " is a nothing." The doctor couldn't see beyond Erin's medical diagnosis. It seems that to the doctor Erin is not a boy, but a diagnosis. Hope seemed so fragile as it flowed out of his Mother. In her despair, she cries and tightly holds me.

I ask her to watch closely. I lie down next to Erin. I softly call his name and he smiles. He squirms and his body bends out over my arm when I hold him. My hand cradles his head and my arm blends with his spine to support his rapid and unpredictable motions. We move together in spirals until he is close to my chest.

Holding his head, I lower my face until I am close enough for Erin to nibble my beard. Our bodies become still and our eyes find each other.

It is as if we lock in on each other and for a moment we are in what I've come to call a "sweet spot." This "sweet spot" is a time-space of connection during which Erin stops his rapid head bobbing and his eye motions slow to a steady gaze into my eyes. His eyes follow mine as I slowly move them from side to side.

Now I take Erin's mother and hold her head where I had placed mine. With my hands I slowly moved her head so that Erin can follow her eyes. She gasps and whispers, "He sees me."

Erin provides his mother with an epiphany, a small window of divine connection. Their mutual presence belongs to that world of grace which cuts through the center of every human heart. I am reminded of Al Huang's comment about an orchid like flower he found on a walk in the hills following Alan Watts' death.

"I asked the orchid,'What is everyday Tao?' The orchid, ... answered, "Nothing special."

## Enthusiasm: Playing For God's Sake

*The eye with which I see God is the same eye*
*with which God sees me.*
—Meister Eckhart

*When God is gone, I am here. When I am gone. God is here.*
—AA saying

*"I see God in every human being."*
—Mother Teresa

*God became man so that man may become God.*
—St. Augustine

*When I was a child, God also became a child with me*
*to be my playmate.*
—Rabindranath Tagore

Imagine that my first suspicion upon meeting you is that you are a face of God. Could *you* really be a face of God? Imagine. Perhaps I think like Mother Teresa, "Seeking the face of God in everything, everyone, everywhere, all the time, and seeing His hand in every happening—that is contemplation in the heart of the world."

On the other hand, I might think like Hafiz

> *How could that moron over there*
> *Really. Be. God?"*

After all a normal person like me doesn't just go around seeing God. This may be thought to be a sign of psychosis, some sort of delusion or hallucination. Or it may be a sign that I need to get confirmation from a religious authority.

Perhaps it's merely evoking an identity crisis of sorts, as when the boundary between self, other, and divine disappears. Or perhaps this is the wonderful problem that Rumi warns us about. "How are we and God to keep from fainting when we encounter each other?"

"Well, what does He look like?" This was a question from a friend after I mentioned that I had seen a face of God while playing with a child. "Who?" I asked. "God, of course." I could tell him that there is nowhere God isn't, or I could say that there is nowhere God is.

Oh well, there was really nothing for me to say. What can I say about seeing a face of God. Not much. In fact, nothing. How do I know that I saw a face of God? I know but I don't know how I know. What proof do I have? None. I didn't take a photo.

It doesn't take long before intellectuals and religious guardians wear themselves out debating whether I could actually "see" a face of God. I recall, for example, a triumvirate of Catholic priests becoming disappointed and frustrated that they couldn't force me to do penance for my sin of "seeing God." Since I am not Catholic their pressure was ineffective. Nothing the priests could say changed the fact that my sense of belonging experienced in play was enthusiastic.

Children neither ask such questions of me, nor do they seek to impose sanctions. My mentors understand that this essence slips through our minds as water through a sieve and so do not get bogged down by quibbling over the nature of God. The children know that their original play is a theophany, or a behavioral manifestation of the one face of God in the many faces of God.

Where is this face of God? Nowhere and everywhere. We peer out into the world through the "peephole" of our finite humanity hoping to see the infinite face of Creation. We use our newest telescopes and microscopes to look for God in the vast emptiness of inner and outer space. In doing so we have made visible things that are invisible to the unaided eye.

Throughout human history, theologians, poets, scientists, and philosophers have struggled eloquently to make sense of the universe, find our place in it, and peer ever so fleetingly into the face of God. It was once imagined that to gaze into the heavens was to see Creation. The French mystic, Simone Weil once said that, "We cannot take a single step toward heaven. If, however, we look heavenward for a long time, God comes and takes us up." And on a more earthly scale, "With a face penetrating through the darkness of pain, Mother Teresa could move beyond appearances and perceive the face of God."

Fortunately for us as Robert Johnson exclaims, "God is loose! God is out and is now appearing everywhere." As Thomas Merton put it, "God isn't someone else." As Ken Wilbur points out, "The stunning message of the mystics is that in the very core of your being you are God."

Carl, a ten-year-old boy in Poland looks at a Catholic priest who is playing on the floor with us and exclaims, " I am playing with God." We laughed and smiled at both the symbol and the reality of Carl's words.

A kindergarten teacher from Austria shared with me his experience in his initial play sessions with the children in his class. One very touching moment was when I asked a 3-year-old boy after the play what he enjoyed the most . He said "the sun," and when I asked him who the sun was, he told me the name of a boy who usually plays the role of the outsider in the group. When I looked over to that very boy I saw how proud he was and that his smile was shining brighter than the sun."

Carl and the three-year-old are enthusiastic in its original sense of "engoddedness," being filled with God. This young boy felt what Indian poet Rabindranath Tagore spoke of, "In this playhouse of infinite forms I have had my play and here have I caught sight of him that is formless." God's face is immanent and transcendent, internal and external, composed and compassionate. I see the face of God—in Lindsay, a blind girl; in the eye of Holly, a dolphin; in the blinding fierceness of Nala, a lioness; in the stunning gaze of a wolf named Sybil; in Katie's soft smile; in Paul's fierce courage; in Danny's shimmering joy. This is like the analogy of a flame passed from one candle to another; however different the candles may be, it is the same flame. These faces express what the Chinese master Hui Neng spoke of as the "Original Face." The Christian mystic Nicholas of

Cusa described it as, "the Face of faces discernible in all faces, veiled as in a riddle..." My mind shuffles words—grace, gnosis, suchness, God, Tao- like cards in a deck searching for a label to end its frustration. But all of these are only pseudonyms. My efforts to convey my experience resemble so much stammering, like too many words on the tip of my tongue.

St. John of the Cross asks, "Who can describe in writing the understanding he [the Beloved] gives to loving souls in whom he dwells." St. Thomas Aquinas, three months before his death wrote, "I can no longer write, for God has given me such glorious knowledge that all contained in my works are as straw—barely fit to absorb the holy wonders that fall in a stable."

Where does that leave me? I feel so much less adequate to describe such an encounter than St. Teresa, St. John of the Cross, and St. Thomas Aquinas. Yet, I remain faced with the same task as they had. I am constantly faced with the "I don't know how I am going to explain this." That nonetheless, strives to be articulated. I agree with St. Thomas Aquinas who very explicitly said that God cannot be named. Perhaps there is nothing so eloquent to express God as silence, or the enthusiasm of children. Enthusiasm is what makes original play original.

Original play's enthusiasm is not conveyed in categories of the mind, but ineffable and mysterious as the one-kindness that fills the whole world. Enthusiasm is a pattern of belonging deep in life that has access to energies of growth and renewal that only it, and no other pattern, possesses.

> *How beautiful*
> *This form of heaven and earth*
> *Created from the source—*
> *We are members of one family.*
> —Morihei Ueshiba

By including me in their conspiracy children reawaken in me their love affair with the world. Children make it clear to me that we are not here to guard earth as our fortress, but to care for it as our garden.

The initiation I underwent It was as if the children smiled at me saying with Hafiz, "I knew it would not take me long to turn you back into God."

And they were conveying their truth in a compelling manner. They haven't made my life easier; they've made it more holy—and that is more difficult. Children do not offer me spiritual tranquilizers. They bring instead, a vocation, that which the Gods call upon me to do. In doing so they give me little of what I expect, but quite a bit of what proves later to be what I need. I often feel as Tagore put it, "like a stray line of a poem, which ever feels that it rhymes with another line and must find it, or miss its own fulfillment."

It is as if Creation hears me and conspires with children to help me awaken so that I might rhyme with the other lines of life's poetry that make up our world. I wonder where I will be when as Hafiz, asks, "God reveals Himself inside of me.

Enthusiasm is a moment when being alive is chosen over simply living. But the choice is so clear that in fact there is really no choice in the matter. There was no one and no thoughts to limit me. In fact, there is no doubt, because there was no "I" to doubt. Perhaps this is what Mother Teresa spoke about with conviction, "There was no doubt.... The moment you accept, the moment you surrender yourself. Then there is no doubt." In Japanese it is called *Ichi-go, Ichi-e* meaning "one encounter, one opportunity." It is the realization that I never play with the same playmate twice. And, I always play with the same face. When I enthusiastically feel my belonging I let go of practicing and begin playing by heart. Which is nothing special.

God said to me," But for me, you would not be here."

"I know that Lord," I answered, "but were I not here, there would be no one for you to play with."

# CHAPTER 7

# Gift/Disciplines of Original Play

*To make the love in your heart the play of your hands.*

*Do not flinch from a task, which by its very nature
cannot be completed.*
—Rabbi Tarfon

## The Doves of Peace

Birth is an outsourcing of life from Creation to earth. In this process we are provided with two gifts: You are lovable, and there is nothing to be afraid of. Together these gifts provide a code of kind-fullness that has access to energies of growth and renewal that only it, and no other pattern, possesses. Together they imprint a new order of relationship into our bodies, minds, and spirits. These gifts are not social mores nor are they intellectual or ideological concepts, but intrinsic core competencies in original play. These gifts cannot be achieved, only received. When we live these gifts we revitalize the hidden symmetry of original play that creates a sense of belonging to all life.

This is the *Godsend Conspiracy*. This is like the principle in Jewish mysticism called *tikkun olam*, literally meaning "world repair." "The idea is that God created the world by containing divine light in vessels, some of which shattered and got scattered all over. It is the job of humanity to help God by finding and releasing those shards of light—through good deeds and acts. In crafting a human being original play's gifts restore God's vessels. Pope John XXIII spoke about the necessity of just such a new order of relationships when he opened the Second Vatican Council in 1962.

These gifts have an ecological rhythm. It comes into being through a sort of graceful engineering that takes place between oneself and the world. Here is how is works. Brian Swimme points out that the sun gives four

196

million tons of itself per second as energy and light to us. He continues, "In the cosmology of the new millennium the Sun's extravagant bestowal of energy can be regarded as a spectacular manifestation of an underlying impulse pervading the universe. In the star this impulse reveals itself in the ongoing giveaway of energy. In the human heart it is felt as the urge to devote one's life to the well-being of the larger community." Cole points out that recently physicists proved experimentally that once subatomic particles interact, they become so entangled that they cease having separate identities. Likewise in original play we carry with us the touch and spirit of all those with whom we play. When someone plays with me, for example, they touch the lioness, and the grizzly, the butterfly and the elephants, the street kids in Cape Town, the autistic boy in Seattle, the cancer patient in California. This lineage widens our circle of compassion to embrace all life. Then we are as Buber put it, "in service to the universe." This is to serve without self-serving.

Original play's seven discipline/gifts are a system of whole hearted practice as well as a set of heartfelt principles that enable us to feel the underlying unity beneath our diversity. Paradoxically, original play's gifts comprise a developmental path for achieving that which we already have! The principles come of themselves, when nobody is practicing, or striving, or winning. Our challenge is to recognize that if we make conscious efforts and strive to become experts, our efforts will be in vain. And yet we must continue. To be effective, these seven gift/disciplines must disappear into the fabric of our lives. Here are two stories from Japan that illustrate this graceful principle of original play.

Japanese potter, Shoji Hamada, was asked why he built a huge kiln, which would hold 10,000 pots. His answer was something like: "If a kiln is small, I might be able to control it completely, that is to say, my own self can become a controller, a master of the kiln. But man's own self is but a small thing after all. When I work at the large kiln, the power of my own self becomes so feeble that it cannot control it adequately. It means that for the large kiln, the power that is beyond me is necessary. Without the mercy of such invisible power I cannot get good pieces. One of the reasons why I wanted to have a large kiln is because I want to be a potter, if I may, who works more in grace than in his own power. You know nearly all the best old pots were done in huge kilns." Like Shoji Hamada I know that I do not control play and it is best when "I" disappear and play in grace rather than in my own power.

A friend in Japan recently sent me the following account of how the touch of her children saved the life of their grandfather. "I recently encountered a miracle of "touch" and of children. A couple of weeks ago, I received a call which informed me that my father-in-law was in a very serious situation and was going to die. He could not even drink, so his medications were also stopped. The doctor in charge told me that his illness itself was not so serious, but his loneliness—the lack of family love sapped his power to live. He added that he would die the next day.

It was when a family member visited him to ask him for money, that they saw him. Most of his senses, except for hearing and touch were leaving his body. My children noticed his condition was the same as that of a newborn baby, and started to stroke him gently and to sing songs which he knew well. After repeated visits he could nod to answer my children's questions, could move his hands freely, and finally he tried to drink water. The nurses exclaimed 'It's miracle!' I was reassured how touch and young people's *ki* power give us an energy to live."

The more connected we are the safer we are. Original play supports the fundamental neurobiology that connects us and demonstrates that there exists a larger compassionate principle which suffuses life. As Richard Davidson points out, "It seems that mental training that cultivates compassion produces lasting changes in these circuits, changes specific to the response to suffering. The message I've taken from this is that there are virtues that can be thought of as the product of trainable mental skills." As Newberg and Waldman add, "This is precisely the kind of neural change we need to make if we want to solve the conflicts that currently afflict our world." In short it is to be a different kind of person.

In this sacred ecology stillness gives depth to trust; trust gives gentleness to touch; touch gives expression to love; love gives permanence to belonging; belonging gives strength to peace; peace gives substance to grace. And grace is what brings the others to fruition, "nothin' special"— merely preparing one to withstand an encounter with a face of God. It is best to think of these skills as strands woven into a braid rather than as separate threads.

> *Wisdom hath builded her house, she hath hewn*
> *out her seven pillars.*
> —Proverbs 9:1

# The Seven Gifts of Original Play

*Stillness*
with stillness we can re-hear our original story and come to

*Trust*
with trust we can give and receive, reaching out to

*Touch*
with touch we are hand crafted by

*Love*
with love we can feel our

*Belonging*
with belonging comes

*Peace*
within which we realize Creation's

*Grace*
and thereby fulfill childhood's dream.

With commitment and discipline, play's original gifts can become disciplines. I call these gift/disciplines the *Doves of Peace*. While I present them separately for descriptive clarity, together their synthesis forms a covenant —the *Godsend Conspiracy*. The Doves of Peace are an inherent and indelible blueprint built into life. This is kind-fullness, a one-pointed concentration of mind-body-spirit in coherence with others and the universe. In original play my body becomes an instrument informed by Creation. It is not enough to regard it as a spiritual approach, nor is it sufficient to think of it as a form of movement. The former is apt to leave one with a shell of philosophical abstraction, while the latter devolves into mere motor activities.

## The Seven Core Disciplines of Original Play

*Stillness*
Stillness is the heart of motion.

*Trust*
Expect nothing, be ready for anything.

*Touch*
Touch to heal, not to defend.

*Love*
Give love at the point of attack.

*Belonging*
Self-disappearance

*Peace*
No revenge.

*Grace*
Touch the face of God in all life.

## Stillness

*Discipline: Stillness is the heart of motion.*

*Let silence be the art you practice.*
—Rumi

*Silence, and non-action*
*Are the root of all things.*
—Chuang-tzu

*"In the silence of the heart God speaks."*
—Mother Teresa

*It is emptiness that makes possible all forms of play.*
—Michael Adam

Stillness is built into life. There are times when life seems held together by the delicate strength of silence. In the heart, for example, diastole is prelude to each resurgent systole. There is also a moment of stillness between inhaling and exhaling. For all of its rambunctiousness original play exhorts us to slow down and take notice.

There are many kinds of stillness in original play ranging from simple quiet or silence to immobility, emptiness, serenity and tranquility to communion and benediction.

While play's *roly-poly* rambunctiousness captures our attention, it is also replete with a repertoire of pauses or still-points that enable its vigorous, creative action. Original play's stillness is not a trance state; it is not a loss of consciousness, awareness, or vitality. It is not a formal convenience, like a "time-out" in sports. Quite the opposite is true. Stillness is time-in. Such moments of stillness are the Sabbaths of original play serving to remind me that there is something sacred and enduring in even the most exuberant of play's movements.

Play's spiraling forms are derived from its still-points. Just as in music whose continuity depends upon the silence of empty spaces, it is the stillpoints that weave original play's action into a well knit whole, providing moments of transition and connection that help stabilize and provide continuity and fluidity to play's movements. For example, trying to figure out the right action does me no good. It is better to be still until the right action arises by itself.

*Figure 8: Forms of Stillness*

Mitchell tells a story. Someone once asked a Zen Master, "What is the essence of wisdom?" The Zen master said, "When spring comes, the grass grows by itself." Such stillness happens from the inside out. For example, when a child runs to jump on my back there are a number of still points in our encounter. As the child lands on my back his or her arm encircles my neck. I reach up and gently and firmly press their arm to my chest. This still-point stabilizes us and prepares us for the next movement. I lower my shoulder that is on the same side as the elbow on their encircling arm. The child rolls down my outstretched arm and there is another still point as I use gentle, firm touch to briefly place him or her on the floor.

Children and animals understand that it is the still-points that communicate a quiet essence of belonging in original play. When I was tired, for example, Kim a young girl with Downs syndrome used to come and sit behind me on the grass at VIP–Tots. She would reach up and rub my neck. After a few minutes she would scamper off without saying a word. In her understanding she could sense that I needed some quiet time and touch. We were just being peaceful together. St. John of the Cross describes a similar experience. He was sad one day on a walk when a rabbit came near and gazed with his "marvelous understanding."

There were two wolves, Sybil and Hambone, who understood the same need in me. Often Sybil would saunter over and rest her head on my lap for a few minutes. Then she would lift her head and jog off to join the other wolves. One day Hambone, a dominant male wolf, allowed me to hold him in my lap. This moment of communion is captured in a photo on the cover of my book, Playing By Heart. Here is no specialized technique, no teaching. Simply a straightforward one-to-one disappearance of human and wolf. In such moments Kim, Sybil, and Hambone and I absorbed stillness like rice paper absorbs ink. At its deepest, play's stillness is a sense of kinship or communion. Paradoxically, the more still I am, the less "I" there is to do the feeling.

Often stillness reflects a lightness of spirit that is a benediction. I have felt such stillness in Hawaii, South Africa, and in the Absaroka mountains of Montana. This is a moment of quiet which allows me to be fully present. I have learned to take time for stillness before entering a playground. For example, I have a special time/place of stillness before I go into the ocean on the Big Island of Hawaii. I drive down the coast and walk out to a sacred shallow circular pool carved in the lava along the shoreline. During high tide the waves submerge the pool, but most of the time the waves just feed it with enough water so that the sun and the lava heat the water to a wonderful warmth. The pool is lined with a soft blanket of beautiful green lichen. I sit in this sacred circle to ask permission to swim and to allow myself a silent quiet time to become present on the island.

We arrived at dusk at our campsite in the South African bush. As the guides prepared dinner, we put out our sleeping bags. Then we all gathered around the small fire to eat dinner and talk. The guides shared with us that it is their tradition that each person takes a turn at night guard duty. This meant standing guard alone at the fire for an hour during the night. The guides told us to shine the flashlight around the camp's perimeter every five minutes or so. When I went to sleep I was not looking forward to my turn as a guard. When I was shaken awake I had wanted to stay snuggled in my sleeping bag. After struggling to put my clothes on and getting a cup of hot chocolate I heard elephants trumpeting, lions roaring, and hyenas yelping.

Strangely enough, silence can deepen even further in the presence of such noise. In spite of the sounds there was a profound concentration of silence that wrapped me in the great dark comforter of the African night.

The silence of the African night lie in the spaces between the sounds.

One day I took a day off from guiding my horse packing group to explore by myself. Leaving behind a world of beaten paths I was riding my appaloosa mare in the Absarokas, a Montana mountain range north of Yellowstone National Park. I came out of the pines along a ridge facing south toward the sky shouldering peaks of the Grand Tetons. I felt like one of the tiny figures in a Chinese landscape scroll.

Basho's haiku captures my moment:

> *My horse clip-clopping*
> *Over a field... Oh-ho!*

I'm part of the picture. There was an ancient quiet here that is a presence of an absence of those who have wandered and rested here before me—mountain men, Absaroka, Lakota, and Siksika. The grass and the flowers; the mountains, and the clouds, actually we are all doing the same thing—being. My horse's ears pricked up, turned his head slightly back toward the forest, and nickered softly. A solitary elk walked slowly out of the trees. Three of us, myself, my horse and an elk shared the stillness. The trees are growing quietly while the rocks and mountains are sitting in silence. At such a time it is easy to understand Carl Jung's thought that, "Solitude is a fount of healing which makes my life worth living."

It's late in the afternoon I dismounted and sat watching the purples of the peaks blend with the orange glow of the sky. I could see the night rise out of the valleys and I wondered why people say that night falls. This moment is an escape into wholeness and holiness as described by Li Po's poem:

> *We sat together the forest and I*
> *Merging into silence*
> *Until only the forest remained.*

There are times in original play when stillness refers to a presence of an absence. Sometimes an animal's absence creates a fullness in an environment that can be felt. I remember feeling this sense of the presence of absence when I was walking "on trail" in a South African game reserve. There were five tourists and two guides. One day we walked and watched for most of the morning only seeing two giraffe in the distance. We relaxed our awareness and spread out as we walked along a dusty road. The two guides were walking together in front and we were strung out behind them along the road. Suddenly the guides stopped and knelt down in the road. We all gathered to see what they found in the dust of the road. It was a fresh lion track. Everything changed. The air itself seemed to become charged. We all looked around us. The emptiness was filled with lioness. Now we walked almost touching each other. No one wanted to be the last in line. We were now feeling the presence of the absent lion. The bush was as "empty" as it had been a few minutes before, but now we felt as if the emptiness was full, teeming with lions.

Perhaps more than anything else stillness confirms a direction of spirit. As Thomas Merton has written, "Life is a spiritual thing, and spiritual things are silent."

# Trust

*Discipline: Expect nothing, be ready for anything.*

*"...Sila ersinarsinivdluge."*

*Be not afraid of the universe*
—Najagneq, Inuit Shaman

*Fear came knocking, faith opened the door, but no one was there.*
—Chinese proverb

Original play is an act of *trust in life*, which was given in trust. I have come to understand that when two hearts meet humble enough to live without fear it is the first faint stirrings of life's kindness seeking flesh and blood expression. Their openness and responsiveness demonstrate that trust is not merely a nice idea nor an ideal, but a no-nonsense way of living one's life. Original play's trust is expressed as expect nothing and be ready for anything. There is no "Let's make a deal" here.

I am fortunate to be mentored by a number of people from very different backgrounds who understand and live such trust. One is an gang member living in Los Angeles, one is a husband and father, one is a Swedish mother and grandmother, one a four year boy, another a middle-aged housewife, and an eight-year-old girl. Each in their own way demonstrates the true nature of original play as sacrifice meaning *sacre facere*, to make sacred which as Ferrucci, describes is —"to rise up vertically in a single act from the profane world of greed and fear, up into the serene, still dimension of the sacred, and to transfigure one's whole life in one moment."

## Paul

Paul was in my kindergarten class. He had leukemia. His doctors and parents were afraid that rambunctious play would hasten his death. So for six months we touched in a variety of ways. For example he liked to snuggle in my lap when I read stories to the class. When we went outside to play I carried him around the playground on my shoulders or he rode on my back when I was a horse.

One day about six months into the school year, Paul came to me and asked me to invite his parents to school for a meeting. The four of us met the following afternoon. Paul was in charge of the meeting. He spoke quietly: "I want to play with Fred. I know that I'm not going to live as long as the three of you. But I want to live my life as if I were." Paul knew what he was asking. There were three crying adults in the room with a four-year-old "therapist." Paul went to each of us and sat in our laps hugging us. I don't know how we did it, because we never talked, but we agreed that Paul could come and play.

When he came to school the following day it was like letting a tornado into the classroom. He was very excited and his play was rambunctious, passionate and uncompromising. He was exhausted by the end of the morning. He stayed home and rested the next day. Because he played so hard when he came to school, Paul could come only every other day. About a month later Paul died of leukemia. At the funeral his parents and I asked each other if we had done the right thing by letting him play. We agreed that it was the right thing to do. That night I thought about what Paul taught me. Paul's trust was not in me, himself or mom and dad; it was how he lived. Some would say that he trusted in God; Paul never used the word. Paul knew what he was doing. He chose to play and die rather than live and not play.

✳✳✳

## Linda

Linda is a middle-aged woman who has cancer. She attended a retreat with other cancer patients. She witnessed me play with another patient's head in an exercise. She asked me if I would do the same with her. I said yes, but she had to agree to play with my head and face first. She laughed and agreed. We sat down in front of each other. I took off my glasses. She began gently rolling my head around between her hands. After a few minutes she stopped. I asked if I could play with her head. She readily agreed. I reached out and held her head gently in my hands. I slowly began to move my hands around her face and head, always staying in touch and caressing it gently and firmly. When I brought my touch to a gentle close she looked at me with tears in her eyes. She hadn't told me that she had cancer in the bones of her neck. She put her head in my hands knowing that if I moved abruptly I could kill her. I held her head "just right."

## Hector

To: Fred    From: Hector

*When you come in June find a message from me. Also I like playing with you and thank you for showing me how to be strong."*

This is a note given by Hector to his school counselor for me. He was one of eight young men in a East Los Angeles junior high. Their school counselor asked me to come and play with them because they never went to class. They spent their days hanging out in her office. I came to be with them for three hours each Friday for ten weeks.

On my first visit I walked into the area where the boys were lounging. I sat down and spread some 8x10 photos of me playing with wolves on the floor. One of the boys looked over and asked if that was me playing with the dogs. I replied that it was, but they weren't dogs. They were wolves. That got their attention. Now, all of the boys came over to look. They got down and passed the photos around. It didn't take long. As if by some pre-agreed upon unspoken cue one of the boys asked me, " How do you do that?"

That was the question I was waiting for. I said, "Come, I'll show you." When I walked by the counselor's desk we shared a knowing smile. She knew what I was up to. I led the boys onto a small area of enclosed lawn. When I got to the grass, I immediately got down on my hands and knees and crawled among them. They laughed, pushed at me and spoke in Spanish. It didn't take long until one-by-one they jumped on me and we began to play on the grass.

On this initial visit, Hector was hesitant. He watched some of the other boys play with me. He smiled and laughed a lot. He was wearing an ankle length black leather coat. This was June in the San Fernando Valley of Southern California. The afternoon temperatures were in the high 90's. Finally, he took of his coat and jumped on me. Hector was a big guy, about six feet and 200 pounds. As we rolled and tussled on the grass he made it clear by his body movements that it was important for him to be on top.

Before I came back for our second play session. His counselor called me and said she wanted to tell me about Hector. She said that he had worn that trench coat every day to school since September. She called it his shield. But after our first play session he left it home. He no longer needed his shield.

## Stark

Growls, thuds, and deep laughter rumbled from the room. From the sounds, one would think that two bears were rampaging about. It was only

Stark and I—two grown men tumbling about on the floor of a bed-and-breakfast inn at a cancer retreat in Northern California.

Stark was in intense pain when we met in January, 1996. He had been informed just a few months earlier that he had pancreatic cancer and was not expected to live more than a few months.

When it came to playtime he became desperately alive like a little boy inside a man who was losing everything. In the midst of one of our play sessions we stopped to catch our breaths. We were quiet for a few moments, just lying on the floor and looking at each other. Stark looked at me and asked, "Fred, what is it that you are trying to tell me."

I replied, "Stark, this is hard for me to say, I am telling you to play with your cancer." I had been thinking about what I would say if a patient asked me why we were playing when their lives were so dangerously serious. I knew that to tell them to play with rather than fight against their cancer would seem absurd. Recalling Einstein's thought that, "If at first an idea isn't absurd there's no hope for it." Perhaps, then there was hope. Anyway, I found the courage to say to people in the retreats that we were going to play with their cancers. In doing so we were going to focus on thriving—being alive while alive—rather than on merely surviving. Obviously surviving is crucial but limiting the focus on it lessens the human adaptive ability and undermines health. Dr. Siddhartha Mukherjee suggests, "This war on cancer may be 'won' by redefining victory." Indeed original play redefines the entire game by focusing on our ability to thrive not merely survive in the midst of adversity.

Stark nodded and smiled as we hugged and continued our roly-poly play like two kids who have wandered off from the fearful eyes of their parents. I don't know how he did it. Cancer had taken over Stark's life and yet when he played there was no indication of the intense pain he was otherwise suffering. Stark portrayed something essential about not just his struggle with cancer but about being human. His fight with cancer had taken him to many places in the world and through many medical alternatives. When Stark was not playing he was intensely preoccupied with his painful cancer, but he once laughingly said that during our play he was like a little boy with no more pain than when he skinned his knee as a child. Following the retreat Stark went home to play with his sons.

Before he died in August, 1996. Stark wrote the following poem:.

*Quietly the spirit and beauty of the mountains fill my heart*
*My heart expands and I open to the awe and*
*sense of discovery offered to me.*
*I feel free and alive and at peace*
*And nearby just inside my heart I hear God saying,*
*"Hello, do you want to play?"*

## Anette

In June 2003 my friend Anette was diagnosed with LAM (lymphangiomiomytosis). The doctor told her that she had a maximum of only one more year to live. She needed a lung transplant. Each month passed with no prospect of a new lung. I remember when we both knew that she had less than two weeks to live. How we knew this I don't know. We didn't talk about it. It was her courage and trust that helped me during this very hard time. Anette never blamed nor did she feel sorry for herself. In fact she never seemed to be going through a trauma. In 2004 she had the good fortune to undergo a single lung transplant. The lung transplant gave her a new and different life, but still rich and rewarding. I realize in sharing with her that Anette's trust is not based on fear, for such a trust would be no trust at all. Her trust was based on not being afraid of the disease LAM. As she expressed it, "To be afraid can limit your possibilities to survive." This is not a philosophy, nor a religion; it is being a loving, alive human being. In 2014 Anette had a second lung transplant and she seems to be doing better now than at any time since her diagnosis. To be with her you would never know that she has had two lung transplants.

The following poem is written by Anette to help others who have come to her for help with a very difficult and at this point incurable disease.

*My advice to you*
*Don't stop living your life.*
*Live your life in the way that's best for you.*
*Enjoy the experience of the little bird's song,*
*a baby's noise, a discussion with a teenager, and listen to the old*
*parent's memories—then you can feel you are still alive*
*and life is still going on around you.*
*You can just do the best with your life, in your own way,*
*as long as it is possible.*
*When the end comes, it comes.*
*Maybe tomorrow or, the day after, but presumably*
*years or decades after.*
*No one knows for oneself or for others either.*
*You can just continue you life and be present as long as you live.*
*And don't leave it prematurely when you still are alive!*
*Still you can live and experience life's beauty,*
*even if the beauty is different than before*
*Feel the grace and knowledge you have in your life.*
*You will always be remembered when the other life comes.*
*Probably it will be a feeling of liberty when it comes.*
*Don't let fear take the beauty from your life*
*When you still can see and smell the flower's message in the spring,*
*notice that small things have their importance*
*But don't be afraid of fear.*
*There is always some friend's warm hand to touch*
*and you will always be remembered*
*And it never ends.*

Anette's poem exemplifies a level of trust in life that is conscious of the reality and inviolability of her own life and at the same time she is able to consecrate her life to the purpose for which it was given to her. She has now lived over ten years with her new lung and has founded a LAM foundation in Stockholm to help others with this disease. With her characteristic wisdom, patience and gracious ways she has recently successfully undergone a second lung transplant. Anette is one of those extremely rare persons of whom Thomas Merton wrote, who is "holding everything together and keeping the universe from falling apart."

***

## Mary

I first met Mary in her classroom. She is a petite eight-year-old. She was playing on a therapy ball. I caught her as she fell off the ball as it rolled. The incident happened so quickly that it frightened her. I was then associated with her fear. For the following few months Mary would move toward her teacher when I came into the room. I played with the other children on the other side of the room. For a number of reasons we didn't see each other for a few weeks. Then one day she came in late when I was already playing with the other children. She walked over and shared her doll and stuffed rabbit with me. When she handed them to me to hold and asked if I would go 'over there." Over there was about five feet away. But this was closer than I had ever been allowed to be to her. After an hour she came over sat in my lap and asked me to read the book she brought with her. When it was time to eat lunch she asked if I would carry her to her seat. I did. As I sat her in her chair she said, "You are a nice boy." How delightful to be a "nice boy" at fifty!

Anette, Linda, Paul, Hector, Mary, and Stark lived trust. Their trust is not an abstraction; it is at the core of their being.

# Touch

*Discipline: Touch to heal, not to defend.*

*How can I withhold my soul*
*When touching yours is its goal*
—Rilke

*The way to save our skins is to get in touch with each other.*
*I have found no delight better than the mix of touch with love.*
—Bahauddin

"Who holds me any more? Nobody!" These were the desperate whispered words of a tearful mother picking up her three-year-old son after school. She was expressing her human hunger to be touched. I was holding her child as she walked up to get him. I often held children or took their hands to meet parents after school. On this day I stepped forward and hugged both child and mother. This mother made me aware that it was not only the children who needed to be reassured of their worth. So, each day I went out to the curb to offer support not only to the children and this mother, but to other parents as well.

Coleridge wrote about just such an experience. His three-year-old child awoke in the night and called for his mother. "Touch me, only touch me with your finger," the young boy pleaded. The child's mother was astonished.

'Why?' she asked.

'I'm not here,' the boy replied. 'Touch me Mother, so that I may be here."

*We touch heaven when we lay hands on a human body*
—Novalis

Jesus said, "The kingdom of heaven is at hand." We don't realize how tangible are his words. Through touch, the signet of Creation is pressed upon our lives. Through touch we feel our belonging. Touch is how we make and structure our world; it is how we feel the other gifts of original play—stillness, trust, love, peace, belonging, and grace. Relearning original

213

play is to get back in touch with the world. This is the mutual touch of life with not only its outward form but its inner spirit. The playmate discerns beneath appearances, understands details, perceives relationships, and senses underlying patterns. Play touch is a craft containing a number of dynamic, childlike principles, each being quite literally a touchstone of reality. It is crucial to realize that progress in these touch skills does not lie in acquiring technical skills alone. The body, mind, and spirit are attuned together. There are no manuals of technique in original play. What is necessary changes at any given moment—expect nothing, be ready for anything.

Touch is the key that unlocks the kind-fullness code of original play. This key has five important properties that distinguish it from other touch.

*First*, it is universal meaning that it is beyond and not bound by social, cultural, religious or even species categories. Original play's touch is personal; it's reach is global.

*Second*, it is based on healing not self-defense, making conflict and contest behavior obsolete.

*Third*, it is tangible, making real such intangibles as peace, love, trust and belonging.

*Fourth*, play's touch is "just right," that is it meets the needs of the being who is touched.

*Fifth*, play's touch connects heaven and earth.

Original play touch is not cultural touch neither is it task touch, therapeutic touch, medical touch, or massage touch. When I play with a child with autism, for example, it is the individual not their social, cultural, or medical categories whom I touch. One day a mother brought her twenty-year-old autistic son to see me. She was sad because whenever he was happy he became excited and he would then initiate rapid stemming motions, hitting himself on the sides of his head with both of his fists. Her son was bigger than she was and she was afraid to try to stop his stemming. She thought her efforts would only serve to escalate her son's excitement. Consequently, she didn't want to do anything that would overly excite him. But, she also felt guilty about her fears.

When she finished I invited her son to play with me. We sat down on the floor near each other. Initially our connection was virtually imperceptible. Quickly, he smiled and became excited; his joy resulted in the rapid stemming motions that his mother mentioned. I reached out my arms and put my hands up next to his head so that when he tried to hit the sides of his head he hit my hands instead. I use the unbendable arm from aikido so that my arms are soft and flexible but strong enough to absorb his force. I began by following his touch. I moved my hands slightly in and out so they absorbed his touch like shock absorbers. When he was used to touching me I changed the pattern from his rapid linear motion to, at first, small then larger circles. His hands would hit my hands and instead of recoiling for the next hit his hands would stay in contact with mine. Now his motions were mirroring mine. I then moved my hands with his hands following to my head. As I did this I reversed the positioning so my hands were now on the outside of and just lightly touching his hands. He lightly touched my head repeatedly. With my hands on the outside and close to his the range of motion was shorter. I then took my hands away and he played with my head while I did the same with his head. This shortly evolved into us playing together like two big kittens.

When we stopped for a rest his mother was surprised and delighted but retained her fear that she wasn't strong enough to do what I had done. After we rested and talked for a while I invited her to join us. I had her sit in front of me with her son facing us. I initiated play and as her son began to reach up to hit his head I took his mother's hands and held them inside of mine. The three of us repeated the process with his mother's hands now being the shock absorbers. As we continued I gradually withdrew my hands so she could feel that not only was his touch not as hurtful or powerful as she had imagined but that her arms were easily capable of handling her son's energetic movements. Now I sat back and watched as mother and son touched.

*The touch of original play is based on healing not self defense.*
There is a training story in the Yagyu martial arts tradition that describes the possibilities when we touch to heal not to defend. Iemitsu, the third Tokugawa shogun, received a tiger as a gift from the Korean court. The shogun dared the famous swordsman Yagyu Tajima Munenori to subdue the beast. Yagyu immediately accepted the challenge, strode confidently into the cage, and whacked the snarling animal on the head with his iron fan just as the tiger was about to pounce. The tiger shrank back and cowered in the corner. The Zen master Takuan, who was also present, chided Yagyu, 'That is the wrong approach." Takuan then entered the cage unarmed, spat on his hands, and gently rubbed the tiger's face and ears. The ferocious beast calmed down at once, purring and rubbing itself

against the monk. Takuan turned to Yagyu and said, "A whack on the head will turn him into an enemy forever; gentle persuasion will make him your friend for life."

No touch does not teach good touch. Contrary to our advertising our "skin hunger" is not satisfied by sex, food,drugs, busy work, frenetic entertainment or other escapes. As Dr. Jim Prescott, among others, has suggested touch deprivation in childhood leads to violence. Safe loving touch changes our nervous systems from a fear based system to a love based system. The touch of original play is a sort of lightening rod for fear absorbing it, neutralizing it, redirecting it as one touches and experiences another as not "other." While I have no problem playing in Poolsmoor Prison in South Africa, I am told that touch is forbidden in American prisons. When American prison officials tell me this I say that it isn't true. In fact, negative touch is very common in American prisons. It must be that it is only positive touch that is not allowed. Such fear of touch does not serve us well.

*Touch makes real such intangibles as peace, love, trust, and belonging.*

Humans need to touch and be touched. Touch is how we know that we are real. My colleague Jola described that before leaving on a trip she brought her two children, Magda and Michal, together and told them ,"You have my love every time and everywhere." Her seven-year-old son, Michal said, "Yes Mom, but we need your touch." Julian of Norwich said that in addition to "seeings" she had "touchings," by which she means forms of understanding that are not merely cerebral at all. Such touching, for example, has been found to provide health benefits to mothers and infants in the postpartum period. Dr. Ann Bigelow and her co-authors in a recent study point out that with skin-to-skin contact between infants and mothers, both mothers and infants experience positive impacts. The women experience less depression and stress and more empowerment as parents. The infants show better growth, more stable body temperatures, heart rates and respiratory rates, and reduced pain and crying.

I often say to beginners that there is no grabbing in original play. While this may sound simple it is not easy for someone raised in a culture that teaches one to grab what you want and hold on to it for dear life. It is easier to be hard, loud, and forceful than to be soft, clear, and powerful. One of the more difficult issues for beginners in original play is letting go. In life we practice grasping, in original play we practice letting go. Grabbing in original play is like holding one's breath, the harder you hold on the more dangerous it is.

The touch of play is a matter of heart-hand coordination, focusing on a tranquil spirit which enables one to use minimum force and then let go. My colleague, Jola's touch has been described by both children and adults as being "like the wind." It reminds me of how Awa Kenzo the master Japanese archer said to hold the bow, "Your grip should be like autumn leaves blown by a storm." The use of minimum force requires learning to use one's fingers, hands, arms and body weight in such a way that allows for one's movements to touch "just right." This is the ability to withdraw force in the microsecond after it is applied making the gesture more precise, more accurate, and less forced.

I have felt such touch from Nala, the lioness, and the wolves Hambone, Sybil and Windsong. All four at different times held me with their teeth. Even though they all held me firmly I had no feeling of being grabbed; it was more like being embraced by teeth. Their touch is made safe by the combination of minimum force and by letting go. It is as if the letting go is not only part of the minimum force, it's that the release is prepared for in the application of the touch itself. It's this *prehension* (taking hold), in which the body anticipates and acts in advance of sense data that gives me no feeling of being held against my will. This is the art of giving and receiving fully. When done correctly there is no residual grabbing.

Dr. Lewis Thomas commented that touching is the oldest and most effective tool in doctoring. "The scientific study of touch reveals the tactile modality to be an ideal medium in which individuals spread goodness to others." Jules Older relates a playful encounter between an osteopath and an elderly patient: " the patient says "I've been waiting for you to tell you that it is because of you that I am still alive," The osteopath says, "What are you talking about?" The old man says "Well every morning you pinched my toe when the others weren't looking." The physician says "Yes, but what does that have to do with... ." The patient answers "Nobody plays with the toes of dying men. So I decided I must not be dying after all."

*Play's touch is "just right," that is it meets the needs of the being who is touched.*

We are touched into existence and through touch we share our lives with others. Even the briefest touch leaves a trace, an impression as we let each other know that we are safe and loved. I once worked as a consultant for Toyota in South Africa. One day as I was walking through the office a woman manager stopped me and asked me to come into her office. She told me that she was one of eleven managers, all the rest of whom were men. She related that she was having a great deal of difficulty communicating her ideas during their management meetings. She was frustrated and sad because she felt excluded and she couldn't quite identify how it was being done. She didn't think it was a conspiracy, but nonetheless she felt the presence of some kind of male bonding that excluded her. She was worried that this would affect not only her ability to work at Toyota but her references. She said that she had tried to be one of the guys but that didn't work. She also tried to be feminine and that didn't work. She was at a loss and didn't know what else to do.

I told her that I had an idea. It wouldn't be easy and she probably wouldn't like it, but I was going to share it with her anyway. I told her that she was to enter the next management meeting and touch each of the ten men before she took her seat. She had to touch all the men in the same meeting. She could not use "man" touch, this meant, for example, no hand shakes and no slaps on the back. Her touch could not convey that she was intending to win their approval. That would engage them in a contest. Instead, her touch had to give two messages: you are lovable and there's nothing to be afraid of. She was distraught with my suggestion.

I shared with her a hint. I asked for a pen. First I handed it to her holding it upright between my thumb and forefinger. She took it. I repeated the exercise, but this time I laid the pen in the palm of my open hand and she picked it up from my hand touching me as she did so. In the second example she could not retrieve her pen without touching me. She smiled and understood the hint. A couple of weeks later I was walking through the office when she motioned for me to come into her office. She was beaming. "It worked!', she exclaimed. "They never knew what happened to them."

"Of course. They were afraid. Even if they were conscious of what they were doing to you they didn't have the courage to act on it." I replied. "Your touch made them feel comfortable. You let them know that they were safe." Two years later she called me and said that she no longer worked for Toyota but how good it felt to have left as a strong woman rather than as a victim of those ten men.

What happened in that conference room? Her touch disarmed them. So, they no longer needed to defend themselves.

Sometimes in the most unexpected ways original play's touch counteracts the mind's automatic tendency to perceive threat, danger, and competition and shifts the nervous system away from its potent, trigger happy fight/flight tendencies toward a physiological profile more conducive to cooperation and kindness. As Newberg and Waldman point out meditation and belief may not be sufficient to eradicate the effects of fear. It's not enough to think kind thoughts, these values must be translated into action.

Some years later my urologist asked me what I do for a living. I gave him a brief synopsis of original play. He asked me if I could help him learn to use touch with his patients. Wonderful, I thought to myself. 'I'll give you two choices. One will be very hard, the other quite easy. You can choose." First, I described the difficult alternative. I suggested that he buy a rocking chair for his office. And each time he has to tell a patient that they have cancer he is to sit in the chair and hold them. I could tell from his expression that this was asking too much of him. So, I gave him a second choice. I told him that he was to make sure that he touched every patient before they left his office. And that his touch was to convey the message: you are lovable and there's nothing to be afraid of. As a hint I demonstrated the exercise with the pen that I had given to the Toyota manager. He replied that he could do this.

*Original play's touch connects heaven and earth.*

Touch is an essential part of connecting human and divine. Mother Teresa tells of a girl who came to India to join the Missionaries of Charity. On the girl's first day Mother Teresa told her that she must go to the Home for the Dying. After three hours the girl returned to Mother Teresa with a big smile and said, "Mother, I have been touching the body of Christ for three hours."

Mother Teresa replied, "How—what did you do?"

The girl continued, "When we arrived there, they brought a man who had fallen into a drain, and been there for some time. He was covered with wounds and dirt and maggots, and I cleaned him and I knew I was touching the body of Christ."

Touch is the primary language of original play, its rich vocabulary communicates heart-to-heart. I recall, for example, a two-year-old who was described as being tactilely defensive. He didn't like to touch things like Jello, whipped cream, shaving cream, or apple sauce. I noticed that whenever we played he liked to sit on my chest with his legs next to my neck and play with my beard. One day I asked his teacher to bring over all the things he didn't like to touch. One by one I put the apple sauce, Jello, whipped cream, and shaving cream in my beard. He touched all of them as he played with my beard. Original play's vision of trust, love, belonging, and peace is a lived practice—here and now. This is both our potential and our reality. Nothing else will do.

*Oh, grant me my prayer that I may never lose the bliss of the touch of the one in the play of the many.*
—Rabindranath Tagore

# Love

**Discipline: Give love at the point of attack.**

*"For only love—which means humility—can exorcise the fear which is at the root of all war."*
—Thomas Merton

*"Love is the strongest force the world possess and yet it is the humblest imaginable."*
—Gandhi

*"Without love the world will never improve."*
—Morihei Ueshiba

*The important thing is not to think much but to love much; and so do that which best stirs you to love.*
—Saint Teresa of Avila

*Look inside and find where a person loves from. That's the reality not what they say.*
—Hypocrites

*Men and women were once whole but were torn in two, and the pursuit and desire of that whole is called love.*
—Plato

I n the midst of our play six-year-old Travis looks up at his Mother sitting near us and exclaims, "Look Mom I'm falling in love."

After his play session a five-year-old boy in Warsaw, Poland says that, "Real play is when no one is crying and no one has a broken heart."

Recently I played with young deaf children at an Austrian school. Following the session a mother who watched me play with her daughter said to me with tears in her eyes, ""there's just so much loving in this play."

This mother and two boys capture the essence of original play and in doing so grasp what Viktor Frankl described as the greatest secret that human thought and belief have to impart: *The salvation of man is through love and in love.* (italics author's). Original play's love as Siegel points out "...is a re-creation because children early on have this receptivity, this playfullness of being."

Original play is an urgent, practical love, actively lived heart by heart in the small round of a unique life and is simultaneously an inclusive love as big as all life. "When a child loves you for a long, long time, not just to play with, but really loves you, then you become real." says the Skin Horse in Margery Williams' *The Velveteen Rabbit.* That's it! That's what the children have been doing with me all along—making me real. Children have been finishing the job that Creation began.

Playing for real allows one to spread love beyond limits to include even enemies. Buddha said, 'Spread thy thoughts of love beyond limits." Christ said, 'Love thine enemies." Then playing for real as Thomas Merton points out, "...in so far as a man returns to his own roots, he becomes able to resist exterior violence with complete success and even, after a certain point, invulnerability." The Skin Horse agrees, "When you are real you don't mind being hurt." We have been told that love "bears all things" and "endures all things." Such admonitions seemed to be the stuff of saints, sages, and children's stories but not realistic suggestions for me. I know what I don't want to know—that I must love with all my heart, but I don't want to acknowledge this so I fight to hide from the fact that love is the survival benefit that comes with the gift of life. Then I met Danny who taught me the living meaning of such love.

When I met Danny he was an abused boy of about four. He had been forced to live with the family dogs. He ate and drank out of the dog dishes and slept in the dog house. When he first came to the school he could not handle the group activities, nor could he sit quietly and wait for his turn. When he was upset he scratched and bit. He was too aggressive for the teachers. So, I was assigned to be with him throughout his half day at school. We spent much of our time playing outside. When he or I felt he could handle it he went inside to join his class. In time he was able to manage the routine of kindergarten.

One day I was carrying him to his school bus. He didn't want to go back to the institution where he was living. Out of anger and frustration he lunged forward and bit through my cheek. I felt instant and intense pain but somehow immediately gave him love through my injured cheek. He raised his head and looked at me and put his head on my shoulder. All of this happened so quickly that it was as if it was only one moment. We looked into each others eyes and I was aware of our deeper connection, our deeper humanity. I hugged him and carried him to his seat on the school bus. I buckled him in and sat with him until the bus had to leave. When I walked into the school I was crying. Seeing my blood and tears a staff member looked at me and commented, "Fred really got it this time." The staff was used to seeing me with a bloody nose or bite, but they had not seen me crying. I sat down and realized that my tears were not from the pain but from a realization of the lesson Danny gave me about love. As soon as I loved him he stopped biting. At the point of loving there was no more pain in my cheek. No attack, no victim.

Danny shared with me the pattern that is at the very heart of original play—giving love at the point of attack. What happened? Was it that as a Stanford Medical School Study points out, "Intense, passionate feelings of love can provide amazingly effective pain relief." "It turns out that the areas of the brain activated by intense love are the same areas that drugs use to reduce pain," said Arthur Aron, PhD, a professor of psychology at State University of New York at Stony Brook. Or... was it that my tears were ones of humility as I realized that through no efforts of my own I had received a great gift that I did not understand. St. Teresa of Avila describes so well what I felt, "The will is fully occupied in loving, but it doesn't understand how it loves. The intellect, if it understands, doesn't understand how it understands; at least it can't comprehend anything of what it understands. It doesn't seem to me that it understands, because, as I say, it doesn't understand—I really can't understand this!"

Danny and I had established for ourselves in a real way what H.H. The Dalai Lama pointed out that, "the importance and efficacy of the attitude of loving-kindness toward other human beings has now been established from the scientific viewpoint." Danny taught me that the efficacy of loving kind-fullness was established from a personal experience. Danny taught me this lesson in the only way he could; perhaps the only way that I could learn it. Original play is not an abstract ideal, but a flesh and blood response to the world. My cheek was bleeding, but not my heart.

The application of love at the point of attack is the heart's wisdom. Danny demonstrated in a most compelling way the meaning of Jesus' teaching of his often quoted admonition to his followers in the Sermon on the Mount to "turn the other cheek"(Matt.5:39). By literally "turning the other cheek" I bring to bear on my injury not the hurt side of myself, but a fresh, uninjured, aspect previously unknown. This is not as some would imagine that I am inviting a second bite. In fact, as Danny's reaction demonstrated we now had a new relationship. This is what I call giving love at the point of attack. I realized then that flesh and blood needs a loving, compassionate heart far more than a just, punishing mind. Danny and I made conflict obsolete and in so doing we had discovered the true roots of our shared humanity.

To those who have the courage to allow love to guide their actions love has a fierce clarity and certainty that no cross-examination by pure reason can shake. I walked into a classroom at 9am. Sitting on the floor were a teacher, a mother and a small boy who was crying very hard and desperately holding on to his mother. This was his second day at school. The teacher took him and he tried to reach to hold his mother who was also crying. She told him that she would come back at lunchtime. She left the room. The teacher stood with the little boy. He was two and a half. He and his family were from Southeast Asia. He has autism. As the teacher walked near me, the boy reached out with his arms to me. I took him and walked outside.

As I came to the door another teacher walked past me and whispered, "I hope you are not going to do that for long. We don't have time for that." She's right and she's wrong. According to the school's daily plan. There's no place in his IEP (Individual Education Plan) for giving love. She's also very wrong. For without the feelings of love and safety the little boy's ability to learn is impaired.

I took the time. We walked outside and I held him until his sobbing quieted and his hold on me softened. Then I sat on the ground with him cuddled in my lap. In time he shifted his position so he could look around the playground. Other kids came by to say "hi" and hug me. He stood up and walked a few steps away and quickly turned to see if I was still there. I was still there. I waved. He smiled and ventured a little further. Little by little he walked further away to explore and return for a hug. Each time going a bit further. Eventually he replaced his return trip to me with a reassuring look. We played together for two hours. When I returned him to his teacher he scampered off to join his class. Each day I came to his class, he spent less and less time with me and grew increasingly comfortable in the classroom. By the second week he would wave to me as he walked to class with his mother.

My acceptance of the little boy's invitation to love invariably strikes the institutional world either as some sentimental foolishness or as a subversive impulse. The question is not whether there is time for love. Rather, it is to say "first things first." Play's perspective does not deny the culture's interest, but it sees beyond it to the truest expression of life's spirit. The point of my response is that the very process will produce a different way of living in this world. Albert Einstein in an exchange of letters with Sigmund Freud posed a question, "Is it possible to control man's mental evolution so as to make him secure against the psychosis of hate and destructiveness?" My experience with children in original play provides an emphatic "Yes!" to this question.

Love is the funeral pyre on which all of my fears are devoured. I know now, and this knowledge has grown considerably, that the only true human progress is a widening of my ability to love. Then I will be who Creation has willed me to be from the beginning; not myself, but love. I now know that life is a journey out of love in search of love. For one human being to love another is the toughest test and proof of original play's sanctity. Original play is Creation's highest spiritual expression. Like an invisible hand on the tiller original play points the heart's compass to the way to heal our hurts and help us find our way back to peace.

Original play is about loving—loving so much that I disappear from myself. Julian of Norwich wrote about such love when she found in the palm of her hand something small. She said, "I looked at it with the eye of my understanding and thought: What can this be? I was amazed that it could last, for I thought because of its littleness it would suddenly have fallen into nothing. And I was answered in my understanding: It lasts and always will, because God loves it; and this everything has being through the love of God."

# Belonging

## Discipline: Self-disappearance

*...to him that is joined to all the living there is hope.*
—Ecclesiastes 9:4

*!ke e: /xarra //ke San language for*
*"Those who are different joining together"*
*(motto on coat of arms of Republic of South Africa)*
—Lyall Watson

One day I was arranging some thin mats on the concrete floor in a corner of a corridor in Pollsmoor Prison, in Cape Town, South Africa. Small groups of prisoners walked by. Most took no outward notice of me. One tall young man in a blue prison jumpsuit stopped. He looked at me as if I were totally out of place. In the prison everyone knows their place. Here is a white guy all alone sitting on the floor in a secluded hallway. No guards were around. He asked me, "Who are you? Do you know who we are? We are murderers, rapists, drug dealers." I just smiled and crawled toward him and nudged his legs. He smiled a huge smile. I tackled him and we rolled together on the mats. He laughed and squirmed out of my grasp. When he stood up he laughingly said, "OK! OK! I get it." We shook hands and he ran to catch up with the other prisoners. I never told him who I was. I showed him who I am. My sudden behavioral answer to his question brought us out of our categories. What is it that he got? For the briefest of times we were without categories, no prisoner, no stranger, no American, no South African. Original play short-circuited our differences and helped us regain our humanity. I experienced this sense of belonging in other play sessions with a group of young men in Pollsmoor Prison in Cape Town, South Africa.

Following our play together, Cedrick, Jeremy, Ricardo, Lionel, Mava, Kenneth, Maurice, Johnny, and David spoke excitedly in Afrikaans about what it meant to play. Each was anxious to share. One said that the play made him feel loved and valuable. Another added that he had never played. One twenty-one-year-old young man who described himself as a gang leader in the prison spoke quietly as he told us that he had not wanted to leave prison because in prison he was a leader but back home in the township he was nothing. After playing he admitted that he wanted to go home and see his mother. Original play's belonging replaced their sense of loneliness and abandonment. We walked back together into the prison building with our arms around each other. There were no congratulatory high-fives, just silence. We understood the difference. In our play these young men felt their belonging to something greater than a gang membership. This is what Archbishop Tutu describes as *ubuntu*, the compassion evident when one's humanity is caught up in another's humanity. Original play dissolved our categories. Garmezy & Rutter indicate, and I could feel, that a loving and affectionate connection to even one person can limit or counteract much of the damage done by negative environments. Belonging changes the scheme of things.

In my graduate school days as a geographer we used to say "location, location, location" as a tried and true principle of prime importance in geography and planning. In social relationships the principle is "connection, connection, connection." The more connected we are the safer we are. Lown reminds us that we know that adults who are more intimately connected with family, friends and life interests experience less heart disease. For those who live alone pets lessen the risk. I recall visiting a home for elderly in Seattle, Washington. I dressed in my play clothes, which were sweat pants and rugby shirt. I was led into a small conference room attached to the dining area of the home. I was surprised at how nice the home was. It seemed like a fine hotel. There were twenty women waiting for me, some were in wheelchairs and others had walkers near them. They were all dressed as if they were going to church. I silently said to myself, OK, so much for getting on the floor. I spoke for a few moments and then did something that I had never done before. I began to crawl on my hands and knees to the first woman on my right. Without talking I put my head in her lap. I then went to the second woman and continued until I had laid my head on the laps of all twenty women. I crawled back and sat in my chair. There was silence in the room. As I looked around the women were crying. Soon, one of them, an elegant and charming person, spoke. She said through her tears, "Fred, you must understand that we have not been touched like that for years."

One day while playing with a group of young children on the Navajo reservation a Navajo elder stopped and observed our play. When I was finished he motioned for me to join him. He smiled and said that "watching you play with the children is like watching flowers grow." The elder understood that original play is a new "Theory of Relativity" in which we feel a pattern of relatedness within the human spirit, charged with a cosmological sacrament. Bahaddin said that, "There is only one living being, only one."

In original play I am turned inside out. St. Paul said that, "we are members of one another." Robert Oppenheimer, Neils Bohr, Carl Jung, John Lilly, Albert Einstein and Edwin Schrödinger are among the prominent scientific figures who felt this sense of belonging. Their work related to them a unity in the universe beyond the material world. Einstein referred to a "cosmic religious feeling." Schrödinger describes a oneness of all things in which individual life and all other conscious beings "are all in all." Biologist Edwin Chargaff adds that, " If [a scientist] has not experienced, at least a few times in his life, this cold shudder down his spine, this confrontation with an immense, invisible face whose breath moves him to tears, he is not a scientist."

When we belong, we feel our proper place in the scheme of life. Playmates are not simply individuals—they are lineages. I am a thread in an elegant tapestry of playmates woven with earnest meticulousness, whose strands are durable and ancient, delicate and intricate. Together we trace an elaborate and impeccable, sacred pattern, a lineage or lifeline, that belongs to all. There is an analogy from physics called the "world line" of a particle that fits well here. The "world line" of a particle refers to its path in space-time, including all of the energy exchanges which the particle has undergone since birth, which it brings to bear at this moment. Likewise, my play-line refers to the energy exchanges that I have undergone in my play which are all brought to bear at this one moment.

It is January in the northern Rocky Mountains, a time of white landscape and gray skies when the grizzly, the marmot and the willow bud are all snuggled under a deep blanket of snow, waiting for spring. It is a time when the howling of wolves echo from mountain peak to mountain peak, rolling down the valleys and the spines of any solitary human who might be out and about. Such is January, the time of the wolf moon, when cold pierces the lungs as deeply as the wolf's howl pierces the soul.

There are three of us here somewhere in the northern Rocky Mountains, myself, Grandfather, and a wolf. Darkness rises and unfolds around us. Up here darkness rises from the valleys; it doesn't fall from the sky. The campfire shoots its sparks aloft like shooting stars going in the opposite direction. In this luminescence Grandfather's spirit is enlivened. No words pass between us as we sit. He knows that translating one's meaning to another is difficult and best done with as few words as possible. Our relationship has been fine tuned during many long, quiet times together.

In the firelight, I see that his face, framed by two thin gray braids, is deeply furrowed like the bark of an old cottonwood tree. I don't know how he lives up here, perhaps he has a grizzly's cave or an old trapper's cabin. But I would rather imagine him being able to slip in and out of some seam in the mountains. He is mountain-born and raised, variable as the winter winds and like the gnarled pine, seared burnt sienna by the wind and sun. His experience is more than his own, immutable, passed on as certainly as his silver hair and the cast of his quick piercing blue eyes. His stature is reckoned by the distance he sees, which has nothing to do with horizons and eyes. He is both burdened and enlivened with a long memory. Utterly synchronized to his place and time, his movements flow like tracings with the efficiency, ease, and grace of a wolf's trot. When he stretches in the warmth of the morning sun, he does so like the earth creatures at the crests of their burrows. The mountains are for him charms, like silver tokens on a woman's bracelet, each animal, stream and cliff caressed first by his spirit, then his hands, and now by his memory,.

He sits quietly on his buffalo robe, aware of something that most of us would miss, lurking beyond the limits of logical sensibilities, where no image registers. He says more than he talks. Nodding toward the aspen grove, he whispers that he is afraid that, like the wolf, the wisdom of belonging will disappear. His dancing eyes penetrate me as he tells me that I must keep the wisdom alive and pass it on to those who wish to share it. He invites me to look beyond where I can see. He sees the wolf with the eye of his awareness, utterly simple and direct.

I feel the wolf, but I don't see her. She waits, one look beyond my view, standing silently just inside the edge of the aspen grove, where the white radiance of the moonlight blends with the velvet black of the forest and makes a zone of almost ephemeral silver-blue where shadow and substance appear and vanish.

She gazes from among the trees—solid, erect, and purposeful. Her silver-gray body flits among the metallic blue-black of the trees like a ghost. Her oversized paws move over the earth with the quietness of feathery snowflakes. And then she is gone.

Grandfather sees differently; he belongs. He is as much a part of the Northern Rockies as the wolf and the winter snows. His is a different order of relationship in which earth, wolf, weather, and self are of one root. I've learned not to strain my eyes to see what Grandfather sees. I've been told about wolves being "two looks away.": the first being eyesight, the second being insight. Grandfather whispers," First you learn to see the tree in front of you, then the rock behind the tree, then the wolf behind the rock, behind the tree, then the spirit of the wolf, behind the wolf, behind the rock and behind the tree." I'm still learning to see the tree in front of me.

"Grandfather, tell me about your wolf."

Grandfather sits and begins to sing an ancient melody, telling of a time when life was woven together by grandfathers and grandmothers. There is something inherently sacred in the sound. His words wisp by me like aspen leaves carried on an autumn breeze—not meant to be caught and held but allowed to finish their natural journey to the earth.

"When I was a young man my father and his father took me to a sacred place in these mountains. I sat alone, silently with my grandfather's wolf robe. During the night a wolf came to me and said, "I am chief of the mountains and I respect you; therefore I am going to give you something that will preserve you and your path and take care of you in times of danger. You have a road within, called the wolf road. If you keep your spirit on that path, you will, at the end of your days, merge with the wolf trail in the sky." Then she left, softly loping away, disappearing into the night. When the sun rose, I looked at the ground near my feet and lying in front of me was a gift.

After Grandfather came to get me we sat quietly with my father. Grandfather prepared his pipe. We smoked. I told them of my experience. Grandfather listened, nodded his head and looked far off. Then he said, "She gave her gift to you to be passed on so that the wolf-nature will not disappear."

Grandfather returns to the present and rises effortlessly, his sinewy body still lithe and strong. He touches my shoulder in benediction and looks directly and ceremoniously into my eyes. With his eagle feather fan he tidies my mind and sweeps my soul. He walks away softly, each step a prayer, into the nearby aspen grove. He concentrates his mind and his spirit on the earth, a landscape he cherishes. We are together and yet he is alone, beyond my reach. The stars dance and grow from pinpoints to blurs as sleep softly settles upon me.

Awakened by an untroubled touch and the faraway warmth of the morning sun, I am aware of an immense stillness and an absence. Grandfather is gone. How and where I don't know. I walk among the aspens and find a necklace. I, in turn, am left with the gift of wolf nature to pass on to those who follow me. What is this wolf nature Grandfather received? He never said. It is not accessible through words. I was allowed to live for a time in the midst of a secret. Now in its afterglow I become conscious of the presence of a mystery, satisfied to be a part of it. I may not be able to touch Grandfather but he is still touching me. Like the wolf, snow, and mountains Grandfather belonged. He knew that he lived with a bounty not of his own making. His impeccable regard radiated from him, so that it was impossible to say where he ends and nature begins. Through this rootedness in place he asserted his connections backward and forward in time. His lessons were both hallowed and haunted.

## Peace

Discipline: No revenge.

*There are no contests in the Art of Peace.*
—Morihei Ueshiba

*"Until he extends the circle of his compassion to all living things, man will not himself find peace."*
—Frederick Franck

*"the greatest prayer of man does not ask for victory but for peace*
—Erik Axel Karlfeldt

*"When the power of love overcomes the love of power, the world will know peace."*
—Jimi Hendrix

I recall in high school getting algebra and geometry tests back with points subtracted from my score with underlined directions in red that said: SHOW STEPS! This, of course, was directed at those of us who only memorized answers and had no idea how we got them. The right answer alone wasn't enough. I had to show the steps in the geometric and algebraic proofs to get credit.

Adults have the same problem with peace that I had with algebra and geometry. We know that peace is the right answer. But we've only memorized this; we don't know the steps to get there.

$$War, Conflict, Contest + ????? = Peace$$
—Algebra of War & Peace

We've always assumed that the correct solution to the equation was simply to add more war. If not war we substitute other types of contests, like politics. In his speech to the 27th Soviet Communist Party Conference in 1986, Gorbachev applied this principle to the nuclear arms race saying that, "the task of insuring security is more and more taking the form of a political task and can be resolved only by political means...." But the social contract in politics is hardly a solid foundation for a lasting peace. As Carl von Clausewitz famously put it, "War is the continuation of politik by other means."

It has not yet occurred to us that such an equation is not one for peace but for continual war. Such an algebra of war ended in suicide on July 23, 1943 for Adam Czerniakow the president of the Jewish Council in Warsaw. The previous day he was confronted by SS Major Hofle, SS Untersturmfuhre Brandt and Oberscharfuhrer Mende and given an order to sign the documents ordering the "resettlement" of "the unproductive element" of the Warsaw ghetto population.

"And the man behind the desk [Adam Czerniakow] a mathematician by training and inclination, performed some calculations and postulated some equations: (1) Jews under German rule do not equal life, (2) Germans as rulers do not equal the fundamental ideals and principles of contemporary Christian civilization, (3) the present development equals a death sentence for the ghetto. And then, like a good mathematician, after he considered each of these equations, he arrived at the conclusion that x could never equal y, where x stood for the bankruptcy of his belief that the vessel could be steered into port and y represented Adam Czerniakow, alive and holding office as president of the Jewish Council. It was then he reached for the cyanide."

Just like me in my math class world leaders try to get away with merely knowing the right answer. But it isn't enough. As Adam Czerniakow knew our equations don't add up. Peace is not merely a recess from war.

I am reminded of a story told by Orlinska in an airline magazine of a young journalist who met an elderly Jew at the Western wall in Jerusalem. The old man had lived in Jerusalem since he was born and would go to the Wall and pray three times a day for peace between Israel and Palestine. One day the journalist asked him what it felt like praying so consistently for so long. The old Jew thought for a moment and answered, "'I feel like talking to a wall." Talking about peace to warring human beings remains just that—talking to a wall.

When I was a child I often went outdoors to play war with my friends. We never played peace. It never occurred to us to play peace. Playing war was easy, we all knew what to do. Society provided the toys and the role models for us to play war. But there were no peace movies on Saturday afternoon, no peace toys to buy. Adults did not provide any models of peace with which we could play.

Instead we provide the guns for children to learn early about our wars of peace. For example, Burnett reports, "The ubiquitous Kalasnikov is so light and simple that it is a perfect child's toy." Children learn to pull triggers with the indifference to consequence that we used to exhibit in my backyard playing war. But in my neighborhood, we all got up to hurry home for dinner after our wars.

Not knowing what else to do humans have assumed, however dubiously, that the weapons delivery system used to wage war can also be used to create peace. The fact that it hasn't worked has not deterred us from reusing it. We have also tried words in the form of treaties, charters, models, and laws. Still no peace. Why are such normative measures inadequate? Why do we continue to get it wrong? Even these attempts are part of the ethical codes and behavioral patterns entrenched in the structural violence that created the problem in the first place. In such a survival based system peace is merely a fortunate, though random, event.

Peace is not merely an absence of war. We are good at making war, but we only talk peace. We say that we must *make* peace. The reality is that we don't know how to make peace a verb. It is a central thesis of Playing For Real that our contest system of self-defense is life defeating. Survival is a cynical calculus for disposable people. We need a new delivery system for peace, a delivery system that is outside of our fear based social and cultural structures. A delivery system is defined as a means or procedure for providing a product or service to the public as in a health care delivery system. The respiratory system is an example of a delivery system that supplies oxygen to the blood to deliver to the rest of the body. Each new medical discovery necessitates an effective delivery system. There have been, for example, a number of vaccine delivery systems, including needles, oral, and the patch. As absurd as it seems I am proposing children as that delivery system and their original play as the change agent.

We must approach peace with the same energy that my friends and I played war. Eleanor Roosevelt echoed this idea, "It isn't enough to talk about peace. One must believe in it. And it isn't enough to believe in it. One must work at it." I would add that we must play at it. Then peace will be more than an idea, more than a theory; it will be a "hands on" process. The peaceful truth of original play is transmitted by touch, laughter, tears, dirt, and grass stains; anything less is hearsay. We will have to get down and dirty; we must go out and play with the world just as it is with all of its disorder, aggression, and revenge. Then peace's lessons will seep into you like the scent of warm dark earth steaming after a summer rain.

> *And the peace of God passeth all understanding.*
> —Phillipians 4:7

This book proposes a new choice, a new narrative, and a new conception and way of being in the world, one that reunites us with our original sense of belonging to all life. According to the *Oxford Dictionary of English Etymology* the original Arabic root aljebr means to reunite broken parts. Hazelton expresses something similar in the Kabbalistic ideal of tikkun olam, "repairing the world." There could not be a more accurate description for the purpose of original play. In this re-framing of life we have a new equation.

Peace is a different algebra that heals all of our broken parts. If we re-examine the equation we have the following:

$$Let\ C^n = Contests\ of\ any\ kind\ or\ number$$
$$Let\ U = Unknown$$
$$Let\ P = Peace$$
$$C^n + U = P$$

—The Algebra of Peace

In this equation we know that the contests with which we live vary to the "nth" degree and we know the outcome we desire is peace. What we don't know is the U or the unknown something that transforms our contests into peace. Now suppose we know the U. And suppose that it is a K or constant, such that no matter what the contest or conflict by adding this K or constant the result is peace. (This is truly revolutionary because we have assumed that war is the human constant.) The new equation looks like this:

$$C^n + K = P$$

—The Algebra of Peace

So what is this K or constant that we can add to our conflicts to achieve peace? This sounds too good to be true. Is it in the realm of myth like the philosopher's stone or the fountain of youth? Is it some sort of a mysterious black box or alchemist's quintessence? No, it is something both more real, practical, and surprising. I'm suggesting that K is child's play. So, we can rewrite the equation as:

Let K= (ChOP), where Ch=children, OP =original play.
Then:

$$C^n + [(ChOP) = P$$

—The Algebra of Peace

It is not enough to collect things and take them apart with our reasoning. In so doing we remain remote. Only in the joining do we discover our indispensable humanity. As a living practice original play reunites humanity's broken parts. In so doing we take peace into our own hands.

A number of years ago I received the following note from an Hispanic teenager in an East Los Angeles school. Jose wrote it to me after our first play session.

"To: Fred (the wrestler)

From: Jose

The next time you come ask for Jose. So I can wrestle you one on one. Just don't hurt me. Let me hurt you. Just playing. Be careful with the bears and wolves."

Jose was the smallest of a group of eight teenagers in an East Los Angeles middle school. These boys went to school but didn't go to class. Instead they hung out in their counselor's office almost every day. One day in June the counselor called me and asked if I'd come and play with them. I went for three hours every Friday for ten weeks.

On my first visit I walked into the counselor's office where the eight boys were hanging out. I put some photos of me playing with wolves on the floor and sat down. The boys leaned forward to look at the photos. One of them said, "That's you playing with the dogs."

I replied, "Those are wolves."

They looked closer, "No, wolves eat you."

"No, those are wolves.

Like a fisherman I had put out the bait. Now I must wait for a nibble.

"How do you do that?" There it is. I've hooked them.

"Come I'll show you."

I led them out to patch of grass behind the counselor's office. As they stood around I got down on my hands and knees and crawled among them, pushing against their legs. They laughed and pushed against me. It didn't take long before one of the boys jumped on me. It was Jose. Before long the other boys joined in.

Early the next week Jose's counselor called me to read the above note. She also shared that she called Jose because he had stopped coming to her office. Afraid that he was back on the streets, she asked him where he was. He replied, "In class." Stunned she asked, "What are you doing there?" He said, "After listening to Fred talk about the wolves and playing with him I realized that I didn't need to get into a contest with my teachers." Jose took responsibility for his actions. Something he had not done before. He no longer blamed his teachers. He stayed in class.

In one of our later play sessions Jose stopped me and asked, "why are we doing this? Do you want me to get out of the gang. Do you want me to put my gun down."

"No. "

"Do you understand that everyone on my block is in the gang?" he asked.

I responded, "We're playing to make you safer on the street."

"How's that?" He was obviously confused.

"When you walk down your street and feel unsafe what do you do?"

He reached behind his back and imitated pulling the gun he kept in his waistband. " I pull it."

"And then?"

"I shoot."

" At who?"

"Doesn't matter."

"If you shoot a child or a mother, it's OK?"

He shrugs his shoulders.

"Look. This is why we're playing. I stood up and centered myself. "Did you see it? When you walk down the street and feel unsafe you will move to your center rather than reach for your gun."

"OK, I get it. Let's play."

At our ninth session Jose arrived very happy. He said, "I did it. I did it."

"What?"

"I put it down."

Jose had put his gun down, not because I told him to. Which I never did. But because he felt that safety was a matter of heart not guns. I can't imagine the courage required to do what Jose did. He still lived in the same neighborhood with the same unpredictably predictable violence. Jose also let go of the ego inflation that accompanies a gun. This feeling is described by Masood Azhar, a Pakistani jihadist, when picking up a Kalishnikov assault rifle. "I felt the weapon in my hands .... It was cocked and the bullet was in the chamber. a feeling of ecstasy descended upon me. My joy knew no bounds as I held the loaded gun in my hands.'"

On the tenth week I came into the counselor's office and she was crying. Jose wasn't at school. She told me that in the previous week Jose's mother remarried and her new husband gave her a choice—husband or Jose. She choose husband. This meant that Jose had to go to foster care. At that time in California because I was part of Jose's life before foster care I could not be part of his life in his new foster care home. We couldn't have any contact with each other.

The same was true for his counselor. She didn't know where he was now going to school. She asked, "Why do you do this? You know what the system does to these kids." I replied, "I know. But now Jose knows where real power comes from, his heart and not his gun. I can't change Joses's world but I can give him the experience of choices that he didn't know he had." Original play gave Jose access to a source of strength that no one can take away. I believe this is the kind of choice that Auschwitz survivor, Eva Mozes Kor describes in her book, *Surviving the Angel of Death*. In her case she choose to forgive and in doing so a burden of pain she had carried for fifty years was lifted from her shoulders and she discovered a feeling of power, "that no one could take away."

More recently, I was allowed to play in Pollsmoor, a South African prison. On our first visit Linda and I walked out into the quad with a guard. There were perhaps one hundred young men there. Some were bouncing an old basketball. Most were in small groups talking or jostling each other. When a white woman and a white man walked out into the quad area all attention was riveted on us. The guard spoke in Afrikans and most of them stopped what they were doing and gathered around us. It was unmistakable in their eyes, we were being sized up, appraised by some set of visible and invisible standards. In some manner that I couldn't tell ten young men chose or were chosen to come with us. After an hour another group of ten were chosen. Linda and I spent three hours with thirty young men between the ages of sixteen and twenty-one. On the first day two guards were with us the entire time. The warden came by to watch too.

Ten young men followed us out to a dirt area between the building and the barbed wire. On our way out one of the prisoners walking next to me asked, "What are we going to do?"

"Play, I responded."

"Where's the ball?," he asked.

"No ball," I replied.

He looked confused. I jostled him on the arm and said, "You'll see."

When we got to the small patch of grass and dirt between the prison wall and the fence I motioned for everyone to sit in a circle. Speaking in Afrikans, Linda briefly introduced us. I then went to the center of the group and motioned for them one by one to come out and play with me. They didn't hesitate to play. I began playing with one prisoner at a time, then two at a time. Finally, five young men played with me at once. Our play was very active and rambunctious but never aggressive. At one point, the smallest young man was hit accidentally in the groin. He was in obvious pain and went to the edge of the mat and sat with Linda who hugged him. None of the young men made fun of him nor did he blame anyone. After some rest he rejoined the play.

I wonder if it possible to understand the importance of such a seemingly small, though painful, incident. In such an extreme contest environment as a prison, everything has meaning in terms of win and lose, dominance and submission, attack and revenge. Here was a spontaneous event in which all of these could have emerged. Yet none did.

The young man achieved what Laurens van der Post has called "the only triumph worth achieving in life: that of not being soured by his suffering or even tempted to the ultimate surrender of dignity of spirit into sullen desire for revenge." The conditions that normally set them apart and at each other's throats were erased in our play which transcended and rendered irrelevant their powerful array of prison allegiances.

As we walked back inside the walls of the prison we held hands or hugged and jostled each other joyfully. For a time, we prevented misunderstanding, hatred, and revenge from spreading further on that day. As is the way of great things this was a very small event in the scheme of life. For a moment in the world, the archaic cycle of hurt—hurt avenged and vengeance revenged was cut. A moment existed among all of us which transcends lesser moments wherein all earthly conflicts are resolved and unimportant. We experienced peace not as passive acceptance but rather as a fierce strength of character. That is a gift not granted to all people.

Such peace is not limited to human beings. Two rhinos gave me a realization of the deeper meaning of peace. On a safari in South Africa our party of five tourists and two guides found two rhinos resting under a tree. We went down into a ravine. The guides described how we would proceed so as not to disturb the resting rhinos. The guides told us that they were going up onto the flat and would separate. On their signal we would come up two at a time to view the resting rhinos with one guide then move to the other guide. I was the last of the five tourists to go up out of the ravine. As the guide and I watched the rhinos we heard what sounded like thunder. The sky was bright blue with no clouds. The guide spun around and tapped my leg. I assumed it meant to follow him. Two rhinos were charging from behind us. We ran and stood in front of the others. As the rhinos got closer, I heard the metallic click as the guide chambered a shell in his rifle. But he kept the rifle pointed at the ground. He later told me that he didn't have a kill shot, and even if he did he could not stop them. As the rhinos closed on us I stood in the stance I use when I play. I was still, my head slightly cocked to one side and my arms at my sides in slight curves with my hands open. As I did this the rhinos skidded to a stop a short distance in front of us. The two rhinos stood still facing us. Their gray armored sides billowed in and out with their explosive breaths. In this hot, dusty veld I felt the meaning of peace. I knew no harm could come to any of us, rhinos or humans. We stood facing each other from about five yards away. Suddenly they turned and trotted away into the bush.

How am I to describe what happened? I thought I understood the meaning of peace. With the rhinos what had been an abstract idea became an intense feeling.

A number of months later I was in the bed and breakfast where we conducted cancer retreats and saw a statue in the corner of the living room. I had seen this statue countless times in my life but I had not given it a second look. Now, something made me stop. At first, I couldn't figure out what caused me to stop. Then it finally dawned on me. The woman in the statue was standing in the pose that I used with the charging rhinos. She held her arms out in slightly curved arcs. Her head was slightly tilted. It is, of course, a statue of Mary. I sat down and gazed at the statute as if I were seeing it for the first time. Which in a way I was. I smiled as I realized the importance of Mary and her stance of peace. Mary reminds me that to play is to feel intimately, particularly, fiercely,and reverently. Whenever one treats living organisms as holy they must necessarily behave as such. When life's categories are dissolved the particular is illuminated; the particular when fully known becomes the universal.

That peace is somehow a product of war is an illusion of the most dangerous kind. There is no discernible meaning and no overall and honorable value that can compensate us for the meaninglessness of our groping towards some concept of peace from the viewpoint of war.

As Laurens van der Post puts it, "The human heart, as history proves, I believe, can endure anything except a state of meaninglessness."

When the Nobel committee sits down to award the Nobel Peace Prize and decides to give it to humanity, then that will be a sign that we will be on the right path.

# Grace

## Discipline: Touch the face of God in all life.

*"The You encounters me by grace—it cannot be found by seeking.'*
—Martin Buber

*"These touches of grace where reality opens up and we know
that we are one with reality, no longer estranged,
but belonging, at home."*
—Frederick Franck

*In our human foolishness and short-sightedness we imagine divine
grace to be finite.... But the moment comes when our eyes are
opened and we see and realize that grace is infinite.*
—Isak Dinesen

But for the grace of God, there go I. I recall my parents saying this when we would encounter someone who had an unfortunate accident. But suppose I change the phrase slightly to say: By the grace of God, there go I. Substituting "by" for "but for" changes everything. Instead of the grace of God being some sort of lucky charm that separates me from an unfortunate other, now it is a recognition of our belongingness. I am outsourced by God. This sense of belonging is a debt of honor, a promise I owe to life for being given the gift of life. Original play is life's way of helping me to remember the grace within which I was born and thereby repay my debt to Creation. In my play I must, as Don Quixote in Man of La Mancha said on his deathbed, "Add a measure of grace to the world."

While it can be experienced grace is difficult to define. *Grace* may be felt in the jaws of a lion or in soft touch of a butterfly, or the giggle of a child or the sudden, thunderous charge of a rhino. Saint Thomas in *Summa Theologica* tells us that the reason for such grace is because the divine goodness "could not be adequately represented by one creature alone, he produced many and diverse creatures, that what was wanting to one in the representation of the divine goodness might be supplied by another. For goodness which in God is simple and uniform, in creatures is manifold and divided; and hence the whole universe together participates

241

in the divine goodness more perfectly, and represents it better than any single creature whatever." What an exciting world of playmates Saint Thomas describes.

The ordinary stuff of life is precisely the stuff of the sacred. Robert Johnson explains that, East Indian Yoga "teaches that 90 percent of the work toward enlightenment is spent preparing your body and mind to withstand an encounter with God." It is like when you are sitting inside and the sun comes through the window and without thinking you lift your face up like a flower toward the sun's warmth.

Life asks nothing more than I play with the very nature of existence. Original play is supremely personal and is simultaneously universal, elemental, real, and sacred. What I cannot do by my own power grace always does with me; but the little things which I can do, Grace leaves for me out of courtesy, so that I can have the joy of cooperating. I, however, miss the point and the play if I strive to be graceful.

With grace one does not see or experience any specific thing differently; rather one sees and experiences everything differently. My play with cancer patients, children, whales, and butterflies is always play with God. By endowing every act with immense significance original play is the realization of the preciousness of all life in a single meeting. To realize grace is to realize the infinite in the finite, and the giver in the gifts.

It has been said repeatedly that humans can never, try as they will, get around to the front of the universe. We are destined to see only its far side, to realize nature only in retreat. Yet, animals and children invite me to come around to life's front door. They share with me a direct and unequivocal experience expressed in Japanese as *kokoro no kamae* or posture of the heart. The result is an opening of unconditional kindness in which the ephemeral coalesces in a tangible moment of grace—the realm of life in which we feel the contagion of authenticity deep within the heart of life. Selves, like embers in a fire, are consumed in such moments. These encounters penetrate to that place where the boundaries of self and other are effaced and heaven and earth have not yet divided.

Many years ago a wolf named Sybil gave me one such gift. She often walked up to me when I was sitting on a tree stump and put her head in my lap. If I stood up she put her paws on my arm that I held out in front of me in an horizontal arc. In this position we would jostle each other's head. At one point she moved over slightly; as I turned my head to look at her, she disappeared. And I disappeared. Everything disappeared. There was no inside, no outside. For a heartbeat, a moment, an hour, a lifetime all I saw was golden light. Then just as abruptly Sybil and I reappeared. I sat down and held her for a few minutes and she walked away. As I left Wolf Haven that day I cried. What happened? Was this the experience of insight when sanity becomes sanctity? Is this the pure intuitive awareness about which Christ seems to speak in the Gospel of St. Thomas: "You cannot take hold of it, yet you cannot lose it." I wanted to know if Sybil experienced what I experienced and felt what I felt. I said to myself, if Sybil was human I would call her or write a letter to ask her. I smiled to myself realizing that Sybil already knew. I was the one who was unsure.

When the universe swings in some fantastic fashion around to present me its face the visage whether wolf or human is the face of one family of life. When life faces life and the compelling torque of meaning is compressed into each moment it's not that I know more, but feel more deeply. The questions vanish, yet I can't point to answers. I can't say what happened with Sybil. But for a moment my soul breaks open, like a shaft of bright sunlight searing through expansive gray clouds leaving bright the ground around, providing a glimpse of life's possibility.

Original play is the immense encoded memory of all the life that has ever been to help the life that is, who, can, in turn, pass it on to all the life that will be. Original play is not a skill to memorize but one that is acquired slowly by the body, mind, and heart. Anything less, however, smooth, is merely a form of posturing. The Buddhist monk, Ittokusai in his kendo instructions speaks of something higher than correct technique. He writes, for example, "that when mind and vital energy are united in emptiness, right action takes place of itself, independently. 'It is,' he says, 'as if a god acted through YOU." Some might say that he's a Buddhist, he's not supposed to believe in God. But "he uses such words because that is what it feels like." In this abandonment of self reality is transfigured and we are transformed, made capable of vision beyond our ken and action beyond our strength.

"Would you show me some ways I can still play with my son? He is fifteen. We used to play together. But now I do not have the energy to play the way we used to. Is there something we can do in a chair or on a bed?" These questions were asked by Mary, a young mother with cancer. She attended a retreat in which play was one part of a holistic approach to life with cancer that involved diet, traditional, and alternative medicine, art, massage, and discussion. She asked me these questions during our one hour play session. I suggested a few ways that she and her son could share the benefits of original play without tiring her. When I finished, I stopped and smiled. She looked at me and asked, "What is it?"

"I have an idea," I replied. "I'm going to suggest something else for you and your son to do." I'll demonstrate it and you can decide if it will be too much for you."

"Let's see it."

"I'm going to take the part of your son. He sits on the floor like this." I sat in the position used to teach beginning aikido students how to initiate a stationary back roll. Then I rolled backwards to show her what her son would do.

"Now you sit in his lap. He holds you snugly and rolls backward and back up to his starting position.

"Can we do it?"

"OK."

I sat on the floor. Mary sat in my lap. We arranged the cord to her oxygen tank so it would not fall out or get tangled. Then I hugged her snugly and asked her to count to three and say go.

"One, two three, go!" she exclaimed.

We rolled backwards and returned to our sitting position. She giggled like a young girl.

"More. More!" she exclaimed.

We did the back roll three more times. Each time she said go and giggled out loud. Then we stopped to rest and I held her. For a few moments we giggled together.

Later that day she became increasingly ill and it was necessary for her to go home to be with her family. When she went to the car I went out to say good-bye. We hugged, and looked at each other through the tears in our eyes. I knew then that our back rolls were not done for Mary and her son. They were done for the two of us. Mary showed me that grace is the divine influence upon one heart and its reflection in the heart of another.

This is not a vague, abstract attitude toward humanity in general, but a single meeting in which the miracle we call life is shared. Some words from Rabi'a al-Adawiyya, an eighth century Islamic saint, expresses my feelings as I watched Mary, her husband and son drive away:

*How can you describe the true form of Something*
*In whose presence you are blotted out?*
*And in whose being you still exist?*

How can I prepare to play with a lion? I don't. I wondered about such things as I drove toward Tigertown, a reserve for big cats in Nevada's high desert. It was a clear late December morning, and the sun was quickly melting the brittle cold of the previous night. I have long ago discovered that my mind in its search for meaning comes dishearteningly fast to its frontier of understanding and promptly turns to my heart to carry me beyond my last "why."

I was excited by my invitation to visit Tigertown. I hadn't yet played with mountain lion, lynx, lion, or tiger. Each new playmate brought me closer to an understanding of play as a universal pattern of belonging and love. Over the years my body and spirit have been molded by them, putting something of the nature of each animal in my body and character.

John and Barbara, the owners of Tigertown, had heard about the man who plays with animals from a mutual friend. They wanted to meet and introduce me to their cats. At first glance, Tigertown didn't look any different from the other homes in this high desert community. Each was a ranch style or mobile home, surrounded by open space, with outbuildings, and a horse corral in the back.

Only on getting out of the car did I notice that the fences here were higher and the outbuildings smaller. Walking up to the door, I passed a mountain lion resting in an enclosure next to the walk. Barbara and John welcomed me warmly and we sat down at the kitchen table to talk. It wasn't hard to notice that their furnishings were sparse. They told me that because of the cats they keep the furniture to a minimum.

I noticed a shy cat eying me from around the corner in the living room. Another larger cat was walking around the kitchen table. She jumped onto the table, walked toward me, and touched her forehead to mine. "Peggy Sue is checking you out," Barbara warned with a big grin. She is a Siberian lynx.

After tea, John showed me around their reserve. He released the cougar, who walked around our legs like a giant house cat. John introduced me to the Siberian and Bengal tigers and the two Barbary lions. Except for the lioness these cats were eager and friendly, coming up for touch through the fences of their enclosures. Only the lioness stayed back, lying on the ground intently gazing at me with an expression in her archaic, gold eyes that caught my attention. It was hard to turn away from her. I felt that I had to turn away from her fierceness and simultaneously invited by the depth of her intimacy. I sensed that she had anticipated me, foreseen my coming and my purpose, but greeted me now on her terms, not mine.

John, Barbara and I were unsure about how my interactions with the bigger cats should proceed so we decided that they would sleep on it and tell me in the morning. I was fine with leaving it to them. I returned to my hotel for the evening. Of all the cats I met during the day it was Nala, the lioness, who both captivated and frightened me. It was as if I knew already who would be chosen.

I was right. When I arrived the next morning John and Barbara suggested that I go in with Nala, the Barbary lioness. I agreed. I wanted to get film of my interaction so I began to set up a camera pointing in the direction of where I imagined we would be. My attention was on the camera and I didn't see Nala lunge at the fence knocking both me and my tripod backwards. She calmly walked away. At the time I didn't know whether she was responding to the camera or my lack of awareness. Her message was clear, however. "Fred, pay attention. No Camera. Be here."

First, John and I entered the small safety enclosure and sensed how everything felt. It was quiet and calm. Nala was resting on the ground to the right, perhaps twenty feet away. I entered the large enclosure alone. John went back outside and watched with Barbara. I walked in and quickly knelt down in the khaki-colored dirt about 20 feet away from Nala. She did not move but was watching me intently with eyes that shone like brass, her tawny coat gleaming in the early afternoon sun.

As soon as I was kneeling on the ground, Nala gathered herself and stood, then trotted unhurriedly toward me. She quickly and silently closed the distance between us. Suddenly I lost sight of her. I was to find out later from John that the reason I didn't see her was that when she got to within six feet of me she leaped in the air. The next instant she was on top of me. She had pounced on my back and enveloped me with her body. I was surrounded, swaddled by lioness. The speed with which this happened was bewildering. She landed on me as gently as settling dew.

Her front legs completely encircled me, gathering me firmly against her. I could feel her body not as weight but as presence. I recall my fingers feeling the softness of the fur and the roughness of the pads on her large left paw that was a few inches from my face. I was amazed that not only were her claws retracted but that there was no tension in her paw as I played with it. I recall having heard in South Africa that the more powerful the animal, like the lion, the more gentle and tender were its natural ways.

At the same time she landed on me she grasped my head firmly in her jaws. She caught me from behind so only my face was visible. She smelled dusty and pungent. Except for my eyes I couldn't move my head. Even my thoughts seemed caught in her teeth. All around me, the stillness intensified and in the acute sensitivity with which confrontation with death equips one, it sounded loud. A thought pierced through me like an arrow: *pay attention Fred, this is the razor edge of life and death.* In contrast to her firm, gentle hold of my head her teeth plunged deeply into my mind. For a month afterwards the feeling obstinately persisted of those four yellow-white canine teeth holding so firmly and precisely at the right base of my skull, behind and below my left ear, on my forehead above my right eye, and in my left temple.

Nala's presence filled me; not missing a single nook or cranny— every brain cell, every muscle invaded. I experienced, in being engulfed by her, simultaneously a quickening with the decisiveness of a lightning strike, the snugness of a tree bud, and the gentleness of a breath of spring breeze on my cheek. She held me like some oversized, misplaced cub. I sat still; so still that I ceased to discern where I ended and Nala began.

After a few moments John pulled the trigger on a fire extinguisher and walked into the small enclosure that led into the large fenced area. The hissing sound caused Nala to release me and jump off. We stood in silence next to each other for a moment. We walked to the gate. She lay next to the fence and licked my hand before I left.

When I went back to my hotel that night I had much to think about. First, when I replayed my encounter with Nala I realized that I had not felt her land my back. She weighs hundreds of pounds. How did she pounce on me without my feeling her weight? How did she grasp my head in her teeth without leaving a mark?

Then I recalled some thoughts I had had on the drive from southern California to Nevada. Following a recent divorce I was thinking to myself that I needed a hug. Of course, I imagined it would be from a woman. But I couldn't imagine who this would be. Now as I recalled my thoughts I smiled and remembered the saying "be careful what you wish for." I had received my hug from a female. I had assumed it would be from a human, not a lioness. It was a hug like none other.

I realized that Nala gave me a lesson in touch and ferocity. Her touch was adjusted to meet my ability to receive it. Fierceness was a presence that she communicated with her gentle touch. Nala was fierce and gentle at the same time. She taught me that with a fierce, clear heart I can have a gentle hand. When we had finished our play I said to myself, "I want her skill. I want to be as good with touch as Nala."

Nala entered my core. She had as Ace Atkinson, my aikido sensei, said "taken me to the heart of the universe." She struck with such fierceness and gentleness that I was for a time suspended on a razor's edge between life and death—a world of infinite and terrible beauty. Here lion and I were in the pattern of creation which has at its disposal the greatest energy of transformation and renewal of which life is capable.

It is as if there was in us an ecology of meaning, an environment of soul and spirit, heart and body, as crucial for the lion as for me. There is an ancient monastic concept known as compunction. The word has numerous meanings. At its heart it is being touched by the awareness of my true state with Creation. This touch "pricks" me to feel enthusiasm, that is, to be "en-Goded" or infused with God. This is how Creation comes to feel play and it is how we feel Creation as Saint Catherine of Siena describes it, "life is a miracle of inclusion."

# Part IV:
# The Dream of Childhood

*O man, remember!*
—Upanishads

*Dare to dream.*
—Janusz Korczak

*God waits for man to regain his childhood in wisdom.*
—Rabindranath Tagore

*Tell me what a man dreams and I will tell what he is.*
—Arab proverb

*"The Child so dear to God who, from the beginning, was playing in His sight all days, playing in the world."*
—Thomas Merton

*There can be no keener revelation of a society's soul than the way in which it treats its children.*
—Nelson Mandela

# CHAPTER 8

# A Circle With No Circumference

*"We are cradled close in your hands—*
*and lavishly flung forth."*
—Rainer Maria Rilke

*"Only those who see the invisible can do the impossible."*
—Dr. Bernard Lown

*"O, Please O Please, Come out and play."*
—Hafiz

*Is the universe a friendly place?*
—Albert Einstein
(Here is Mother Teresa's answer:)

*Take Time To play.*
*Take Time To Love and Be Loved.—*
—Sign on wall of Mother Teresa's children's home in Calcutta

The sign in Mother's Teresa's children's home in Calcutta is a Zen-like reply to Einstein's question. Instead of answering the question the sign tells us what to do in order to discover the answer for ourselves.

Asked by the photographer, Philippe Halsman whether he thought there would ever be lasting peace, Einstein replied, "No, as long as there will be man there will be war." Is there an antidote to war's perennial seductiveness? Yes, I add to Einstein's thought, as long as there will be children there will be the possibility of peace. Children are the real resurrection. A child raised to believe in Creation's Dream of *One* will be a profoundly different human being than a youth brought up to fight as if the world must be won. This is a resurrection not only of flesh and blood but of a deeper rebirth that reaches deep into the heart and soul.

If childhood's dream seems like nothing more than a castle in the air, all is not lost. Along with Rumi, Hafiz, Mother Teresa, Pope John XXIII, we each can be irrationally crazy about childhood's dream. How much life is abandoned each time childhood's dream is disregarded? To take a child's hand and join in play is like voyaging to the unknown regions of the human heart, where, like early explorer's maps, firm cartographic boundaries become first dashed lines, then disappear altogether. In the adult world I must be cleared by customs and emigration on the frontier of my native land as I set out for a new world beyond my accustomed borders. But play's journey is different; it is beyond boundaries. Fortunately, childhood's playgrounds are places where visas, passports, and border guards are unknown. The circle without circumference, like childhood's dream, doesn't end; it is renewed with each birth.

Make no mistake to play in a world in which the Duchess' Game is "played" on a vast scale is terribly difficult. The astonishing thing is that no matter how harsh their lives children are capable of living childhood's dream. No matter how nightmarish and distorted it may seem at times childhood's dream remains a taproot whose depth is as indestructible as the heart of the child within whom it is concealed. This is why as Nelson Mandela put it, "In South Africa children should be allowed to play again." Jeremy Hayward expands on this thought, "So we need to help others to play. That could be the best purpose in life—to learn how to feel living space and to play together." The most vulnerable are the most courageous. Original play is to:

*Gamble everything for love.*
*If you're a true human being*
*If not, leave this gathering*
*Half-heartedness doesn't reach into majesty.*
*You set out to find God,*
*But then you keep stopping for long periods*
*at mean-spirited roadhouses.*

—Rumi

We've been half-hearted loiterers at our mean-spirited roadhouses long enough. It's time we expand our moral universe and gamble for love. What we don't realize is that contrary to our fears love is no gamble; it is a sure thing. Original play is a visceral one not merely as an idea, but as a heart and gut feeling in which the energy of *One* replaces the adrenalin of *Won*.

I began life as a child in quest of a man and somewhere along the way I have become a man in search of a child. Years ago children tugged on my pants and seized my imagination. They have led me off the map of my experience encountering a whole new world and exploring a great mystery within my own spirit. I often feel like the 17th century Japanese poet, Matsuo Basho who likened himself to "a travel-worn satchel," a creased leathery bag of bones so thinned by heat, wind and rain that it tumbles along the roads as helplessly as the clouds scud across the sky. Perhaps the most terrifying of the effects of exploring off the map has been my sense of bewilderment at what I had unknowingly lost and my surprise at my puzzling discoveries. Never has it been so important if I am not to fail in the purpose for which my life is created, to continue an ancient quest of seeking to feel my aliveness and in so doing I see the face of God in another being. The goal is not a giant step backward but the regeneration of one's original play, whose playground is everywhere. So here it is the deepest pattern in life, unalterable and irrevocable, this adventure began in childhood, the way of first and last resort, when I am sure of nothing and curious about everything.

The children in this book stand for the childhood that is in all of us, a presence which beckons us to share a reality that has been all but eroded. Loving-kindness is more than a head trip. The thousands of children who have played with me are indeed living proof of the absurd reality that— peace is child's play. Original play is compassion in action. And as Gandhi pointed out,

*If we are to reach real peace in this word and if we are to carry on a war against war, we shall have to begin with children; and if they grow up in their natural innocence, we won't have to struggle; we won't have to pass fruitless, idle resolutions, but we shall go from love to love and peace to peace until at last all the corners of the world are covered with the peace and love for which consciously or unconsciously the whole world is hungering.*

*Children are life.*

—H.H. The Dalai Lama

Childhood is the regenerative power of life. A child is like a cherry tree in Spring: If we are not to miss their fruits we must allow them time to blossom. It is only in the conservation of childhood that human life can be sustained and thrive. With each new birth the Godsend Conspiracy is renewed carrying with it the potential to remake humankind. It's not enough to cherish our children; we must irrationally cherish *all* children. Children are the world's heritage. Childhood is a nonrenewable resource. Childhood is universal and belongs to all the peoples of the world.

The wonderful thing about dreams is that there's always the possibility they can come true. I end the book with hope kindled not by the wishful thinking of childish dreams, nor the melancholy memories of old age in which dreams fuse with reality but by the fierce determination of children who have the courage to live the human dream of peace. Here are statements of some children who confirm this dream. Anna, age 10 writes, "Play is being able to tell the world that you don't like what it is doing to you, and not harming anyone while you do it." Elijah, age 6, asks his teacher, "Can we practice playing? Because if we practice we will get good at it and learn how not to hurt others and how not to get hurt." Hannah age seven tells her mother, "You know mom I'm getting on much better with the boys than I used to. Actually they are my friends now." Her mother asked her what had changed. Hannah replied, "Well, you know, I just listen to my heart now." After a play session with me an eight-year-old boy with autism comments, "I wish I had a normal life. I wish I had a normal life. [Sigh!] This play is my reminder of a normal life."

These children do not write from the perspective of one who dreams about something that might happen. They write from the experience of having lived what they speak about. They have played by heart and in so doing become more real. Childhood's dream does not belong to us but to life itself; no matter how much we may ignore it, it does not abandon us. Children tugged on my pants and spirit years ago as if they instinctively knew that what they would share with me would touch me at a primal level. They were right. Children, with their inherent wisdom and compassion, have given me the courage to live childhood's dream—which makes war obsolete not to me, but in me.

This book began with the absurd idea that *Peace is child's play*. But is it so absurd? Original play is not a condiment added on to sweeten an otherwise bland life. Peace is not an add on, nor is it a recess from the constant stress of conflict. The improbable connection between children and peace is the defining human paradigm. This is a whole new way of relating to reality whose sense of belonging is finite and yet infinite.

Original play is not a vision of paradise, nor an ideal to be sought after; it is instead a *lived* blessing to be accepted as a inherent property of one's life. We can become children's co-conspirators.

It is time to marshal our courage and launch ourselves, like a child on the first day of summer, out into the world as personal emissaries of Creation. The vital importance of original play lies in its ability to revive the behavior needed to feel the inherent sanctity of all life

The issue is not whether nations and peoples are ready, but whether you and I have the wisdom and courage to invest in children as a covenant of faith in the future. I cannot do this for you, only with you, for to do otherwise turns the visceral into the vicarious. Over the past forty years I have encountered thousands of children who were ready to play in the face of their fears. I am asking the same of you, the reader. We each seek the experience of being alive before we die. The difficulty is that for us to find it, we must not be afraid of life. We must not abandon living just to stay alive.

Make no mistake to come out and play with the world requires courage. This is not the courage to face death. The courage to face death is insufficient to bring peace—it never has. The peace of original play requires more. Forbidding as it may seem, we must find the courage to love. When we discover the truth of this we discover not an idea, but we meet God, face-to-face in the proportion that reduces us to our proper scale.

The one thing that attracted me to children is not a educational or social theory, it was not a formula for peace, nor a collectivist panacea for the evils of the world: it was children themselves, the truth that was in them, their simplicity, their direct contact with life, and the fact that they are full of the only force that is capable of replacing fear: they are full of love. In original play's love the divine and human meet as the pattern that connects. This meeting reveals the ultimate meaning and significance of life. This love is original. It is as the Upanishads say "unreachable yet nearer than breath, than heartbeat."

The more I follow the thread of play's meaning, the greater the ethical charge imposed on me. Increasingly, I come to realize that my play in the world is not an escape from the rigors of life but a way of entering into them more lovingly and thereby more effectively. I now have an obligation which I can never disown without serious consequences for not only my consciousness but the welfare of the world. I am part of a conspiracy which is both my soul's deepest longing and a clear bond of infinite sympathy which neither diversity of species nor character nor even sheer being can prevent or erase. For support I am reminded of Dag Hammarskjold's poem in which he instructs his playmate body not to flinch when it comes time for him to do the impossible.

Albert Einstein warned us that, "We shall require a substantially new manner of thinking if mankind is to survive." This book presents such a new manner of thinking. In the end, this is about accepting an invitation to return to the sanctity in which we were born. It is an invitation to love and thereby join the *One* who loved us into being. As Mother Teresa put it, "Holiness is not the luxury of the few. It is everyone's duty: yours and mine."

As always this new meaning has to be lived before it can be known. So here it is, irrevocable and unalterable—Original play is a pact with Creation, a secret sympathy, hidden in the profusion and diversity of life, and so pledged to reproduce its underlying connective pattern, on however small a scale, so that the original design is there for the spirit to discover and follow. This is the meaning of the indestructibility of Creation's gift of Love. Such is the preamble of life, a immutable provision of belonging in which Creation is a play of immense diversity to which you and I and even the immense star spray we call the Milky Way bears witness.

And for all of those who seek to follow in my footsteps—Good Luck! For I don't leave any! Whew! There is nothing and no one to live up to. There is only a passion to explore, to touch the world, and let the world touch you, and an awareness that the masters are alive and well ready to mentor a mind that knows nothing, a body ready to take flight, and a heart whose nature is kindness.

This means that you will have to come out and play as if your life depends upon it.—It does.

## Fred's Contact Page

ofreddybear@aol.com

Originalplay.eu

## USA
2 Colony Ave. Trumbull, CT. 06611 USA

tel. 203 400 1874

## Sweden
DeGeersgatan 10, Stockholm SE115 29 Sweden

## Austria
Kirchenplatz 7, 4483 Hargelsberg, Austria

# Appendix 1

# The CREDO of Original Play

Whereas,
Love is the reason for the creation of the world and me in it; and
original play is Creation's way of allowing me to feel my love's contribution
to the grace of the world; and
I have no option but to choose between living out this enlarged awareness
of life's meaning, or evading it and seeing it and I diminish lethally as a
result.

I hereby vow
to play as if life depends upon it.
My charge is to use up all of the love Creation has invested in me in this
life; and
to play so that I might disappear from myself, so that I am able to love, to
love so much that I no longer realize that I am loving.

Then,
I will be who Creation has willed me to be from all eternity; not myself,
but love.
and grace will be fulfilled in me.

# Appendix 2

*The Metacortex: Playing Myself Into A New Brain.*
*O. Fred Donaldson. Ph.D.*

*There ain't no rules around here!*
*We're trying to accomplish something!*
—Thomas Edison

I am often asked about what happened to the Playmate Project described in *Playing By Heart*. It has gone through several modifications. This is an outline of the newest version and what can be done to create a service, research and training program using original play to eliminate conflict and cultivate kind-fullness. This is a work in progress that focuses on insights and actionable findings from three areas of inquiry: my forty years of play with children and animals, hints from sages and scientists, and recent findings in neuro-science.

The assumption has been that while our brains have evolved from a brain stem to a cortex to a neocortex, we remain largely subject to a reptilian contest brain that is reflexive and unchangeable. Consequently we firmly believe the conflict, aggression, and war are deeply seated, normal, natural, and necessary for human creativity and for life itself to survive. We are blind to the fact that such a contest brain believes that our differences make a difference. This results in our inability to see others as ourselves. Our impaired vision destroys life. I'm suggesting, however, that we have a different as yet unexplored choice. We can not only change our minds about conflict but change our brains and in so doing advance our understanding of what peace means. Peace need not remain a romantic Utopian ideal. Indeed, as children make clear to me, it is part of us. Winning and losing are not our only choices. We can make compassion more than a mission statement. The ability to not only conceive of and perceive the harmony of our universe but to act accordingly is an integral part of who we are.

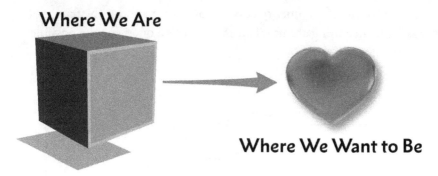

**Where We Are**

**Where We Want to Be**

FEARFUL CONTEST BRAIN — LOVING PLAYFUL BRAIN

We know that we want a loving brain. We don't know how to get from where we are to where we want to be. The question has been how do we get from one kind of brain—a fearful contest brain—to another kind of brain—a loving playful brain?

It is not surprising that a fearful brain has a different neural profile than a loving brain. Suppose, it is not only possible to change our minds about conflict and war, but it is also possible to change our brains? Nature has endowed the human brain with a plasticity that allows it to adapt to the world in which it finds itself. The contest brain is not immutable, neither are the conflicts we create necessary. Original play has the potential to not only change our minds about war but activate our mind's infinite resources for peace. This means that not only can we de-condition the fearful *I-Me-Mine* aspects of the brain we can restructure the brain to be more humane. Original play demonstrates that the world is truly *One*, children are imbued with an inherent kindness code, and the brain can be trained to choose love over fear. I call this brain/mind the metacortex, meaning beyond the cortex. The metacortex is the basis for the emergent seamlessly interconnected whole I call original play. An emergent phenomenon is one whose characteristics and/or behaviors cannot be explained in terms of the sum of its parts.

This is our original graceful mind which is characterized by wonder, awe, and compassion. It is an expression of mutual gratitude in recognizing each other as a face of God. This enthusiasm celebrates our embedded-ness within the whole of reality. This interdependence accounts for the structure, coherence, and intelligibility of the universe. It's all play, and its original. Simply put original play is a relational world of potentials and possibilities. Yes, but is it scientific? I like what Matthieu Ricard said, "A science is exact if it comes to correct conclusions about the nature of things." The nice thing about science is that it is a quest for the possible within the impossible.

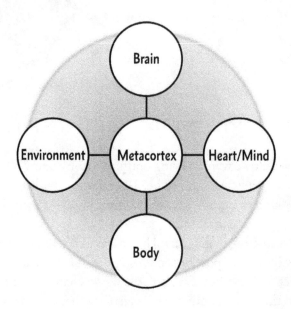

*Original Play's Seamless System*

The essential transformation made by the Metacortex has been stated by Zen master Hakuun Yasutani, "The fundamental delusion of humanity is to suppose that I am here (pointing to himself) and you are out there. The metacortex refers to a mind/brain connection that is neither self centered nor other centered. I'm suggesting a third possibility a gnosis-centered brain in which one brain is paired with another causing an extraordinary external field of connection coinciding with internal patterns of coherence sufficient to produce the state of belonging inherent in original play. This is the state of oneness in original play that was described by five-year-old David, *Fred, play is when we don't know that we are different from each other*. David's insight is not different from what Aryadeva wrote in the Four Hundred Verses,"he who sees the ultimate nature of one thing, sees the nature of all things.'"

## Three Core areas of Experience and Ideas
The idea of a unity that underlies the immense diversity of life on earth

is certainly not new. The ground-breaking approach suggested here brings together for the first time three unique and informative areas of inquiry. By bringing together three approaches to understanding the nature of reality I suggest that we can achieve a more complete picture of human potential. These cores areas are: hints from scientists and sages; play with children and animals; and research in neuro-science. Each of these three areas sets forth a number of principles that when taken together provide the basis for a new brain, what I call the metacortex. I propose a new area of research which can profoundly shift not only how we view children and childhood, play and contest, and war and peace, but serve as a foundation for a choice for humans to thrive not merely survive. At the heart of this synthesis is the idea that original play is an experience of an inherent code of kindness in life. With practice this code of kindness is reflected in a playful brain, increasingly compassionate behavior, and a change of mind. The transformation of our mind/body/brain creates a coherence with our surroundings that not only changes our moment-to moment response to the world, but provides a practical basis for a sustainable peace.

## Metacortex

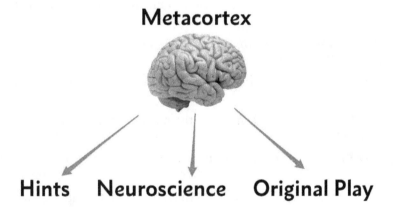

## Hints    Neuroscience    Original Play

## Hints

Looking back now it is possible to see the hints about the nature of the world that have been laid out for us like "breadcrumbs" along a trail by sages and scientists from a wide variety of cultures.

# Children

*I am His messenger sent to tell you the way to Him....*
*If you respect me, and leave me as I am,*
*And do not seek to seize me with a full and selfish possession*
*Then I will bring you joy:*
*For I will remain what I am.*
—Psalm 104, verse 2-4

Jesus thanks God for revealing life's secrets to children: "I bless you Father, Lord of heaven and earth, for hiding these things from the learned and the clever and revealing them to little children."

While sitting under the pippala tree, Siddhartha "was happy to see how unschooled children from the countryside could easily understand his discoveries." He then attained enlightenment.

Meister Eckhart writes that, "If I was alone in the desert and feeling afraid, I would like to have a child with me, for then my fear would disappear and I would be strengthened—so noble, so full of pleasure, and so powerful is life itself."

Nelson Mandela wrote that, "In South Africa, children must be able to play again."

Graca Machel has called children "the nucleus of sustainable human development."

Janusz Korczak wrote that children can indeed be "the salvation of the world."

Psychiatrist Robert Coles declares that children have a lot to teach us.

## Unity

H.H. The Dalai Lama describes a feeling of interdependence, in which he is connected in such a way that his personal boundaries dissolve.

Jung called such a feeling "all-belonging."

Physicist David Bohm agrees saying, "Deep down the consciousness of mankind is one."

Another term for this sense of being consecrated is *ipseity*—our essential way of being beneath the layers of culture, thought and reaction, identity and adaptation. It is the essential self prior to the autobiographical self. This "ipseitious" self is universal.

Ken Wilbur points out that, "The stunning message of the mystics is that in the very core of your being, you are God."

H.H. The Dalai Lama argues that the basic human nature is compassionate, loving kindness and that its importance and effectiveness have now been established from the scientific standpoint.

Noam Chomsky claimed that the human brain is predisposed to recognized and generate language. Similarly the brain may be predisposed to recognize in others, kindness as a code of conduct.

## Principles:

The above statements set forth two fundamental principles that serve as hints about the true nature of life on earth:

1. The world is *One*.
2. Children have something valuable to offer.

## Original Play

*We know truth not only by reason, but also be the heart, and it is from this last that we know first principles.*

—Blaise Pascal

My play with children and animals for the past forty years has provided a wealth of anecdotal data on the emotional and physical principles inherent in original play. The principles listed here are ones that have re-occurred numerous times in different play situations. Some of these experiences are elaborated in *Playing By Heart*, in this book and in my other writings.

In addition these principles have been replicated and described in the writings of others, including Jolanta Graczykowska, Suellen, Inwood, Jan Donaldson, Linda Copley, Katja Gerkensmeyer and Douwe vander Zee, Daniel Caron, Stefan Heitzer, Uwe Reisenauer, and Christoph Blumberg, among others.

Our play has established a number of principles:

1. Original play is a universal, inherent pattern of kindness that can be experienced, shared, and communicated.
2. Original play is an optimal learning model.
3. Original play is inherent, a gift from Creation, not an artifact of culture.
4. Original play provides a choice to safely disengage from the contests of our lives.
5. Love is stronger than fear.
6. The more in touch you are the safer you are.
7. Original play is loving kind-fullness in action.
8. One's safety increases as one's sense of I-Me-Mine is replaced by the experience of belonging.

## Neuroscience

Interest and research in neuroscience has dramatically increased in the past few years revealing a number of findings that are important for original play. Some of these discoveries about the brain/mind follow:

1. Iacobini has called mirror neurons the cells in our brains that make our experience of others deeply meaningful. He contnues, "They show that we are not alone, but are biologically wired and evolutionarily designed to be deeply interconnected with one another."
2. Daniel Goleman says that, " The social brain's wiring connects us all at our common human core."
3. Research has now shown that "the resonance circuits have been shown to not only encode intention, but also to be fundamentally involved in human empathy, and also in emotional resonance, the outcome of attunement of minds" This means that at a neural level our brains can encode not only what we physically see, but the intention that we imagine. Daniel Siegel continues, "In the next now, what happens actually matches what our mirror neuron system anticipated and the coherence between that anticipation and the map of what actually came to be creates a profound state of coherence."
4. Siegel adds that, "This is a re-creation because children early on have this receptivity, this playfullness of being."
5. Original play is a coherent state in which our fight or flight

mechanism of the sympathetic nervous system is reduced while simultaneously promoting the healthier, growth potential of the parasympathetic nervous system.

6. H.H. the Dalai Lama points out that "the brain cannot develop properly and people cannot be healthy in the absence of human affection."

7. Newberg and Waldman point out that words such as anger, fear, and punish are neurogically unpleasant, activating the amygdala. While words like love trust, and compassion activate the striatum and other parts of the brain.

8. When there is no self-defense there is no sense of "I" at all. Such a brain becomes as Dr. James Austin points out, "a resource which could serve as the basis both for our long range biological survival and for our cultural advancement."

9. David Bohm writes, "If somebody is perceived as an enemy, matter is organized differently than if he is perceived as a friend."

10. Bruce Lipton says, "The simple truth is when you're frightened you're dumber." In fact, a sustained self-defense response inhibits the creation of life-sustaining energy.

11. Lipton describes the brain functioning as a light switch—off and on, fear and love. Newberg & Waldman say the same thing in different words: "Love goes up, and fear goes down. Anger goes up and compassion goes down."

## Principles:

1. An individual can change their mind and in so doing choose to activate one brain state or another.

2. Synapses that are used become part of enduring circuits that underlie thinking, feeling, responding and behaving.

3. When the prefrontal cortex sends inhibitory signals to the amygdala, bounce-back time decreases.

4. Mental force or energy acts on the brain by amplifying newly emergent brain circuits responsible for healthy behavior.

5. Conscious cerebral activity blocks volitional activity so no motor action occurs. In this case the possibility of an alternative action is not theoretical. The essence of directed mental force (quality of attention) is to stop the fear reflex from acting, then the wisdom of the prefrontal cortex can be actively engaged.

6. The choice or quality of attention and awareness of the mind acts as a gatekeeper knowing which thoughts to block and which to activate.
7. The prefrontal cortex is central to making choice.
8. Mental activity can clearly and systematically alter brain function; willful effort generates a physical force that has the power to change how the brain works and even it's physical structure.
9. The attentional state of the brain produces physical change in the structure and future functioning of the brain.
10. The brain is wired by experience. Changes in how a person interacts with their environment result in changes in connectivity and vice versa.

***So, from these three sources, hints, play and neuroscience, what can we use as a basis for further exploration?***

1. The world is a unity which remains largely unexplored.
2. We belong. The kindness that is at the heart of our world can be discovered and experienced by us.
3. Children remain an unexplored resource for the living practice of kindness.
4. We are not stuck with a fearful brain; we can change our minds and thus our brains.
5. We have access to a mental force, ( love) that can change the world as we know it.
6. Connection, connection, connection. Whether in the brain or in the world the more connected we are the safer we are.

But, we have to ask again what Einstein asked...

## *"Is the universe a friendly place?"*

Again I refer to Mother Teresa's answer:

*Take Time To play.*
*Take Time To Love and Be Loved. —*
(Sign on wall of Mother Teresa's children's home in Calcutta.)

That sign, in Mother's Teresa's children's home in Calcutta is a Zen-like reply to Einstein's question. Instead of answering the question the sign tells us what to do in order to discover the answer for ourselves.

We say that we want a safe, peaceful world. But even with all of our science we don't know how to achieve our goal or if it is even possible. The Adverse Childhood Experiences (ACE) Study, one of the largest investigations ever conducted to assess associations between childhood maltreatment and later-life health and well-being, suggests that some of the worst health and social problems in the United States can arise as a consequence of early childhood experiences. The question has been not only how do we get from one kind of brain—a fearful *contest* brain—to another kind of brain—a loving *playful* brain, but even more fundamentally should we even try?

Here is how some scientists express these concerns:

Anthropologist, Gregory Bateson asks: "What pattern connects the crab to the lobster and the orchid to the primrose and all four of them to me?"

Philosopher Jiddhu Krishnamurti's inquires, "Is it possible for a human being, living psychologically in any society to clear violence from himself inwardly? If it is, the very process will produce a different way of living in this world."

Professor History of Science, Anne Harrington poses the matter this way: "Is there some way of thinking about life being precious that could go beyond thinking about survival?"

Writer & editor Sharon Begley wonders, "whether it is possible to cultivate virtue through the way we construct a society, raise children or even train our own brains."

M.D. Andrew Newberg and Mark Waldman ask the question differently: "So is there something more definitive that we can do to tame our selfish brain?"

We can answer a resounding "Yes!" to the above questions. It may seem absurd but the answer to all of these questions is to be found in the original play of life. So, with such a seemingly absurd idea as peace is child's play we have hope!

We can tame our selfish brain. We can construct a society to train our brains for kindness. We can move beyond thinking about mere survival. We can move beyond the psychosis of hate. We can clear violence from ourselves inwardly. The pattern of kind-fullness connects us all and original play activates the pattern within and between us.

## How Do We Get From A Fearful Brain to a Playful Brain?

Up to now our quest for belonging and safety has been so narrowly focused as to give us tunnel vision. Our old certainties with which we have lived for centuries have remained unchallenged. Consequently we have been left with the insanity of conflict. As Donald Pfaff puts it, "...we are not very good at preventing violence."

What is required is a much broader vision of life's possibilities. Original play provides such an inspiration.

We know that adverse childhood experiences(ACE) are major risk factors for leading causes of illness and death in adulthood. Suppose we turn this problem on its head as I make the obvious suggestion that by providing positive childhood experiences we promote health and wellness in adults. Then truly the children shall lead us. What is required is an entirely new way of approaching the problem. This new approach requires a unique, and innovative partnership between adults and children.

H.H. The Dalai Lama has repeatedly suggested that we work with children. Can children actually lead us to a new answer to an age old problem? Could conflict be viewed as a faulty brain mechanism? Could there be a choice by which a person can opt out of conflict altogether? Is it possible that a person could learn a practical, self-directed approach to life that would give them the power to strengthen and utilize the healthy parts of their brain? I believe that the answer to these questions is "Yes."

Psychologist Paul Ekman writes, "We need a loving-kindness exercise room." An exercise room of loving-kindness or playground is exactly what original play provides. Fortunately original play taps into implicit, hard-wired capacities of our native intelligence dropping out the psychic and social, and even species self, and in the process disrupts our automatic fear response and transforms what constitutes our self-defense relationship with reality.

This approach differs from the research that has focused on adults using directed mental force (meditation). We substitute children for adults and use their original play as a non-directed energy. This has the benefits of; (**1**) using a process with children that is inherent and not taught; (**2**) because the play is intrinsic to children the energy does not come from an external source; (**3**) original play is universal and independent of language, culture, and medical issues; (**4**) there is no thinking during the play. This approach is in line with the suggestion made by Dr. James H. Austin that it would seem worthwhile for investigators to extend their studies toward the more spontaneous, non-task-induced behaviors, because this would more closely correspond with the way one's experience naturally unfolds and there is no-thinking and this long moment of non self-conscious mental silence in clear awareness corresponds more closely with the psychological concept of an authentic "baseline."

Here are the research plan differences in chart form.

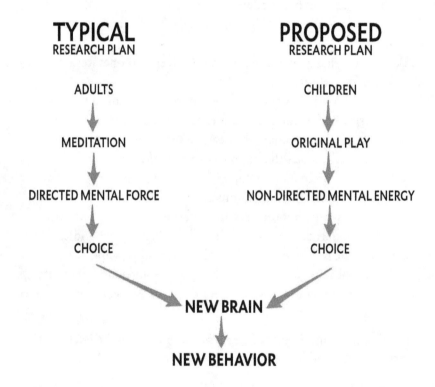

## Hypotheses For Future Research

In addition to the ongoing work with trained meditators I believe we can add children who do original play as a second group to gain insights into brain function and compassion. Original play is a dynamic pattern of relations in which one can experience the kindness pattern underlying all of life. Original play remaps and replaces the habitual and reflexive brain circuit for fear and self-defense with a new circuit of loving-kindness. With practice the regular activation of the safety circuits produce systematic changes in the neural structures that replace the fearful messages and new behavior patterns become stabilized.

Such a major research and training agenda implies serial, repeated and longitudinal studies of many and varied subjects. Based on research in neuroscience and my years of play with thousands of children and animals, we can take two complimentary approaches: (1) first person reports of play with children and adults; and (2) an array of neuro-imaging techniques such as MEG (magnetoencephalography) FMRI (functional magnetic resonance imaging) and other relevant tools.

With these two approaches in mind I make the following working hypotheses:

1. Because original play is inherent and universal it operates without our thinking about it.

2. Play and contest, fear and love are different patterns of neuro-connections. The fearful contest reflexes we assumed to be set not only can be modified, they can be replaced. Original play's "remapping" enables the brain to process information much differently than in contest consciousness, re-channeling fearful, aggressive energies toward compassion.

Original play is an embodied attentional state that functions as an internal cartographer; destructuring, deprograming and deconditioning fear, disrupting the reflexive segue from the fear response and the pathological brain states associated with it promoting neural plasticity and strengthening specific neurological circuits that generate peacefulness, awareness, and compassion.

- Since the signaling circuits of fear work so quickly, to be effective those of original play and love must operate even faster.

- Original play opens the brain to a range of behavioral choices simply unavailable to the contesting brain.

- With practice the emotional temperament to contest with the world can be altered in a positive direction without the need for drugs or invasive procedures.

- Original play is a coherent state in which our fight or flight mechanism of the sympathetic nervous system is reduced while simultaneously promoting the healthier, growth potential of the parasympathetic nervous system.

- Original play increases choice but does not increase what is clinically called decision paralysis.

- Original play reduces the negative influence of the amygdada and de-conditions the limbic system and frontal regions of their more maladaptive responses while liberating some of the most highly evolved associative functions represented farther forward in the frontal pole and temporal pole.

- Original play increases activity in the fusiform gyrus and lowers activity in the amygdala.

- Original play enhances and increases activation and strengthens connections in and between the prefrontal cortex and other brain areas, increasing resilience.

- Original play systematically eliminates synapses used in fear and replaces them by stimulating synapses used in love.

- Original play's pattern of choice alters the gating function of caudate nucleus in a way that changes neural circuitry.

- With practice, seconds of kind-fullness can be stabilized into temperaments as they become familiar and effortless.

- Original play provides behavioral evidence that the body has been de-conditioned from fear and conflict and spontaneous fluid movements arise from liberated sensorimotor pathways.

## SUMMARY:

Original play provides a vision and a practice that moves us closer to who we really are. It is what St. John of the Cross described as being continuously in the presence of ultimate reality. It is to be enthusiastic in its original sense of "engoddedness."

Training in original play produces a sense of compassionate coherence that can be instantaneously activated and communicated to others.

Original play is a simple, inherent, and practical relationship that decreases fear and aggressive behavior and replaces these feelings and actions with wisdom and compassion so that at the deepest experiential level we reach a universal truth. Such a brain-heart/mind-body-environment system serves not only as the basis both for personal movement away from fear and contest behavior to love and a sense of belonging but also serves as a basis for social advancement and long range biological thriving, not merely surviving.

# Appendix 3

## Keepsakes

- *Humans have been devoted to a dying world story, a tale of tragic distortion of consciousness in which we believe ourselves to be strangers in a dangerous world where our only hope for survival is self-defense.*

- *The dying world story is based on the Duchess' Game, a culture of war in which fear is the organizing principle and life is a contest for survival accepted not only as normal and natural, but necessary.*

- *In the Duchess' Game a Faustian bargain is made between adults and children and in the process life's original play is adulterated into cultural play.*

- *In the Duchess' Game children are expendable and childhood is null and void.*

- *But we have an unexplored choice of a living world story in which we can choose to thrive not merely survive. This is a profound shift in human consciousness, unlike any that has come before.*

- *The living world story is based on a conspiracy hidden within childhood that restructures the social contract between humans and life.*

- *Children's enthusiasm delivers Creation's message—life is to be lived as one. This pact with the divine is the genesis of original play in which the divine and human meet as the pattern that connects, a secret sympathy, hidden in the profusion and diversity of life, and so pledged to reproduce its underlying connective pattern, on however small a scale, so that the original design is there for the spirit to discover and follow.*

- *Original play is a code of peace whose wisdom is at once biological and spiritual, ecological, and ecumenical.*

- *Original play's breathtakingly ingenious neural pattern recognition system is an innate ecological intelligence or pattern of kindfullness that not only recognizes that all life is of only one kind, but embodies an emergent pattern of behavior that sustains this sense of life's deep belonging.*

- *Original play is an ongoing process of open-heart surgery in which whole-hearted practice as well as a set of heartfelt principles enable us to feel the underlying unity beneath life's diversity.*

- *Original play bestows upon children a latitude of freedom that they know exactly what to do with. Come join them and play as if your life depends upon it—it does.*

## The Seven Gifts of Original Play

*Stillness*
with stillness we can re-hear our original story and come to

*Trust*
with trust we can give and receive, reaching out to

*Touch*
with touch we are hand crafted by

*Love*
with love we can feel our

*Belonging*
with belonging comes

*Peace*
with which we realize Creation's

*Grace*
and thereby fulfill childhood's dream.

# The Seven Core Disciplines of Original Play

*Stillness*
Stillness is the heart of motion.

*Trust*
Expect nothing, be ready for anything.

*Touch*
Touch to heal, not to defend.

*Love*
Give love at the point of attack.

*Belonging*
Self-disappearance

*Peace*
No revenge.

*Grace*
Touch the face of God in all life.

# Acknowledgments

This book is a collaborative enterprise. I have written it, but it is my playmates who have made it possible through their patient, loving handcrafting. It is one thing to carve an object or paint a picture, it is quite another to craft the very being through which we experience life.

Richard Stengel shares the Zulu word *ubuntu* from the proverb *Umuntu ngumuntu ngabantu* that may be translated as 'a person is a person through other people." I have become a person through the humanity of others. This book is then a gesture of *ubuntu*, of gratitude to all of my playmates who have come in so many forms to help me craft my life. For its beauty, trust, and belonging I have only them to thank, for its contradictions, faults, and imperfections I have myself to challenge, discipline, and smile at. For all of the people and animals, named and unnamed, who have guided and supported me on my journey I thank you.

This book is about *moments of influence*, moments when I was being touched inside and out. There are moments of choice and moments of chance. Such moments became a momentum with the force to bring together other such moments. Most often these moments were like the slow drip of water from a leaking faucet; at other times they coalesced into what seemed like a tsunami of experience.

While I do not recall that my parents ever played with me they both gave me wonderful gifts. My mother and father paid me the compliment to consistently expect from me intelligence and kindness. My mother's gifts were curiosity, a passion for reading and scholarship, and exploring outside established boundaries. My father's gifts were patience, stillness, and kindness.

Because this book is grounded in my play experience with specific people I have many hundreds of debts around the world. For forty years I have put myself into the hands of tens of thousands of playmates, both people and animals whose wise hearts and loving hands reaffirmed a direction of spirit, a sense of belonging, a way of being and living that I call *original play*.

Over the years of playing I have come to be a wanderer, but not an exile. I have left one place called home only to discover that the world has become my home. So a hearty and heartfelt thank you to my worldwide family.

Thank you to Roselle, Anthony, and Etienne Rippo my first family and my first mentors of so many of play's lessons. They taught me the importance of play in a family.

There are many other families who have included me and in so doing helped to make me feel at home around the world.

Thank you to Vicki, Robert, Brian, and Ross Williamson for being my family for so many years, especially to Vicki for taking me to meet my first animal playmates, the wolves of Wolf Haven.

Suellen and the Inwood family, Becky, Jamie, and Tim, have provided another home away from home.

To Linda Stokes-Copley, Marisa Sharlto and Donovon in South Africa; Maria-Luisa and Heinz Nuesch, Luzia Iten, Therese Ballmoos and Nina Moreva Schaerer in Switzerland; Steve & Priska Heitzer in Austria; Noraini Mahmood, Maja Al Mannal, and Rawan Al Husseini in Bahrain; Mariah Dodd and Barbara DeFranco on the Big Island of Hawaii.

To Keiko, Hirata and Mizuma Ichihara my Japanese family whom I've never met for your many inspirational words and gifts.

My great appreciation goes to many individuals who have had a hand in shaping me. My hand-crafters include in the United States; Insui Ghiel, Sally Lew and Craig McEwen, Bill Shaul, Alok Hsu Kwang-han, Eko Noble, Kazuaki Tanahashi, Lorenzo Hyland, Kri Schlafer, Mark Dansereau, Peter Rennert, Shirley Stafford, Michael Mendizza, William Evans, Dan Noonan, Virginia Veach, Michelle and Joel Levy, Karen Malik, Walkin' Jim Stoltz, Stuart Brown, C.J. Rogers, Adam Blatner, Jack Travis, Heather Heliger, Wendy Palmer, Richard Srozzi-Heckler, Lynda & Michael Sexson, Bill Serdahely, Pamela Curlee, Tawni Lawrence, Beverly Hunter, A.J. Thompson, , Koelle Simpson, Al Chung-Liang Huang, Jim & Myra Bull, and Melissa Nogues: in Sweden: Allan Scharf and Suzanne Bruchfeld, Eva Ullen and Ulf Ahrberg, Jennie Elevall, Emma Gran, Neela, Gerda Salis Gross, Vidar Vetterfalk, Torsten Grind, Kenneth Wide and Lena Hero; Douwe van der Zee and Shan Ellis in South Africa, Li-Anne Tan and Shao Em Huang in Singapore, and Robin Reiss, Sonja Mille and Rainer Deutner, Katja Gerkensmeyer, Uwe Reisenauer, Christoph Blumberg, Mathias Stuflesser, Kerstin, Hannah & Georg Eichberger-Sonnberger in Europe.

And to Vince Duff, for our coffeehouse talks when your green eighteen-wheeler would cross my path in California. Thanks to Ray Napolitano who always seemed to know when or where to phone and give his steadfast support to me in so many ways. To all the families and staff of Camp Hope, especially to Ted and Margie Klontz for taking a chance on me and play, to Josh White jr., Tim and Anne Cusack, Marion Simms, Brad Klontz, Brenda Klontz Anderson, Karen Allen, Jerry Harmon, Herman Humes for creating such wonderful summer camps. I thank Joan Almon of the Alliance for Childhood and Carol Artigiani of Global Kids, Dr. Richard Harper of University of Brigeport, and Lienhard Valentin of Arbor-Verlag for their support.

A very special thank you to Wes and the Native American Grandfathers and Grandmothers whose lives demonstrated there's nothing to be afraid of.

A special thank you to Daniel Caron for his friendship, integrity, courage, and years of devotion to the ideals of original play.

Mark Heliger, with his help and patience, he understood that my writing this book was like cleaning one's house; it is never done.

A heartfelt thank you to Sensei Ace Atkinson who, through his numerous lessons in stillness, and motion, giving and receiving you made the love inherent in aikido real for me. In doing so I found the blend of original play and aikido.

I owe a big debt to Steve and Linda Kuntz and Jack Laufer of Wolf Haven who showed me so much courtesy and trust when I began my play with animals. In a world of fear, blame, and litigation I began my play with wolves at Wolf Haven with the trust of a handshake with Steve.

A most special *dziekuje* (thank you) to Jola Graczykowska, Michal, and Magda for helping me to feel at home in Poland. I thank you Jola, for your wisdom, loving gentleness, astute management, and clear dedication to original play. A special *dziekuje* (thank you) to many others in Poland including Urszula Foks, Agata Godawa, Aleksandra Jastrzebska, Robert Czeslaw Pioro, Dorota Liss, the Koczyk family (Malgosia, Krzysztof, Ania, and Janek) and Mrs. Hanna Konwinska and her staff and the children of Primary School Nr. 92 and Jadwiga Boguszewska and the staff and children of Zespol Szkol Specjalnych Nr 100 in Warsaw, Poland. *Dziekuje* to Professor Andrzej Gofron Dean of Pedagogy Department in Academy of Y. Dlugosz who opened the opportunity for scientific dialogue in original play in Poland.

To Robert Johnson thanks for scaring me into silence. When I was writing this book I re-read your book, *Balancing Heaven and Earth*, I laughed at what I had written in the margin on page 125 next to your description of your relationship with Dr. Jung. I wrote "just like me."

This is what you wrote: "Dr. Jung saw the potential in me as well as the dangers ahead. I remember sitting there thinking, 'This man is just like me, except infinitely wiser. He understands me completely. He understands." Well, Robert that's how I think about you. You were always so direct and loving with me. You always seemed to know why I came to see you even when I didn't.

To Björn Wrangsjo for his twinkling eyes and gentle wisdom, and our many talks and walks through Stockholm which remind me of that wonderful combination of scholarship and compassion that I had hoped to find in universities.

A most special thank you to Anette von Koch who lives courage and shares a trust of which poets speak. Thank you for helping me to understand all things Swedish.

A special loving thank you to Jan Donaldson for being a best friend and mentor, for sharing her graceful care of special needs children, for years of reading my "stuff" with red pen in hand, constantly haranguing me to write for "real people," and for her patience and steadfast, though challenging, encouragement to write what I know.

# References

## Acknowledgments

Johnson, Robert. *Balancing Heaven and Earth*. San Francisco: Harper, 1998, 185.

Stengel, Richard. *Mandela's Way: Lessons on Life*. London: Virgin Books, 2010, 231.

## Introduction

Avoth, Pirkei. quoted in Melissa Fay Greene. *There Is No Me Without You*. London: Bloomsbury, 2006, 28.

Bobbit, Philip. *Terror and Consent*. London: Penguin, 2008, 5.

Bradley, General Omar. quoted in P.W. Singer *Wired For War*. New York: Penguin, 2009, 426.

Crutzen, Paul. "Can We Survive the "Anthropocene" Period?" *Science and Society*. http://www.project-syndicate.org/commentary/crutzen1/English.

Dower, John W. *Cultures of War*. New York: W.W. Norton, 2010, 45.

Durant Will and Ariel. quoted in Mark Kurlansky, *Nonviolence*.

New York: Modern Library, 2006, 165.

Einstein Albert. quoted in Austin, James. *Selfless Insight*. Cambridge, MA.: MIT Press, 2009, 135.

France, Anatole quoted in Mark Kurlansky, *Nonviolence*. New York: Modern Library, 2006, 182.

Gat, Azar, *War in Human Civilization*. London: Oxford University Press, 2006, 473.

Graczykohski, Michal. Personal communication, August, 2013.

Keegan, John. *A History of Warfare*. New York: Alfred A. Knopf, 1993, 385.

Korczak, Janusz. quoted in Lifton Betty Jean. *The King of Children: The Life and Death of Janusz Korczak*. New York: American Academy of Pediatrics, 1988, 5.

Machel, Graca. quoted in "Mandela and Machel to lead global children's initiative." UNICEF http://www.unicef.org/newsline/00pr36.htm. 2000.

Rivkin, Jeremy. *The Empathic Civilization*. New York: Jeremy Tarcher Penguin, 2009, 96.

Siu , R.G.H. *A Neo-Taoist Approach To Life*. Cambridge,MA.: The MIT Press, 1974, 25-6.

Swimme, Brian *The Hidden Heart of the Cosmos.* Maryknoll, NY: Orbis Books, 1996, 36.

Tuchman, Barbara W. *The March of Folly.* New York: Abacus, 1984, 486.

Woolf, Virginia. *A Room of One's Own and Three Guineas.* London: Oxford University Press, 1993, 141.

## Prologue

Becker, Ernest *The Denial of Death.* New York: The Free Press, 1973, 277.

Berry Wendell. *A World Lost.* Berkeley, CA.: Counterpoint, 2008, 43.

Booker, Christopher. *The Seven Basic Plots.* New York: Continuum, 2004.

Camus, Albert. quoted in Robert Fisk. *The Great War for Civilization: the Conquest of the Middle East.* London: Harper Perennial, 2006, 1285.

Churchill, Winston. quoted in Virginia Woolf, *A Room of One's Own and Three Guineas.* London: Oxford University Press, 1993, 197.

Elahi, Nur Ali quoted in Carter, Richard Burnett. *The Language of Zen.* New York: Sterling, 2010, 111.

Fauliot, Pascal. *Martial Arts Teaching Tales.* Rochester,VT.: Inner Traditions, 2000.

Hafiz quoted in Daniel Ladinsky. *The Gift.* New York: Penguin Compass, 1999, 28; 290.

Heschel, Abraham Joshua. quoted in Diane Ackerman. *The Zookeepers Wife.* New York: W.W. Norton, 2007, 157.

Holmes Jr. Oliver Wendell. quoted in Thomas, Evan. *The War Lovers.* 2010, 2.

Keegan, John. quoted in William T. Vollmann. *Rising Up and Rising Down.* New York: Harper Perennial, 2004, 49.

Merton, Thomas. Quoted in Lucinda Vardey. *God In All Worlds.* New York: Vintage, 1995, 161.

Picasso quoted in Zizek Slavoj. *Violence.* London: Profile Books, 2008, 9.

Pope John XXIII quoted in Frederick Frank. *A Passion For Seeing.* New Paltz, New York: Codhill, 2002, 38.

Powell, Thomas quoted in Thomas Carroll, *House of War.* Boston: Houghton Mifflin, 2006, 267.

Roosevelt Theodore. quoted in Thomas Evan. *The War Lovers.* 2010, 2.

Rumi quoted in Khaled Hosseini. *And The Mountaiins Echoed.* London: Blumesbury, 2013.

Thomas, Evan. *The War Lovers.* New York: Little, Brown & Co., 2010, 2.

van Creveld, Martin. *The Culture of War.* New York: Ballantine, 2008, xi.

van der Post, Laurens. *About Blady: A Pattern Out of Time.* Orlando,FL: Harcourt Brace Jovanovich 1993, 159.

van Schlieffen, Alfred von. quoted in Cleveld, Martin. *The Culture of War.* New York: Ballantine, 2008, xv.

# Part 1

## Chapter 1

Abbey, Edward. quoted in Berry, Wendell. *Citizenship Papers.* Washington, D.C.: Shoemaker & Hoard, 2003, 150.

Amdur, Ellis. *Dueling With O-sensei.* Seattle, WA.: Edgework, 2000, 188.

Armstrong, Karen. *The Great Transformation.* London: Atlantic Books, 2006, 391.

Ashkenas, Ron. "Why Leaders Play Chicken. Forbes. (6/19/2012) http://onforbes.es/MpXZFo.

Bachmann, Michele. "Michele Bachmann Silent On Teen Suicides In Her School District, Opposed Anti-Bullying Bill."(2011,p.1) http://www.huffingtonpost.com/2011/07/26/michele-bachmann-silent-o_n_910040.html

Bakan, Joel. *Childhood Under Siege.* London: The Bodley Head, 2011, 89-91.

Becker, Ernest. *The Denial of Death.* New York: The Free Press, 1973, 221.

Berry, Wendell. Citizenship Papers. Washington, D.C.: Shoemaker & Hoard, 2003, 150.

Bosch, Andrew quoted in Jonny Steinberg. The Number. Johannesburg: Jonathan Ball Publishers, 2004, 9.

Brinkley, Joel. "Lethal Game of 'Chicken' Emerges for Israeli Boys," *New York Times.* (April 3 1989).

Browning, Christopher. *Ordinary Men.* New York: Harper Perennial, 1998, 182.

Buddha, Gautama, quoted in Quoted in Stephen S. Hall. *Wisdom: from Philosophy to Neuroscience.* New York: Alfred A. Knopf, 2010, 215.

Burke Edmund. quoted in Howard Kirschenbaum & Valerie Henderson. (eds.), *Carl Rogers Dialogues* Boston: Houghton Mifflin, 1989, 240.

Carcaterra Lorenzo *Sleepers.* New York: Ballantine, 1995, 37.

Carroll Lewis. *Through The Looking Glass.* New York: Macmillan, 1885.

Carroll, James, *House of War.* Boston: Houghton Mifflin, 2006, 354.

Chao-chou. quoted in Hyers, Conrad. *Zen and the Comic Spirit.* Philadelphia: The Westminister Press, 1973, 14.

Chol, Mun. quoted in Briefing. *Time.* Vol. 181 (February,25, 2013), 5.

Christie, Tom. quoted in Mark Thompson. "The Most Expensive Weapon ever Built," *Time.* Vol. 181 (February, 25, 2013), 30-35.

Coalition To Leverage And optimize Sales Effectiveness. *Wall Street Journal.* April 8, 2008, 3.

Compton, Arthur. quoted in Brian VanDeMark, *Pandora's Keepers: Nine Men and the Atomic Bomb.* New York: Back Bay Books, 2003, 185.

Davies, Norman. *Rising'44: The Battle for Warsaw.* London: Penguin, 2003, 192.

Dawkins, J.L. "Bullying, physical disability and the paediatric patient. *Developmental Medicine and Child Neurology.* 1996; Vol. 38, 603-612.

Diem, Sergeant quoted in Frederick, Jim. *Black Hearts.* New York: McMillan, 2010, 242.

Dobbs, Michael. *One Minute To Midnight.* New York: Arrow Books, 2008, 192.

Donaldson-Evans, C. *Children With Food Allergies Often Victims of Bullying.* AOL Health News. http.//aolhealth. com/2010/09/28/children-with-food-allergies-o... icid=main%7Cmain%7Cl10%7Csec1.Ink3%7C174144&a_ dgi=aolshare_email.September 28, 2010.

Fosdick, Dr. Harry Emerson *Journal of Creative Behavior.* V. 14 (2), 75-76, 1980.

Franklin, Benjamin. quoted in John Fabian Witt. *Lincoln's Code.* New York: Free Press, 2012, 43 & 45.

Friedlander, Saul. *Nazi Germany and the Jews, 1939-1945: The Years of Extermination.* New York: Harper, 2007, 469.

Gandhi, Mohandas K. quoted in Arthur Herman. *Gandhi and Churchill.* New York: Bantam, 2008.

Hachenburg, Hanus. quoted in *I Never Saw Another Butterfly...* New York: Schocken Books, 1993. 20-21.

Hall, Stephen S. *Wisdom: From Philosophy to Neuroscience.* New York: Alfred A. Knopf, 2010, 13.

Hallie, Philip. *Lest Innocent Blood Be Shed.* New York: Harper Perennial, 1994, 275.

Hammer, Joshua. "Inside the Danger Zone." *Newsweek.* (April 11, 2011), 28-33.

Hatzfeld, Jean. *Machete Season* New York: Farrar, Straus & Giroux, 2005.

Hegel, George. quoted in Greene, Robert. *33 Strategies of War.* London" Profile Books, 2007

Herbert ,Frank. *Dune* New York; Berkley Medallion Book,1965.

Higley, J. Dee. quoted in Jeffrey M. Schwartz & Sharon Begley, *The Mind and the Brain: Neuroplasticity and the Power of Mental Force.* New York: Harper Collins, 2002

Holmes, Oliver Wendell. quoted in Jack Higgins, *Touch The Devil,* NY: Signet, 1983, 7.

Holmes, John. quoted in Nossiter, Adam." Rights and rituals clash in Africa". *International Herald Tribune.* (September 14, 2010), 2.

Janssen, I. Craig, W.M. Boyce, W. F. & Pickett, W. "Associations between overweight and obesity within bullying behaviors in school-aged children." *Pediatrics* (2004) Vol. 113 1187-1194.

Junger, Sabastian, *War.* New York: Twelve, 2010, 145.

King, Gary. quoted in Fahrenhold, David A. 27% of communication by members of Congress is taunting professor concludes." *The Washington Post.* (April 6, 2011), 1.

Kondo, Hajime. quoted in Laurence Rees. *Their Darkest Hour.* London: Ebury Press, 2008, 59.

Kor, Eva Mozes. *Surviving the Angel of Death.* Terre Haute, IN.: Tanglewood, 2009, 98.

Krehic, Tarja "Dragon's Feet" *Time, 1995.*

Laing, R.D. *The Politics of Experience.* New York: Ballantine, 1967, 183.

Langer, Lawrence I. *Art from the Ashes.* London: Oxford University Press, 1995, 155.

Lemonick, Michael D. "The Bully Blight". *Time.* (April 11, 2005).

Levi, Primo. *Survival in Auschwitz.* New York, The Orion Press 1958, 19.

Lipton, Bruce. *The Biology of Belief.* Santa Rosa, CA.: Mountain of Love/ Elite Books, 2005, 147.

Lown, Bernard. *Prescription For Survival.* San Francisco, CA.: Berrett-Koehker Publishers. 2008, 19.

Montagu, Ashley. *Touching.* New York: Harper & Row, 1986, 85.

Niemöller, Martin. quoted in *The World Must Know.* Washington, D.C.: The U.S. Holocaust Memorial Museum, 2006, 37.

Overbye, Dennis. *Lonely Hearts of the Cosmos.* New York: Perennial, 1991, 277.

Peck, M. Scott. *People of the Lie.* New York: Touchstone, 1983, 286.

Pope John XXIII. quoted in Thomas Cahill, *Pope John XXIII: A Penguin*

*Life*. London Penguin, 2002, 156.

Rees, Laurence. *The Dark Charisma of Adolf Hitler.* London: Ebury Press, 2012, 126-7.

Roosevelt, Theodore, quoted in Evan Thomas. *The War Lovers.* New York: Little Brown & Co., 2010, 199.

Sachs, Andrea. "How To Bully-Proof Young Girls." *TIME.* (August 25,2010). 1. http://www.time.com/time/health/article/0,8599,2013184,00.html?artId=2013184?contType=article?chn=sciHealth

Safire, William. Quoted in Wendell Berry. Citizenship Papers. Washington, D.C.: Shoemaker & hoard, 2010, 124.

Scurlock, James D. "How To Get the Best of The Fear Economy." *AARP The Magazine.* (Jan.-Feb., 2009), 44-49.

Shirer, William quoted in Srargardt, Nicholas. *Witnesses of War.* New York: Vintage, 2005 , 25.

Smith, Steve. quoted in Scooby Axson. "Ravens WR Steve Smith on team mentality: 'we build bullies' SI wire, (August 15,2014).http://www.si.com/nfl/2014/08/15/baltimore-ravens-steve-smith-we-build-bullies

Steinberg, Jonny. *The Number.* Johannesburg: Jonathan Ball, 2004, 185.

Steiner, Jean-Francois. *Treblinka.* New York: Meridian, 1994, 53.

Storch, Eric. "Bullying Keeps Overweight Kids Off Field," *Medical News Today.* April 24, 2006. P.1-2. http://www.medicalnewstoday.com/printerfriendlynews.php?newsid=42038.

Synkova, Alena. Quoted in... *I Never Saw Another Butterfly...* New York: Schocken Books, 1993, 69.

Thomas, Cal & Bob Beckel, "How to end an idiotic game of chicken," *USA Today* (July 28,2011), 7A.

van der Post, Laurens. *About Blady: A Pattern Out of Time.* Orlando,FL: Harcourt Brace Jovanovich 1993, 159.

VanDeMark, Brian. *Pandora's Keepers: Nine Men and the Atomic Bomb*. New York: Back Bay Books, 2003, 191.

Weisel, Elie. *Night.* New York: Bantam, 1960, 105.

Yeats, W. B. quoted in Booker, Christopher. *The Seven Basic Plots.* New York: Continuum, 2004, 455.

Yogananda, Paramahansa, quoted in Lucinda Vardey. *God In All Worlds.* New York: Vintage, 1995, 56.

## Chapter 2

Adams, John. quoted in Sahlins, Marshall. *The Western Illusion of Human Nature*. Chicago: Prickly Paradigm Press, 2008, 77.

Ahtisaari, Martti. Peace Nobelist: "Mideast peace failure a disgrace". *USA Today*. http://www.usatoday.com/news/world/2008-10-25-mideast-peace_N.htm – October 26, 2008.

American Medical Association. "Doctor's group opposes public health insurance plan,"*International Herald Tribune*,(June 12, 2009), 4.

Andreas, Dwayne. Quoted in Derrick Jensen. *A Language Older Than Words*. White River Junction, VT.: Chelsea Green Publishing Co., 2004, 135.

Annan, Kofi. quoted in Traub, James. *The Best Intentions: Kofi Annan and the UN in the Era of American World Power*. New York: Farrar, Straus & Giroux, 2006, 240.

Arendt, Hannah. quoted in Zimbardo, Philip. *The Lucifer Effect*. New York: Random House, 2007, 484.

Armstrong, Jim. Cheating Doesn't Seem to Faze Fans. Aol. Feb.23, 2007. http://sports.aol.com/nascar/story/_a/cheating_doesn't_seem_to_faze_fans/20070222162609990001.

Bakan, Joel. *The Corporation: The Patholgical Pursuit of Profit and Power*. Toronto: Penguin, 2004, 88-89.

Bauman, Zygmunt. *Liquid Times*. Cambridge: Polity Press, 2007, 6.

Berry, Thomas. *The Dream of the Earth*. San Francisco: Sierra Club Books, 1988., 216.

Betancourt, Ingrid. Interview by Larry King. "Some Kind of Wonderful," *CNN Traveller*. (September-October, 2008), 135.

Bohm, David. Quoted in Weber, Renee. *Dalogues With Scientists and Sages*. London: Routledge & Kegan Paul, 1986,107.

Boo, Katherine. *Behind The Beautiful Forevers*. New York: Random House, 2012, 29.

Booker, Christopher. *The Seven Basic Plots*. New York: Continuum, 2004, 654.

Brown, Robert McAfee. quoted in Paul Farmer. *Pathologies of Power*. Berkeley: University of CA. Press, 2005, 157.

Burke, Edmund. quoted in Jon Meacham, *Thomas Jefferson: The Art of Power*. New York: Random House, 2012, 64.

Bush, President George. Quoted in Jehl. International Herald Tribune. 2005, 30.

Cain, Holly. "Carl Edwards Delivers Drama for NASCAR, but When Is

Enough, Enough? http://motorsports.fanhouse.com/2010/07/19/carl-edwards-delivers-drama-for-nascar-but-when-is-enough-eno/

Cain, Holly. NASCAR's Missed opportunity. http://motorsports.fanhouse.com/2010/03/09/nascars-missed-opportunity/

Carroll, James. *House of War*. New York: Houghton Mifflin, 2006, 211.

Carcaterra, Lorenzo. *Sleepers*. New York: Ballantine,1995, 84.

Cavafy, Constantine. quoted in Soloman Hughes. *War on Terror, Inc.* London: Verso, 2007, 223.

Chen, Stephanie. "Teens locked up for life without a second chance." CNN.com (April 8, 2009), 1.

Chretien, Marc. quoted in Rajiv Chandrasekaran, *Little America: The War Within The War For Afghanistan*. New York: Alfred Knopf, 2012, 208.

CNN Wire Services. "Despite Gulf oil spill, rig owner executives get big bonuses. http://edition.cnn.com/2011/BUSINESS/04/03/gulf.spill.bonuses/index.htlm?

Coalition To Leverage And Optimize Effectiveness. *Wall Street Journal*. April 8, 2008, 3.

Darby, Joe. quoted in Zimbardo, Philip. *The Lucifer Effect*. New York: Random House, 2007, 476.

Deming, Dr. W.E. quoted in Senge, Peter M. *The Fifth Discipline*. New York: Random House, 2006, xii.

Dobbs, Michael. *One Minute To Midnight*. New York: Arrow Books, 2008, 114

Doctorow, E.L. *The March*. New York: Random House, 2005, 187.

Dyson, Freeman. quoted in Carroll, James. *House of War*. New York: Houghton Mifflin, 2006, 90.

Easterbrook, Judge Frank. quoted in Bakan, Joel. *The Corporation: The Pathological Pursuit of Profit and Power*. Toronto: Penguin, 2004, 79.

Einstein, Albert quoted in Eric Schlosser. Command and Control. London: Allen Lane, 3013, 124.

Eisenhower, General and President Dwight. quoted in Mark Kurlansky, *Nonviolence*. New York: Modern Library, 2006,140.

Eitan, Michael. quoted in Teibel, Amy. Israel "May Get Second Female President". *AOL News*. Associated Press. (September 4, 2008).

Escriva, Monsignor Josemaria. quoted in Yallop, David. *The Power and the Glory*. London: Constable, 2007, 625.

Farmer, Paul. *Pathologies of Power*. Berkeley: University of CA. Press, 2005, 138.

Fisk, Robert. *The Great War for Civilization: the Conquest of the Middle East*. London: Harper Perennial, 2006, 713.

Friedlander, Saul. *Nazi Germany and the Jews, 1939-1945: The Years of Extermination*. New York: Harper, 2007, 479.

Gandhi. quoted in Feldman, Christina, & Jack Kornfield. (eds.) *Stories of the Spirit, Stories of the Heart*. San Francisco: Harper Collins, 1991, 144.

Gardner, Daniel. *The Science of Fear*. New York: A Plume book, 2009, 24.

Gates, Robert. quoted in Richard Rhodes. *The Twilight of the Bombs*. New York: Alfred A. Knopf, 2010, 4.

Gordon, Michael R. & General Bernard E. Trainor. *Cobra II: the Inside story of the Invasion and Occupation of Iraq*. New York: Vintage, 2007, 72.

Gourevitch, Philip. *We Wish To Inform You That Tomorrow We Will Be Killed With Our Families*. Stories From Rwanda. New York: Picador, 1998, 222.

Gray, J. Glenn. *The Warriors: Reflections on Men in Battle*. Lincoln: University of Nebraska Press, 1970, 132.

Greene, Robert. *33 Strategies of War*. London" Profile Books, 2007, 3.

Glover, Jonathan *Humanity: A Moral History of the Twentieth Century*. London: Jonathan Cape, 1999, 56, 131.

Hamilton, Alexander. quoted in Sahlins, Marshall. *The Western Illusion of Human Nature*. Chicago: Prickly Paradigm Press, 2008, 76.

Hatzfeld, Jean. *Machete Season*. New York: Farrar, Straus & Giroux, 2005, 144.

Haval, Vaclav. quoted in Lucinda Vardey. *God In All Worlds*. New York: Vintage, 1995, 19.

Howard, Michael. *The Invention of Peace & the Reinvention of War*. London: Profile Books, 2001.

Huizinga, Johan. *Homo Ludens*. Boston: Beacon Press, 1950.

Ikeda, Daisaku. quoted in Arnold Toynbee & Ikeda, Daisaku. *The Toynbee-Ikeda Dialogue*. Tokyo: Kodansha, 1976, 93.

Ilibagiza, Immaculee *Left To Tell: Discovrng God Amidst the Rwandan Holocaust*. Carlsbad California; Hay House, 2006, 13.

Jefferson, Thomas. quoted in Derrick Jensen. *Endgame Vol. II Resistance*. New York: Seven Stories Press, 2006. 515.

Jefferson, Thomas. quoted in Jon Meachan, *Thomas Jefferson: The Art of Power*. New York: Random House, 2012.

Jones, Jonathan. *The Lost Battles*. London: Simon & Schuster, 2010, 253.

Levi, Primo. *Survival in Auschwitz*. New York: Touchstone, 1996, 92.

Lewis, Ray. quoted in Staff Report. "Ray Lewis says crime will rise without NFL labor settlement." http://aol.sportingnews.com/ nfl/story/2011-05-22/ray-lewis-says-crime-will-rise-without-nfl-labor-settlement#ixzz1NCI4dqbM, 2010, 255.

Katha Upanishad. quoted in Booker, Christopher. *The Seven Basic Plots*. New York: Continuum, 2004, 593.

Kagame, Paul. quoted in Dallaire, Romeo. *Shake Hands with The Devil*. London: Arrow Books, 2003, 156.

Khouri, Rami. quoted in Singer, P.W. *Wired For War*. New York: William Morrow, 2009, 313.

Kirkpatrick, Jeane. J. *Making War To Keep Peace*. New York: Harper Collins, 2007.

Kohn, Alfie. *No Contest*. Boston: Houghton Mifflin, 1986, 97.

Kurlansky, Mark. *Nonviolence*. New York: Modern Library, 2006, 112.

Leggett, Trevor. *Encounters in Yoga and Zen: Meetings of Cloth and Stone*. London: Routledge & Kegan Paul, 1982, 57.

Lengyel, Olga. quoted in Friedrich, Otto. *The Kingdom of Auschwitz*. New York :Harper Perennial, 1994, 39.

Levitt, Arthur Alter, *Newsweek* collected articles 2002, 25.

Lilenthal, David. quoted in Carroll, James. *House of War*. New York: Houghton Mifflin, 2006, 174.

Lincoln, Abraham. quoted in William T. Vollmann. *Rising Up and Rising Down*. New York: Harper Perennial, 2003, 368.

Lombardi, Vince. quoted in Miedzian Myriam. *Boys Will Be Boys*. New York: Dounbleday, 1991, 73.

Lown, Dr. Bernard. *The Lost Art of Healing*. New York: Ballantine, 1999, xi.

Madison, James. quoted in Sahlins, Marshall. *The Western Illusion of Human Nature*. Chicago: Prickly Paradigm Press, 2008, 74.

Maske, Mark. *War Without Death: A Year of Extreme Competition in Pro Football's NFC East*. New York: The Penguin Press, 2007, 6.

Merton, Thomas. quoted in Lucinda Vardey. *God In All Worlds*. New York: Vintage, 1995, 130, 138.

Miller, Bob. quoted in K.C.Cole. *Conversations With The Cosmos*. Orlando: Harcourt,Inc., 2006, 74.

Montefiore, Simon Sebag. *Jerusalem: The Biography*. London: Orion Books, 2011, 563.

Nasrudin. quoted in Feldman, Christina & Jack Kornfield. (eds.) *Stories of the Spirit, Stories of the Heart*. San Francisco: Harper Collins, 1991, 252.

Nitze, Paul. quoted in Carroll, James. *House of War*. New York: Houghton Mifflin, 2006, 325.

Obama, President Barack. quoted in Jeff Zeleny." Obama confronts 'necessity' of war." *International Herald Tribune*. (December 11, 2009, 1, 4).

Obama, President Barack. Quoted in "Line Drawn on Guns." *USA Today*. (January 17, 2013), 1.

Obama, President Barack. Quoted in Jeff Zeleny. "President Obama's speech at Nobel ceremony.", 2009, 1&4.

*Reuters*. http://www.reuters.com/assets/print?aid=USTRE5B92KK20091210.

Orwell George quoted in Bernard Lown, *Prescription for Survival*. San Francisco, CA.: Berrett-Koehler Publishers, 2008, 203.

Orwell, George. *1984* New York: Plume, 1983.

Palmer, Chris. quoted in Dan Solomon. "Wildlife Filmmaker Chris Palmer says Nature Documentaries Are Manipulative," AOL Original. (October 1,2010). http://blog.moviefone.com/2010/10/01/wildlife-filmmaker-chris-palmer-says-nature-docs-are-manipulative/?a_dgi=aolshare_email

Pearce, Joseph Chilton. quoted in Bruce Lipton & Steve Bhaerman. *Spontaneous Evolution*. Carlsbad, CA.:Hay House, 2009.

Pellegrino. Edmund quoted in Paul Farmer. *Pathologies of Power*. Berkeley: University of CA. Press, 2005, 163.

Podvig, Pavel. quoted in Peter Baker. "Quirky logic of arms talks: Reductions without cuts. *International Herald Tribune*. (April 1,2010), 1&5.

Pope John Paul II, quoted in Yallop, David. *The Power and the Glory*. London: Constable, 2007, 30.

Potter, Wendell. *Deadly Spin*. New York: Bloomsbury Press, 2010, 73.

Powell, Thomas. quoted in Carroll, James. *House of War*. New York: Houghton Mifflin, 2006, 432-3.

Rees, Laurence. *Their Darkest Hour*. London: Ebury Press, 2008, 4.

Roosevelt, Teddy. quoted in Eduardo Galeano. *Mirrors*. New York: Nation Books, 2009, 250.

Rumi. quoted in Coleman Barks. *The Soul of Rumi*. San Francisco: Harper San Francisco, 2001, 48.

Sagan, Carl. Quoted in Barbara Kingsoler. *High Tide in Tucson.* New York: Harper, 1995, 218.

Shakespeare, William. Julius Ceasar. quoted in Tuchman, Barbara W. *The March of Folly.* New York: Abacus, 1984, 58.

Shakespeare, William. quoted in Booker, Christopher. *The Seven Basic Plots.* New York: Continuum, 2004, 637.

Shawcross, William. *Deliver Us From Evil.* New York: Touchstone, 2000, 193.

"Sidewalk Bump Ends in 2 Deaths," AOL News. (September 30, 2012) http://www.aolnews.com/story/sidewalk-bump-ends-in-murder-suicide-for/694758

Siegel, Kenneth N. quoted in Jena McGregor. "Sweet revenge." *Businessweek Online.* (January 22, 2007), 1-4 http://www.businesweek.com/print/magazine/content/07_04/b4018001.htm?chan=gl

Simon David & Ed Burns. *The Corner.* Edinburgh: Canongate, 2009, 57.

Stargardt, Nicholas. *Witnesses of War: Children's lives Under The Nazis.* New York: Vintage Books, 2005, 81.

Strick, Anne quoted in Kohn, Alfie. *No Contest.* Boston: Houghton Mifflin, 1986. 1986, 162.

Terman, Frederick E. quoted in Friedman, Robert Marc. The Politics of Excellence. New York: A.W.H. Freeman books, 2001, 276.

Tolstoy, Leo. *War and Peace.* London: Penguin Books, 1978, 635.

Twain, Mark. *The War Prayer.* New York: Perennial, 1951.

van Creveld, Martin. *The Culture of War.* New York: Ballantine, 2008.

van der Post, Laurens & Jean-Marc Pottiez. *A Walk With A White Bushman.* New York: William Morrow, 1987, 50.

Vidal, Gore. quoted in Slavoj Zizek. *Violence.* London: Profile Books, 2008.

von Clausewitz, Carl. quoted in Greene, Robert. *33 Strategies of War.* London" Profile Books, 2007, 3.

von Clausewitz, Carl. quoted in Mark Kurlansky, *Nonviolence.* New York: Modern Library, 2006, 140

Weil, Simone. *Waiting For God.* New York: Harper Perennial Modern Classics, 2009, 36.

Weintraub, Stanley. *Silent Night: The Story of the World war I Christmas Truce.* New York: The Free press, 2001, 161.

Wiesel, Elie. *Night.* New York: Bantam Books, 1960, 105.

Witt, John Fabian. *Lincoln's Code.* New York: Free Press, 2012, 63, 342.

Yallop, David. *The Power and the Glory.* London: Constable, 2007, 591.

Yesin, Victor. quoted in quoted in Dobbs, Michael. *One Minute To Midnight*. New York: Arrow Books, 2008, 284.

## Chapter 3

Ali, Nujood. with Delphine Minoui. *I Am Nujood*. New York: Broadway Books, 2010, 117.

Auden, W.H. quoted in Bobbit Philip. *The Shield of Achilles: War, Peace and the Course of History*. New York: Knopf, 2002, 818.

Alberts, Paul. *Some Evidence of Things Seen*. Johannesburg: Open Hand Trust, 1997, 21.

Allen. quoted in Archbishop Desmond Tutu. *Rabble-Rouser For Peace*. New York: The Free press, 2006.

Berry Wendell. *Watch With Me*. New York: Pantheon,1995, 78.

Broyles, William. quoted in Jonathan *Glover, Humanity: A Moral History of the Twentieth Century*. London: Jonathan Cape, 1999, 56.

Burke, Edmund. quoted in Jon Meacham, *Thomas Jefferson: The Art of Power*. New York: Random House, 2012, 64.

Connell, John. quoted in Richard Holmes. *Acts of War*. London: Weidenfeld & Nicolson, 2003, 2003, 6.

Courtney, Bruce. *The Power of One*. New York: Ballantine, 1989, 51.

Dallaire, Romeo. *They Fight Like Soldiers, They Die Like Children*. London: Huthinson, 2010, 3.

Doctorow, E.L. *The March*. New York: Random House, 2005, 187.

Dowden, Richard. "Thousands of child 'witches' turned on to the streets to starve." The Observer. (February 12, 2006). http://guardian.co.uk/world/2006/feb12/theobserver.worldnews11.,p.1).

Garbarino, James. *Raising Children in a Socially Toxic Environment*. San Franciscco. CA.: Jossel-Bass, 1999, 103.

Goethe, Johann Wolfgang. *Faust*. Cleveland: World Publishing Co., 1948.

Gourevitch, Philip. *We Wish To Inform You That Tomorrow We Will Be Killed With Our Families*. Stories From Rwanda. New York: Picador, 1998, 228.

Holden, Chris. Quoted in Whitall N. Perry. *A Treasury of Traditional Wisdom*. Rochester, VT: Destiny Books, 1991, 57.

Hughes, Lucy. quoted in Bakan, Joel. *The Corporation: The Pathological Pursuit of Profit and Power*. Toronto: Penguin, 2004, 122.

Huizinga, Johan. *Homo Ludens*. Boston: Beacon Press, 1950, 11.

Kirkpatrick, Jeane. quoted in Farmer, Paul. *Pathologies of Power*. Berkeley:

University of CA. Press, 2005, 9.

Korczak, Janusz. quoted in Lifton Betty Jean. *The King of Children: The Life and Death of Janusz Korczak*. New York: American Academy of Pediatrics, 1988, 47.

Kristof, Nicholas D. "Terrorism that's personal." *International Herald Tribune*. (December 1, 2008), 9, 7.

Merton, Thomas. quoted in Robert Inchausti ed. *Seeds*. Boston: Shambhala, 2002, 131.

Machel, Graca. quoted in "Mandela and Machel to lead global children's initiative." UNICEF Http://www.unicef.org/newsline/00pr36.htm., 3.

Machel, Graca. quoted in Singer, P. W. *Children At War*. New York: Pantheon, ,2005, 30.

Mandela, Nelson. quoted in Michael Reagan, *Reflections on the Nature of God*. Atlanta: Andrews McNeal Publishing, 2004, 70.

Mydans, Seth. "Khmer Rouge paranoia." *International Herald Tribune*. (March 2,2009), 1&6.

Robertson, Nic. :Sudan soldier: 'They told me kill, to rape children.'" *CNN.com*. (March 21,2009),p.1.http://printthis.clickability.com/pt/ cpt?action=cpt&title=Sudan+so...4%Fdarfur.rape%2Findex.htm. p.1).

Sadako, Ogata. quoted in Shawcross, William. *Deliver Us From Evil*. New York: Touchstone, 2000, 193.

Singer, P. W. *Children At War*. New York: Pantheon, 2005.

Stargardt, Nicholas. *Witnesses of War: Children's lives Under The Nazis*. New York: Vintage Books, 2005, 189.

Sunil. quoted in Katherine Boo. *behind the beautiful flowers*. New York: Random house, 2012, 49.

Tutu, Archbishop Desmond. quoted in Singer, P. W. *Children At War*. New York: Pantheon, 2005, flyleaf.

UNAIDS prediction of the United Nations Program on HIV/ AIDS Melissa Fay Greene. *There Is No Me Without You*. London: Bloomsbury, 2006.

U.N. 1996 report *The Impact of Armed Conflict on Children*. UNICEF and National Children's Rights Committee quoted in Alberts, Paul . *Some Evidence of Things Seen*. Johannesburg: Open Hand Trust, 1997.

Veneman, Ann M. Foreward. *Children and Conflict In A Changing World. Machel Study 10-Year Strategic Review*. Office of the Special Representative of the Secretary-General for Children and Armed Conflict. New York: 2009, iv.

Wiesel, Elie. "Crimes Against Childhood." *We, The Children*. New York: W. W. Norton & Co. UNICEF, 1990, 28.

Wiesel, Elie. *A Beggar In Jerusalem*. New York: Schocken, 1970, 99.

Wines, Michael. "In Africa, hard labor and stolen youth," International Herald Tribune, August 24, 2006, 1.

Wolken, Dr. Otto. quoted in Friedrich, Otto. *The Kingdom of Auschwitz*. New York :Harper Perennial, 1994, 53.

World Bank. quoted in Greene, Melissa Fay. *There is no Me Without You*. London: Bloomsbury, 2006, 389.

Zimbardo, Philip. *The Lucifer Effect*. New York: Random House, 2007, xi.

# Chapter 4

Austin, James H. *Zen-Brain Reflections*. Cambridge, MA.: MIT Press, 2006, 270.

Austin, James H. *Selfless Insight*. Cambridge, MA.: MIT Press, 2009,135.

Bateson, Gregory. *Mind and Nature*. New York, Bantam, 1979.

Begley, Sharon. "Why Do We Rape, Kill and Sleep Around?". *Newsweek* (June 29, 2009), 1-7.

Berry, Thomas. quoted in Deignan, Kathleen (ed.) *Thomas Merton When Trees Say Nothing*. Notre Dame, IN.: Sorin Books, 2003, 182.

Berry, Wendell. *Citizenship Papers*. Washington, D.C.: Shoemaker & Hoard, 2003.

Bohm, David. quoted in Renee Weber. *Dialogues With Scientists and Sages*. London: Routledge & Kegan Paul, 1986, 215.

Booker, Christopher. *The Seven Basic Plots*. New York: Continuum, 2004, 18.

Cahill, Thomas. *The Gifts of the Jews*. New York: Anchor, 1999, 24.

Camus, Albert. quoted in Robert Fisk. *The Great War for Civilization: the Conquest of the Middle East*. London: Harper Perennial, 2006, 1285.

Chuang Tzu. quoted in Henri J, M. Nouwen. *Encounters With Merton*. New York: Crossroads Publishing Co., 1981, 116.

Davidson, Richard. quoted in Hall, Stephen S. *Wisdom: From Philosophy to Neuroscience*. New York: Alfred A. Knopf, 2010, 131.

Eckhart, Meister. quoted in Matthew Fox. *Whee! We, Wee All The Way Home*. Santa Fe, New Mexico: Bear & Co., 1981, 99.

Einstein, Albert Hall. quoted in Stephen S. Hall. *Wisdom: from Philosophy to Neuroscience*. New York: Alfred A. Knopf, 2010, 190.

Ekman, Paul. quoted in Goleman, Daniel. *Destructve Emotions. A Dialogue with the Dalai Lama*. London: Bloomsbury, 2003, 148.

Eliot, T.S. quoted in Reagan, Michael & Sharon Begley. *Inside The Mind of God*.Philadelphia: Templeton Foundation Press, 2002, 99.

Franck, Frederick. *Everyone*. Garden City, NY: Doubleday & Co. 1978, 110.

Frank, Anne. *The Diary of a Young Girl*. New York: Pocket Books, 1953.

Gandhi, M. K. *An Autobiography*. London: Modern Penguin Classics, 1929, 194.

Goleman, Daniel. Social Intelligence. New York: Bantam, 2006, 36.

Goldin, Dan. quoted in K.C. Cole. *Mind over Matter*. Orlando: Harcourt, Inc. 2003, 64.

Griffith, Father Bede. quoted in Renee Weber. *Dialogues With Scientists and Sages*. London: Routledge & Kegan Paul, 1986, 159.

H.H. The Dalai Lama. quoted in Anne Harrington & Arthur Zajonc. Eds. *The Dalai Lama at MIT*. Cambridge, MA.: Harvard University Press, 2006, 15.

H.H. The Dalai Lama. quoted in HH The Dalai Lama and Victor Chan. *The Wisdom of Forgiveness*. London: Hodder & Mobius, 2004, 120.

H.H. The Dalai Lama. quoted in Hayward, Jeremy W. & Francisco J. Varela. *Gentle Bridges: Conversations with the Dalai Lama on the Sciences of the Mind*. Boston: Shambhala, 2001, 254.

H.H. The Dalai Lama. quoted in Goleman, Daniel. *Destructve Emotions. A Dialogue with the Dalai Lama*. London: Bloomsbury, 2003, 277.

H.H. The Dalai Lama. quoted in Begley, Sharon *The Plastic Mind*. London: Constable, 2009, 262.

Hafiz. quoted in Daniel Ladinsky. *The Gift*. New York: Penguin Compass, 1999, 31.

Hammarskjöld, Dag. *Markings*. Translated by Leif Sjöberg and W.H. Auden. New York: Knopf, 1964, 17.

Hanh, Thich Nhat. quoted in James Austin. *Zen and the Brain*. Cambridge. MA.: MIT Press, 1998, 109.

Harrington, Anne. quoted in Richard J. Davidson and Anne Harrington. *Visions of Compassion*. London: Oxford University Press, 2002, 220.

Hedges, Chris. *War Is A Force That Gives Us Meaning*. New York: Anchor, 2002, 1.

Heschel, Abraham. quoted in Stephen S. Hall. *Wisdom: from Philosophy to Neuroscience*. New York: Alfred A. Knopf, 2010, 115.

Hillman, James. *A Terrible Love of War*. New York: The Penguin Press, 2004

Hokusai. quoted in Frederick Franck. *A Passion For Seeing*. New Paltz,

New York: Codhill, 2002, 3.

Huang, Al Chung-liang. *Enbrace Tiger, Return To Mountain.* Real People Press, Moab, UT: 1973, xiii.

Jefferson, Thomas. quoted in Jon Meacham. *Thomas Jefferson: The Art of Power.* New York: Random House, 2012, 336.

Johnson, Robert A. *Balancing Heaven and Earth.* San Francisco: Harper, 1998.

Keegan, John. quoted in William T. Vollmann. *Rising Up and Rising Down.* New York: Harper Perennial, 2003, 49.

King, Jr., Dr. Martin Luther. quoted in Carroll, James. *House of War.* New York: Houghton Mifflin, 2006, 506.

Kornfield, Jack. *The Wise Heart.* New York: Bantam,2009, 219.

Lindgren, Astrid. Pippi Longstocking. London: Penguin, 1978.

Lipton, Bruce. *The Biology of Belief.* Santa Rosa: Mountain of Love/Elite Books, 2005, 202.

Livingston Robert. quoted in Hayward, Jeremy W. & Francisco J. Varela. *Gentle Bridges: Conversations with the Dalai Lama on the Sciences of the Mind.* Boston: Shambhala, 2001, 254.

Magee, John Gillespie, Jr. quoted in Begley, Sharon *The Plastic Mind.* London: Constable, 2009, 79.

Mandela, Nelson. *Some Evidence of Things Seen.* Rivonia, Republic of South Africa: Open Hand Trust, 1997, 19.

McClintock, Barbara. quoted in Piero Ferrucci. Inevitable Grace. Los Angeles: J.P. Tarcher1990, 6.

Merton, Thomas quoted in James Austin. James H. *Zen-Brain Reflections.* Cambridge, MA.: MIT Press, 2006, 69.

Muir, John. quoted in K.C. Cole. *Mind over Matter.* Orlando: Harcourt, Inc. 2003, 233.

Nakai, R. Carlos. CD Liner. *Mythic Dreamer.* Phoenix: Canyon Records Production, 1998.

Newberg, Andrew & Mark Robert Waldman. *How God Changes Your Brain.* New York: Ballantine, 2009, 127.

Panksapp, Jaak. Quoted in Paul Thagard. T*he Brain and The Meaning of Life.* Princeton,N.J.: Princeton University Press, 2002, p.161-2.

Perrow, Charles B. quoted in Eric Schlosser. *Command and Control.* London:Allan Lane, 2013, 461.

Pfaff, Donald W. *The Neuroscience of Fair Play.* New York: Dana Press 2007, 118.

Prigogine Ilya. quoted in Renee Weber. *Dialogues With Scientists and Sages*. London: Routledge & Kegan Paul, 1986, 187.

Pugh, Emerson. Quoted in Reagan, Michael & Sharon Begley. *Inside The Mind of God*. Philadelphia: Templeton Foundation Press, 2002, 61.

Rukeyser, Muriel. quoted in Jack Kornfield. *The Wise Heart*. New York: Bantam, 2009.

Rumi quoted in Lewis. Franklin D. *Rumi: Swallowing The Sun*. Oxford: One World, 2008, 151.

Schrodinger, Erwin. quoted in Renee Weber. *Dalogues With Scientists and Sages*. London: Routledge & Kegan Paul, 1986, xv.

Schrodinger, Erwin. quoted in Jeffrey M. Schwartz & Sharon Begley. *The Mind and The Brain*. New York: Harper, 2002, 323.

Schweitzer, Albert. quoted in David Lorimer. *Whole In One*. London: Arkana, 1990.

Siegel, Daniel. J. *The Mindful Brain*. New York: Norton, 2007, 99.

St. Catherine of Siena. quoted in Daniel Ladinsky. *Love Poems From God*. New York: Penguin Compas, 2002, 199.

St. John of the Cross, quoted in Daniel Ladinsky. *Love Poems From God*. New York: Penguin Compas, 2002, 317.

St. Teresa of Avila. quoted in Kavanaugh, Kieran & Otilio Rodriguez. *The Collected Works of St. Teresa of Avila*. Washington, D.C.: ICS Publications, 1976, 141.

Strogatz, Steven. *Sync*. New York: Hyperion, 2003, 259.

Swimme, Brian. quoted in Begley, Sharon *The Plastic Mind*. London: Constable, 2009, 156.

Tagore, Rabindranath. *Sadhana: The Realization of Life*. Radford, VA: Wilder, Pub., 2008, 24.

Thompson, Francis. quoted in K.C. Cole. *Mind Over Matter*. Orlando: Harcourt, Inc., 2003, 234.

Tutu, Archbishop Desmond. quoted in H. H. The Dalai Lama & Victor Chan. *The Wisdom of Forgiveness*. London: Hodder & Stoughton, 2004, 68-9.

Tutu, Archbishop Desmond. *Made For Goodness*. New York: HarperOne, 2010, 6.

Ueshiba, Morihei. Quoted in Kisshomaru Ueshiba. *The Spirit of Aikido*. New York: Kodansha, 2012, 49.

Varela, Francisco. quoted in Hayward, Jeremy W. & Francisco J. Varela. *Gentle Bridges: Conversations with the Dalai Lama on the Sciences of the*

*Mind*. Boston: Shambhala, 2001, 253.

Watson, Lyall. *Gifts of Unknown Things*. New York: Destiny Books, 1991, 42.

Watts, Alan. quoted in Lucinda Vardey. *God In All Worlds*. New York: Vintage, 1995, 37.

Wiesel, Elie. "Crimes Against Childhood." In *We, The Children*. New York: W. W. Norton & Co. UNICEF, 1990. UNICEF,1990, 27.

White, E.B. *Charlotte's Web*. New York: Harper Collins, 1952.

Whiting, Candace Calloway. "Humpback whales intervene un orca attack on gray whale calf. *Digital Journal* (May 8, 2012) http://www.digitaljournal.com/article/324348.

Wilber, Ken. *The Simple Feeling of Being*. Boston: Shambhala, 2004, 2.

Wilhelm, Richard. quoted in Hayward, Jeremy. *Letters To Vanessa*. Boston: Shambhala, 1997, 194.

Williams, Margery. The Velveteen Rabbit. Garden City. New York: Doubleday, no date.

Wrangsjo, Björn. personal communication, 2000.

Yun-men. quoted in *Narrow Road To The Interior*. Matsuo Basho and Sam Hamill. Boston: Shambhala, 1998.

# Chapter 5

Atkinson, Ace. Personal communication.

Austin, James H. *Zen and the Brain*. Cambridge. MA.: MIT Press, 1998, 567.

Bach, Richard. quoted in Reagan, Michael & Sharon Begley. *Inside The Mind of God*. Philadelphia: Templeton Foundation Press, 2002, 72.

Baker, Roshi Richard. quoted in *The Leadership Dojo*. Berkeley, CA. : Frog Books, 2007.

Barks, Coleman. *Rumi. The Book of Love*. San Francisco: Harper San Francisco, 2003, 65.

Basho. quoted in Amdur, Ellis. Dueling *With O-sensei*. Seattle, WA.: Edgework, 2000, 22.

Berns, Gregory. *Iconoclast*. Boston: Harvard Business Press, 2008, 58.

Cezanne, Paul. quoted in Austin, James H. *Zen-Brain Reflections*. Cambridge, MA.: MIT Press, 2006, 21.

Carroll, Lewis *Through The Looking Glass*. New York:Macmillan,1885,133.

Cummings, e.e. quoted in Stephen Nachmanovitch Free play. Los Angeles: Jeremy Tarcher, 1990, 116.

de Saint-Exupéry, Antoine. The Little Prince, New York 1971, 78-84.

de Waal, Frans. The Bonobo and the Atheist. New York: Norton, 2013, 45.

Einstein, Albert quoted in Evelyn Fox Keller. *A Feeling for the Organism: The life and Work of Barbara McClintock*. New York: A.W.H. Freeman/ Owl Book, 1983, 201.

Feldman, Christina & Jack Kornfield. (eds.) *Stories of the Spirit, Stories of the Heart.* San Francisco: Harper Collins, 1991, 67.

Genro. quoted in Hyers, Conrad. *Zen and the Comic Spirit*. Philadelphia: The Westminster Press, 1973. 1983, 181.

Gibran, Kahlil. *The Prophet*. New York: Alfred A. Knopf, 1966, 79.

Gladwell, Malcolm. Quoted in Sam Sheridan. *The Fighter's Mind*. New York: Grove Press, 2010

Glover, Jonathan. *Humanity: A Moral History of the Twentieth Century*. London: Jonathan Cape, 1999

H.H. The Dalai Lama. quoted in Anne Harrington & Arthur Zajonc. Eds. *The Dalai Lama at MIT*. Cambridge, MA.: Harvard University Press, 2006,157.

H.H. The Dalai Lama. quoted in Anne Harrington & Arthur Zajonc. Eds. *The Dalai Lama at MIT*. Cambridge, MA.: Harvard University Press, 2006, 157.

Hafiz quoted in Daniel Ladinsky. *The Subject Tonight Is Love*. New York: Penguin Compass, 2003, 30.

Hayes, John quoted in Brooks, David. *The Social Animal*. New York: Random house, 2009, 136.

Heitzer, Steve. Personal communication.

Herrigel, Eugen. Zen in the Art of Archery. New York: Vintage,1953, vii.

Ittokusai quoted in Trevor Leggett. *The Old Zen Master*. Totnes, England: Buddhist publishing Co., 2000, 97.

Johnson, Robert. A. <u>Balancing Heaven and Earth.</u> San Francisco: Harper San Francisco, 1998, 58.

Kamata, Shigeo and Shimizu, Kenji. *Zen and Aikido*. Tokyo: Aiki News, 1984, 97.

Keller, Evelyn Fox. *A Feeling for the Organism: The life and Work of Barbara McClintock*. New York: A.W.H. Freeman/Owl Book, 1983, 198.

Krishnamurti, Jiddu. quoted in Jacob Needleman & David Applebaum. Real philosophy. London: Arkana, 1990, 241.

Leggett, Trevor. *Encounters in Yoga and Zen: Meetings of Cloth and Stone*. London: Routledge & Kegan Paul, 1982, 39-40.

Levitin, Daniel. quoted in Richard Sennett. *The Craftsman.* New Haven: Yale University Press, 2008, 172.

Lilly, Antoinette. quoted in Piero Ferrucci. Inevitable Grace. Los Angeles: J.P. Tarcher, 1990, 6.

Nisargadatta, Majaraj. quoted in Carter, Richard Burnett. *The Language of Zen.* New York: sterling, 2010, 12.

Hatsumi, Masaaki. quoted in Akiro Hino. *Kokoro No Katachi.* Akiro Hino, 2013, 187.

McClintock, Barbara. quoted in Keller, Evelyn Fox. *A Feeling for the Organism. The Life and Work of Barbara McClintock.* New York: W.H. Freeman/Owl Book, 1983, 198.

McClintock, Barbara. quoted in Piero Ferrucci. Inevitable Grace. Los Angeles: J.P. Tarcher, 1990, 6.

Merton, Thomas. quoted in Lucinda Vardey. *God In All Worlds.* New York: Vintage, 1995, 848.

Miller, Bob. quoted in K.C. Cole. *Mind Over Matter.* Orlando, FL Harcourt, Inc. 2003, 180.

Mitchell, Stephen. *The Second Book of the Tao.* New York: The Penguin Press, 2009, 75.

Mother Teresa. quoted in Rai, Raghu. *Mother Teresa: A Life of Dedication.* New York: Harry N. Abrams, Inc., 2004, 58.

Mother Teresa. quoted in *Mother Teresa at 100. Time.* New York: Time/Life Books, 2010.

Mother Teresa of Calcutta and Brother Roger of Taize.*Meditations on the Way of The Cross.* New York: The Pilgrim Press, 1987, 45.

Orwell, George. quoted in Jonathan *Glover, Humanity: A Moral History of the Twentieth Century.* London: Jonathan Cape, 1999, 53.

Pfaff, Donald W. *The Neuroscience of Fair Play.* New York: Dana Press 2007

Picasso. quoted in James H. Austin. *Chase, Chance, and Creativity.* Cambridge, MA: MIT Press, 2003, 167.

Pope John XXIII quoted in Frederick Franck. *A Passion For Seeing.* New York: New Paltz, 2002, 78.

Raine, Kathleen. quoted in Hayward, Jeremy. *Letters To Vanessa.* Boston: Shambhala, 1997, 6.

Richards, M. C. *Centering.* Hanover, NH:Wesleyan University Press, 1989,13.

Rilke, Rainer Maria. *Stories of God.* New York: Norton, 1963, 83.

Rilke, Rainer Maria. quoted in David Stendl-Rast. *A Listening Heart: The Art of Contemplative Living.* New York" Crossroads Publishig Co., 1983.

Robson, James. quoted in Whitall N. Perry. *A Treasury of Traditional Wisdom.* San Francisco, CA.: Harper & Row, 1986.

Sexson, Lynda. *Ordinarily Sacred.* New York: Crossroad, 1982, 165.

Simon, Herbert. quoted in Anne Harrington & Arthur Zajonc. Eds. *The Dalai Lama at MIT.* Cambridge, MA.: Harvard University Press, 2006, 157.

St. John of the Cross. quoted in Karen Armstrong. *The Case For God.* New York: Alfred A. Knopf, 2009, 181.

St. John of the Cross. quoted in Daniel Ladinsky. *Love Poems From God.* New York: Penguin Compas, 2002, 322.

St. Teresa of Avila. quoted in Kavanaugh, Kieran & Otilio Rodriguez. *The Collected Works of St. Teresa of Avila.* Washington, D.C.: ICS Publications, 1976.

Steinbeck, John. Quoted in Frans De Waal. The Bonobo and the Atheist. New York: Norton, 2013, 111.

Stevens, John. (trans. & ed.) *The Art of Peace.* Boston: Shambhala, 2002, 84.

Suzuki, Roshi quoted in Jon kabat-Zinn *Coming To Our Senses.* New York: Hyperion,2005, 85.

Suzuki, Daisetz T. *Zen and Japanese Culture.* New York: Princeton University Press, 1959, 92.

Swimme, Brian. *The Universe Is A Green Dragon.* Santa Fe, New Mexico: Bear & Co., 1984, 127.

Tagore, Rabindranath. Quoted in Jacob Needleman & David Applebaum. *Real Philosophy.* London: Arkana, 1990, 237.

Tokitsu, Kenji. *Ki and the Way of the Martial Arts.* Boston:Shambhala, 2002, 88.

Ueshiba, Morihei. *The Art of Peace.* Boston: Shambhala, 2007, 92.

Valery, Paul. quoted in James H. Austin. *Zen-Brain Reflections.* Cambridge, MA.: MIT Press, 2006, 22.

van der Post, Laurens. *About Blady: A Pattern Out of Time.* Orlando,FL: Harcourt Brace Jovanovich 1993, 47.

Wallace, Alan. *Embracing Mind.* Boston: Shambhala, 2008, 176.

Watson, Lyall. *Elephantoms.* New York: W.W. Norton, 2002, 229.

Whittier, John Greenleaf *Child,*1988, 66.

Wilde, Oscar. quoted in Karl F. Friday & Seki Humitake. *Legacies of the Sword*. Honolulu: University of Hawai'I Press, 1997, 100.

Williams, Margery. *The Velveteen Rabbit*. Garden City, New York: Doubleday, No date.

Wilson, Frank. quoted in K.C. Cole. *Mind Over Matter*. Orlando, FL:Harcourt, Inc., 2003, 280.

## Chapter 6

AA. quoted in Rush, Lockwood. *Finding The Way Home*. Unionville,PA.: Ilm House-LLC, 2007, 159.

Armstrong, Karen. *The Case For God*. New York: Alfred A. Knopf, 2009, 17.

Atkinson, Ace. Personal communication.

Austin, James H. *Zen-Brain Reflections*. Cambridge, MA.: MIT Press, 2006, 268.

al-Nasafi, Aziz ibn Muhammad. quoted in Whitall Perry. *A Treasury of Traditional Wisdom*. Cambridge: Harper & Row, 1986, 828.

Basho. quoted in Holmes, Stewart W. & Chimyo Horioka. *Zen Art For Meditation*. Rutland, Vermont: Charles E. Tuttle, 1973, 41.

Bian. quoted in Armstrong, Karen *The Case For God*. New York: Alfred A. Knopf, 2009, xiii.

Bohm, David. quoted in Weber, Renee. *Dalogues With Scientists and Sages*. London: Routledge & Kegan Paul, 1986, 107.

Bohr, Niels. quoted in Hayward, Jeremy. *Letters To Vanessa*. Boston: Shambhala, 1997, 123-4.

Buber, Martin *I and Thou*. Berlin: Shocken,1923, 56 32.

Buscaglia, Leo personal communication.

Degre, Alain & Robert, Sylvia &, *Tippi of Africa*. New Holland, Australia, 1997, p.207).

Descartes, Rene. quoted in Eben Alexander. *Proof of Heaven*. New York: Simon & Schuster, 2012, 149.

Durckheim, Karlfried Graf. *The Way of Transformation*. London: Unwin Paperbacks, 1980, 166.

Eckhart, Meister. quoted in Austin, James H. *Zen-Brain Reflections*. Cambridge, MA.: MIT Press, 2006, 342.

Eckhart, Meister. quoted in Weber, Renee. *Dalogues With Scientists and Sages*. London: Routledge & Kegan Paul, 1986, 3.

Feldman, Christina & Kornfield, Jack. (eds.) *Stories of the Spirit, Stories of the Heart.* San Francisco: Harper Collins, 1991, 345.

Gianotti, Fabiola *Time,* (July 23, 2012), 30.

Hafiz. quoted in Daniel Ladinsky. *The Gift.* New York: Penguin Compass, 1999, 67, 251.

Hafiz quoted in Daniel Ladinsky. *The Subject Tonight Is Love.* New York: Penguin Compass, 2003, 30, 23.

Hammarskjöld, Dag. *Markings.* Translated by Leif Sjöberg and W.H. Auden. New York: Knopf,1964, 89, 213.

Huang, Al Chung-liang. *Enbrace Tiger, Return To Mountain.* Real People Press, Moab, UT: 1973, xiii.

I-Ch'ing. quoted in Mitchell, Stephen. *The Second Book of the Tao.* New York: The Penguin Press, 2009, 46.

Inati, Shams C. Ibn Sina's *Remarks and Admonitions: Physics and Metaphysics.* New York: Columbia University Press, 2014, 147.

Johnson, Robert. A. *Balancing Heaven and Earth.* San Francisco: Harper San Francisco, 1998, 294.

Jung quoted in van der Post, Laurens . *Jung and the Story of our Time.* New York: Vintage, 1975, 57.

Lao-tzu. quoted in *Tao Te Ching.* Gia-Fu, Jane English & Toinette Lippe (Translators) New York: Vintage, 1972.

Lindgren, Astrid & Nyman, Ingrid. *Do You Know Pippi Longstocking?* Stockholm:Rabin & Sjögren Bokförlag, 1999.

Lipton, Bruce & Bhaerman, Steve. *Spontaneous Evolution.* Carlsbad, CA.:Hay House, 2009, 105.

McTaggart, Lynne. quoted in Lipton, Bruce. *Spontaneous Evolution.* Carlsbad, CA.: Hay House, 2009,105.

Merton, Thomas. quoted in David Stendl-Rast, Deeper Than words. New York: Image, 2010,13.

Milne, A.A. & Shepard, Ernest H. *The House At Pooh Corner.* New York: Dutton, 1988.

Mother Teresa. quoted in Rai, Raghu. *Mother Teresa: A Life of Dedication.* New York: Harry N. Abrams, Inc., 2004

Mother Teresa. quoted in Benenate, Becky (ed.) *Mother Teresa: In the Heart of the World.* Novato, CA.: New World Library, 1997, 31.

Mother Teresa. quoted in Brian Kolodiejchuk, M.C. *Mother Teresa: Come Be My Light.* New York: Doubleday, 2007, 259, 297.

Nantenbo, Audrey Yoshiko. *Enso.* Boston: Weatherhill, 2007, 80.

Nouwen, J.M. *Encounters With Merton.* New York: Crossroads Publishing

Co., 1981, 116.

Packer, Toni. *The Silent Question.* Boston: Shambhala, 2007.

Pascal, Blaise. quoted in Austin, James H. *Selfless Insight.* Cambridge, MA.: MIT Press, 2009, 143.

Pascal, Blaise quoted in Austin, James H. *Zen-Brain Reflections.* Cambridge, MA.: MIT Press, 2006, 29.

Picasso quoted in James H. Austin. *Chase, Chance, and Creativity.* Cambridge, MA: MIT Press, 2003.

Rather, Dan. quoted in Packer, Toni. *The Silent Question.* Boston: Shambhala, 2007, 111.

Ricard, Matthieu. quoted in Luisi, Pier Luigi. *Mind And Life.* New York: Columbia Series in Science and Religion, 2009, 44.

Rumi. quoted in Coleman Barks. *Rumi. The Book of Love.* San Francisco: Harper San Francisco, 2003, 124.

Rumi. quoted in Coleman Barks. *The Soul of Rumi.* San Francisco: Harper San Francisco, 2001, 49.

Rumi. quoted in Quoted in Daniel Ladinsky. *Love Poems From God.* New York: Penguin Compas, 2002, 77.

Rumi. quoted in Coleman Barks. *The Soul of Rumi.* San Francisco: Harper San Francisco, 2001, 113.

Schweitzer, Albert. quoted in David Lorimer. *Whole In One.* London: Arkana, 1990, 72.

Shoju quoted in Kamata, Shigeo and Kenji Shimizu. *Zen and Aikido.* Tokyo: Aiki News, 1984, 98-99.

Silesius, Angelus. quoted in Whitall Perry. *A Treasury of Traditional Wisdom.* Cambridge: Harper & Row, 1986, 829.

Singer, P. W. *Wired For War.* New York: Pengiun, 2009, 102.

St. Augustine. quoted in Ken Wilber, *Grace and Grit.* Boston: Shambhala, 1991, 86.

St. John of the Cross. quoted in Kavanaugh, Kieran & Otilio Rodriguez. *The Collected Works of St. Teresa of Avila.* Washington, D.C.: ICS Publications, 1976, 461.

St. John of the Cross. quoted in Christina Feldman & Jack Kornfield. (eds.) *Stories of the Spirit, Stories of the Heart.* San Francisco: Harper Collins, 1991, 97.

Aquinas, St. Thomas. quoted in Ladinsky, Daniel. *Love Poems From God.* New York: Penguin Compass, 2002, 122.

Aquinas, St. Thomas. quoted in Renee Weber. *Dalogues With Scientists and Sages*. London: Routledge & Kegan Paul, 1986, 168.

Stanislavski, Constantin. *An Actor Prepares*. New York: Routledge, 1948, 32.

Susskind, Leonard. quoted in. Quoted in K.C. Cole. *Mind Over Matter*. Orlando: Harcourt, Inc., 2003, 127.

Suzuki, Shunryu. quoted in Sheridan, Sam. *The Fighter's Mind*. New York: Grove Press, 2010, 53.

Tagore Rabindranath. quoted in Jacob Needleman & David Applebaum. *Real Philosophy*. London: Arkana, 1990.

T'sai Ken Ten. quoted in Frederick Franck, *Fingers Pointing Toward The Sacred*.Bostonm: Beacon Point Press, 1994, 252.

Ueshiba, Morihei. *The Secret Teachings of Aikido*.Tokyo: Kodansha, 2007, 16.

Weil, Simone. *Gravity and Grace*. New York: Routledge, 2002.

Wilbur, Ken. *The Simple Feeling of Being*. Boston: Shambhala, 2004, 170.

## Chapter 7

*A Course in Miracles*. Mill Valley, CA.: Foundation For Inner Peace, 2007.

Adam, Michael. *Wandering in Eden*. New York: Alfred A. Knopf, 1976, 135.

Aron, Arthur. Et.al. *The experimental Generation of Interpersonal Closeness: A Procedure and Some Preliminary Findings*. Personality and Social Psychology Bulletin. (April, 1997), Vol.23, 363-377.

Atkinson, Ace. Personal communication.

Auden, W. H. quoted in Goleman, Daniel. *Destructive Emotions. A Dialogue with the Dalai Lama*. London: Bloomsbury, 2003,319.

Azhar, Masood. Quoted in Adrian Levi & Cathy Scott-Clark. *The Meadow*. London: William Collins: 2012, 54.

Bahauddin. quoted in Barks, Coleman & John Moyne. *The Drowned Book*. San Francisco: Harper, 2004, 45 & 129.

Basho. quoted in Holmes, Stewart W. & Chimyo Horioka. *Zen Art For Meditation*. Rutland, Vermont: Charles E. Tuttle, 1973, 49.

Bigelow, Ann. Ph.D. et. al. The Effect of Mter/Infant Skin-to-Skin Contact on postpartum Depressive Symptoms and Maternal Physiological Stress." *Journal of Obstetric, Gynecologic, & Neonatal Nursing*. Vol. 41 (May/June, 2012), 369-382.

Buber, Martin, *I and Thou*. New York: Charles Scribner's Sons. 1970, 62 &67.

Burnett. John. *Where Soldiers Fear To Thread*. London: Arrow Books, 2005, 139.

Chargaff, Edwin. quoted in Andrew Newberg. *Why God Won't Go Away*. New York: Random House, 2001, 154.

Chuang-tzu. quoted in Hyers, Conrad. *Zen and the Comic Spirit*. Philadelphia: The Westminster Press, 1973, 129.

Cole, K.C. *Mind Over Matter*. Orlando, FL.: Harcourt, Inc. 2003.,234.

Coleridge, Samuel Taylor. quoted in Brooks, David. *The Social Animal*. New York: Random house, 2009, 43.

Czerniakow, Adam. quoted in Grynberg, Michal. Translated by Philip Boehm. *Words To Outlive Us*. New York: Picador, 2002,96.

Davidson, Richard. quoted in Sharon Begley. "Adventures in Good And Evil." *Newsweek*. (May 4, 2009), 3.

Dinesen, Isak. quoted in Reagan, Michael & Sharon Begley. Inside The Mind of God.Philadelphia: Templeton Foundation Press, 2002, 35.

Donne, John. quoted in Austin, James H.. *Zen and the Brain*. Cambridge. MA.: MIT Press, 1998, 55.

Einstein, Albert. quoted in Andrew Newberg. *Why God Won't Go Away*. New York: Random House., 2001, 153.

Einstein, Albert. quoted in Walter Isaacson. *Einstein*. New York: Simon & Schuster, 2007, 382.

Ferrucci, Piero. *Inevitable Grace*. Los Angeles: J.P. Tarcher, 1990. Ferrucci, 1990, 313, 30.

Franck, Frederick *Pilgrimage To Now/Here*. New York: Orbis Books, 1974, 11.

Frankl, Viktor. quoted in Lucinda Vardey. *God In All Worlds*. New York: Vintage, 1995, 337.

Gandhi. quoted in Stephen S. Hall *Wisdom: From Philosophy to Neuroscience*. New York: Alfred A. Knopf, 2010, 143.

Garmezy & Rutter. quoted in Richard J. Davidson and Anne Harrington. *Visions of Compassion*. London: Oxford University Press, 2002, 178 .

H.H. The Dalai Lama. quoted in Hayward, Jeremy W. & Francisco J. Varela. *Gentle Bridges: Conversations with the Dalai Lama on the Sciences of the Mind*. Boston: Shambhala, 2001, 254.

Hafiz quoted in Daniel Ladinsky. *The Subject Tonight Is Love*. New York: Penguin Compass, 2003, 8.

Hafiz. quoted in Daniel Ladinsky. *The Gift*. New York: Penguin, 1999, 121.

Hamada, Shoji. quoted in Yanagi, Soetsu. *An Unknown Craftsman*. New York: Kodansha, 1989, 224.

Hazelton, Lesley. *Mary: A Flesh and Blood Biography of the Virgin Mother*.

New York: Bloomsbury, 2004, 11.

Hendrix, Jimi. quoted in Stephen King. *Under The Dome.* London: Hodder & Stoughton,, 2009, 53.

Hypocrites. quoted in Barks, Coleman. *Rumi. The Book of Love.* San Francisco: Harper san Francisco, 2003, 6.

Ittokusai quoted in Trevor Leggett. *The Old Zen Master.* Totnes, England: Buddhist publishing Co., 2000.

Johnson, Robert. A. *Balancing Heaven and Earth.* San Francisco: Harper San Francisco, 1998, 84.

Julian of Norwich. quoted in Sexson, Lynda. *Ordinarily Sacred.* New York: Crossroad, 1982, 125.

Julian of Norwich. quoted in Carol Lee Flinders. *Enduring Grace: Living Portraits of Seven Women Mystics.* New York: Harper, 1993, 86.

Karlfeldt, Erik Axel. quoted in Dag Hammarskjold. *To Speak For The World.* Stockholm: Atlantis, 2005, 57.

Kenzo, Awa. quoted in John Stevens. *Zen Bow, Zen Arrow.* Boston: Shambhala, 2007, 71.

King, Stark. Personal Communication.

Kor, Eva Mozes *Surviving the Angel of Death.* 2009, 132.

Lown, Bernard. The Lost Art of Healing.New York: Ballantine, 1999, 33.

Merton, Thomas. quoted in Pennington, Basil. M. *Thomas Merton, Brother Monk.* New York: Continuim, 1997, 29.

Merton, Thomas. quoted in Shannon, William. H. *Thomas Merton: Passion for Peace.* New York: A Crossroad Book, 1995, 34.

Merton, Thomas *Faith and Violence.* South Bend, IN,: University of Notre Dame Press,1976, 13.

Mitchell, Stephen. *The Second Book of the Tao.* New York: The Penguin Press, 2009, 53.

Mother Teresa. quoted in Brian Kolodiejchuk. *Mother Teresa; Come Be My Light.* New York: Doubleday, 2007, 2.

Mother Teresa. quoted in Mother Teresa of Calcutta and Brother Roger of Taize. *Meditations on the Way of The Cross.* New York: The Pilgrim Press, 1987, 37.

Mother Teresa. quoted in Benenate, Becky (ed.) *Mother Teresa: In the Heart of the World.* Novato, CA.: New World Library, 1997, 45.

Mukherjee, Siddhartha. *The Emperor of all Maladies.* New York: Scribner, 2010, 465.

Najagneq, Knud Rasmussen quoted in Joseph Campbell. *Myths To Live*

*By*. New York: Bantam, 1972, 150.

Newberg, Andrew, M.D. & Waldman, Mark Robert *How God Changes Your Brain*. New YorK: Ballantine Books, 2009, 14 & 127.

Novalis. quoted in Ashley Montagu. *Touching*. New York: Harper & Row, 1986.

Older, J. quoted in Field, Tiffany. *Touch*. Cambridge, MA.: MIT Press, 2001, 17.

Orlinska, Ula. "Israel." *Kaleidoscope*. (September, 2008, 12-21.

Plato. quoted in Think Exist Quotations. "Platoquotes." Think Exist. com Quotations Online. 1 Feb., 2010 6, March 2010. http://einstein/ quotes/Plato/

Po, Li. quoted in Christina Feldman & Jack Kornfield. (eds.) *Stories of the Spirit, Stories of the Heart*. San Francisco: Harper Collins, 1991.

Pope John XXIII quoted in Frederick Franck. *I Love Life: A Living Portrait of John XXIII, Prophet of a World At Peace*. New York: St. Martin's Press, 1967, 13.

Rabi'a al-Adawiyya. quoted in Andrew Newberg. *Why God Won't Go Away*. New York: Random House., 2001, 159.

Rilke quoted in Bert Hellinger. *With God In Mind*. Bischofswiesen, Germany : Hellinger Publications, 2007, 138.

Roosevelt, Eleanor quoted in Bernard Lown Prescription For Survival. San Francisco: Berrett-Koehler Publication, 2008, 213.

Rumi. quoted in Barks, Coleman, Michael Green & Jalai Al-Din Rumi. *The Iluminated Rumi*. New York: Broadway Books, 1997.

St. Teresa of Avila quoted in Kavanaugh, Kieran & Otilio Rodriguez. The Collected Works of St. Teresa of Avila. Washington, D.C.: ICS Publications, 1976.

Aquinas, St. Thomas quoted in Quoted in Daniel Ladinsky. Love Poems From God. New York: Penguin Compas, 2002.

Tagore, Rabindranath. *Sadhana: The Realization of Life*. Radford, VA: Wilder, Pub., 2008, 24.

Takuan quoted in Stevens, John. *Invincible Warrior*. Boston: Shanbhala, 1997, 101.

"The fight for fairness". *Warsaw Business Review*. (October 19-25, 2009), 1.

The Ten Principal Upanishads. Quoted in Wendell Berry. *A Place In Time*. Berkeley, CA.: Counterpoint, 2012.

Thomas, Lewis. Quoted in Lown, Bernard. *The Lost Art of Healing*.New York: Ballantine, 1999, 23.

Ueshiba, Morihei. Quoted in Kisshomaru Ueshiba. *The Spirit of Aikido*. New York: Kodansha, 2012, 4.

van Der Post, Laurens. *Yet Being Someone Other*. London: Penguin Books, 1982, 335.

von Clausewitz, Carl. quoted in Greene, Robert. *33 Strategies of War*. London. Profile Books, 2007, 3.

Von Koch, Anette. Personal communication, 2009.

Watson, Lyall. *Elephantoms*. New York: W.W. Norton, 2002, 229.

Williams, Margery. The Velveteen Rabbit. Garden City. New York: Doubleday, no date.

# Chapter 8

Basho quoted in Holmes, Stewart W. & Chimyo Horioka. *Zen Art For Meditation*. Rutland, Vermont: Charles E. Tuttle, 1973.

Einstein, Albert. Quoted in Walter Isaacson. *Einstein: His Life and Universe*. New York: Simon& Schuster, 2007.

Eliot, T.S. quoted in Reagan, Michael & Sharon Begley. Inside The Mind of God.Philadelphia: Templeton Foundation Press, 2002.

Gandhi quoted in Think Exist Quotations. "Mahatma Gandhi quotes." Think Exist.com Quotations Online. 1 Feb.2010, 6 March 2010. <http://einstein/quotes/mahatma_gandhi/>

H.H. The Dalai Lama. Quoted in Chhaya, Mayank. *Dalai Lama*. London: I. B. Tauris & Co. LTD., 2008.

Hafiz. Quoted in Daniel Ladinsky, *The Gift*. New York: Penguin, 1999.

Hammarskjold, Dag. *To Speak For The World*. Stockholm: Atlantis, 2005.

Hayward, Jeremy. *Letters To Vanessa*. Boston: Shambhala, 1997.

Korczak, Janusz. quoted in Lifton Betty Jean. *The King of Children: The Life and Death of Janusz Korczak*. New York: American Academy of Pediatrics, 1988, 5.

Mandela, Nelson. *Some Evidence of Things Seen*. Rivonia, Republic of South Africa: Open Hand Trust, 1997.

Mother Teresa quoted in James Martin, SJ *Becoming Who You Are*. Boston: hidden Spring, 2006.

Mother Teresa.quoted in Benenate, Becky. (ed.) *Mother Teresa: In The Heart of The World*. Novato, CA.: New World Library, 1997.

Rilke quoted in David Steindl-Rast. *A Listening Heart: The Art of Contemplative Living*. New York: Crossroad Pub. Co., 1983.

Rumi quoted in Barks, Coleman, Michael Green & Jalai Al-Din Rumi.

*The Iluminated Rumi.* New York: Broadway Books, 1997.

The Ten Principal Upanishads. Quoted in Wendell Berry. *A Place In Time.* Berkeley, CA.: Counterpoint, 2012.

## Appendix 2

Austin , James. *Zen and the Brain.* Cambridge. MA.: MIT Press, 1998, 109.

Bateson, Gregory. *Mind and Nature: A Necessary Unity.* New York: Bantam, 1979, 8.

Begley, Sharon *The Plastic Mind.* London: Constable, 2009, 262.

Bohm, David. quoted in Weber, Renee. *Dalogues With Scientists and Sages.* London: Routledge & Kegan Paul, 1986, 107.

Bornstein, David. "Protecting Children From Toxic Stress." Opinion Pages. T*he New York Times.* (October 30, 2013).

Chomsky, Noam. *Language and Mind.* London: Cambridge University Press, 2006.

Coles, Robert. Jay Woodruff & Sarah Carew Woodrruff (eds.) *Conversations With Robert Coles.* Jackson: University Press of Mississippi, 1992, 199.

Eckhart, Meister. quoted in Matthew Fox. *Whee! We, Wee All The Way Home.* Santa Fe, New Mexico: Bear & Co., 1981, 99.

Edison, Thomas. quoted in James H. Austin. *Selfless Insight.* Cambridge, MA.:MIT Press, 2009, 205.

Einstein, Albert. quoted in Austin, James. *Selfless Insight.* Cambridge, MA.: MIT Press, 2009, 135.

Einstein, Albert. quoted in Walter Isaacson. *Einstein.* New York: Simon & Schuster, 2007.

Ekman, Paul. *Emotional Awareness.* New York: Henry Holt, 2008.

Goleman, Daniel. *Social Intelligence.* New York: Bantam, 2006, 36.

H.H. The Dalai Lama. quoted in Anne Harrington & Arthur Zajonc. Eds. *The Dalai Lama at MIT.* Cambridge, MA.: Harvard University Press, 2006. 2006, 15.

H.H. The Dalai Lama. quoted in HH The Dalai Lama and Victor Chan. *The Wisdom of Forgiveness.* London: Hodder & Mobius, 2004, 120.

H.H. The Dalai Lama. quoted in Ekman, Paul. *Emotional Awareness.* New York: Henry Holt, 2008, 223.

Harrington, Anne & Arthur Zajonc. Eds. *The Dalai Lama at MIT.* Cambridge, MA.: Harvard University Press, 2006. 2006, 15.

Iacobini, Marco. *Mirroring People.* London: Picador, 2009, 267.

Korczak, Janusz. quoted in Lifton Betty Jean. *The King of Children: The Life and Death of Janusz Korczak.* New York: American Academy of Pediatrics, 1988, 5.

Krishnamurti, Jiddu. quoted in Jacob Needleman & David Applebaum. Real philosophy. London: Arkana, 1990, 241.

Lipton, Bruce & Steve Bhaerman. *Spontaneous Evolution.* Carlsbad, CA.:Hay House, 2009.

Machel, Graca. quoted in "Mandela and Machel to lead global children's initiative." UNICEF http://www.unicef.org/newsline/00pr36.htm 2000.

Mandela, Nelson. *Some Evidence of Things Seen.* Rivonia, Republic of South Africa: Open Hand Trust, 1997, 19.

Merton, Thomas. quoted in Robert Inchausti (ed.) *Echoing Silence.* Boston: New Seeds, 2007, 110.

Newberg, Andrew & Mark Robert Waldman. *How God Changes Your Brain.* New York: Ballantine, 2009, 127.

Pascal, Blaise. Quoted in James H. Austin. *Selfless Insight.* Cambridge, MA.:MIT Press, 2009, 143.

Pfaff, Donald W. *The Neuroscience of Fair Play.* New York: Dana Press, 2007, 154.

Siegel, Kenneth N. quoted in Jena McGregor. "Sweet revenge". *Businessweek Online.* (January 22, 2007), 1-4.

Wilbur, Ken. *The Simple Feeling of Being.* Boston: Shambhala, 2004, 170.

Yasutani, Zen Master Hakuun. quoted in James H. Austin. *Selfless Insight.* Cambridge, MA.:MIT Press, 2009, 53.

# Index

CPSIA information can be obtained
at www.ICGtesting.com
Printed in the USA
LVHW031344211220
674774LV00039B/588

9 780692 885864